WITHDRAWN

Compiled here are reviews, reports, notes, and essays found in German-language periodicals published between 1783 and 1830. The documents are translated into English with copious notes and annotations, an introductory essay and indexes of names, subjects, works, and periodicals. This volume contains a general section and documents on specific opus numbers up to opus 54, with musical examples redrawn from the original publications.

The collection brings to light contemporary perceptions of Beethoven's music, including matters such as audience, setting, facilities, orchestra, instruments, and performers as well as the relationship of Beethoven's music to theoretical and critical ideas of the eighteenth and nineteenth centuries. These documents, most of which appear in English for the first time, present a wide spectrum of insights into the perceptions that Beethoven's contemporaries had of his monumental music.

Wayne M. Senner is the director of German and Scandinavian studies at Arizona State University. His publications include *The Origins of Writing* (Nebraska 1989).

UNIVERSITY OF NEBRASKA PRESS
Lincoln NE 68588-0484

www.nebraskapress.unl.edu

Number 3 in the series North American Beethoven Studies
Edited by William Meredith

The Critical Reception of *Beethoven's Compositions*

by His German Contemporaries, VOLUME I

Wayne M. Senner, GENERAL EDITOR, COMPILER, AND TRANSLATOR

Robin Wallace, MUSICOLOGICAL EDITOR

William Meredith, MUSICOLOGICAL EDITOR

Published by the University of Nebraska Press, Lincoln and London,
in association with the American Beethoven Society and the
Ira F. Brilliant Center for Beethoven Studies, San José State University

Library of Congress Cataloging-in-Publication Data
The critical reception of Beethoven's compositions by his German
contemporaries / Wayne M. Senner, general editor, compiler, and
translator; Robin Wallace, musicological editor; William Meredith,
musicological editor.
      p.   cm. — (North American Beethoven Studies; no. 3)
Includes bibliographical references and indexes.
ISBN 0-8032-1250-X (cl. : alk paper, v. 1)
      1. Beethoven, Ludwig van, 1770–1827—Criticism and interpretation.
I. Senner, Wayne M.   II. Wallace, Robin.   III. Meredith, William
Rhea.   IV. Series: North American Beethoven studies; v. 3.
ML410.B42C75   1999
780'.92—dc21   98-55462
                                                                                        CIP
                                                                                        MN

Contents

Acknowledgments

Wayne Senner would like to express his gratitude for the kind support and help rendered by the following libraries and archives during the compilation of the documents published in this volume: Bayerische Staatsbibliothek Munich; Beethoven-Haus, Bonn (in particular, Sieghard Brandenburg); Gesellschaft der Musikfreunde Vienna; Hessische Landes- und Hochschulbibliothek Darmstadt; Kreisarchiv und Wissenschaftliche Bibliothek Bonn; Österreichische Nationalbibliothek Vienna; Stadtarchiv Aachen; Stadtarchiv Trier; Stadtarchiv und Wissenschaftliche Stadtbibliothek Bonn; Stadtbibliothek Nürnberg; Stadt- und Universitätsbibliothek Frankfurt; Theaterbibliothek Porzheim; Universitätsbibliothek Bonn, Universitäts- und Stadtbibliothek Cologne; Universitätsbibliothek Freiburg; Universitätsbibliothek Hamburg; Universitätsbibliothek Heidelberg; Universitätsbibliothek Regensburg; and the University of California, Berkeley, Library. He would also like to thank the German Academic Exchange Service and the Ira F. Brilliant Center for Beethoven Studies (in particular, Ira F. Brilliant and Charles Burdick) for their financial support of this project. Special thanks to Arizona State University for the sabbatical leave to undertake the research and compiling in Germany and Austria.

We would like to thank musicologists Maynard Solomon, for his assistance in the earliest stages of the project, and Robert Oldani, Arizona State University, for his suggestions and comments in later stages.

William Meredith and the Beethoven Center would like to thank Ira F. Brilliant and the late Charles Burdick (former dean of the College of Social Sciences, San José State University) for their financial and moral support of this project. Patricia Elliott Stroh, the center's curator, has lent her expertise and research skills to the project on many occasions. Special thanks are due to Ray White, Library of Congress, for his assistance with the *Berliner allgemeine musikalische Zeitung,* and to James Sealey for his fastidious work on the music examples. Finally, many musicologists assisted with answers to queries; special thanks are due to Jonathan Bellman, Geoffrey Chew, David Fenton, Robert Laudon, Fred Maus, Vivian Ramalingam, Ivan Raykoff, and Piero Weiss.

Robin Wallace would like to thank the staff of the Mickel Library at Converse College for their assistance: Darlene Fawver, Miriam Cody, Wendi Arms, Patsy Copeland, Trudy Cox, Becky Poole, Becky Dalton, Camille McCutcheon, and Wade Woodward. A faculty research grant from Converse in 1996 also helped speed the progress of this edition.

Preface

The project of compiling documents for *The Critical Reception of Beethoven's Compositions by His German Contemporaries* began in 1985 under the auspices of the Ira F. Brilliant Center for Beethoven Studies (San José State University) and at the urging of Ira F. Brilliant, the founder of the center. The focus of my search was based on the names of Beethoven's contemporaries provided in MacArdle, Thayer, and Solomon and on Kirchner, *Die Zeitschriften des deutschen Sprachgebietes von den Anfängen bis 1830* (Stuttgart, 1969), as well as Imogen Fellinger, *Verzeichnis der Musikzeitschriften des 19. Jahrhunderts* (Regensburg, 1968). For the next several years I visited archives; state, city, and university libraries; and newspaper collections in Aachen; Berkeley, California; Berlin; Bonn; Cologne; Darmstadt; Frankfurt; Munich; Nürnberg; Regensburg; and Vienna, searching through many hundreds of periodicals and monographic sources. All materials were collected on microfilm, transferred to xerox copies, and then retyped. During the final stage of my search I checked the documents I had gathered against another German collection, which, unknown to me, a team of German musicologists had been undertaking at the same time and which appeared in 1987 under the title *Ludwig van Beethoven: Die Werke im Spiegel seiner Zeit,* ed. Stefan Kunze (Laaber). The Kunze collection was useful for double-checking my own results. A few documents were also provided by William Meredith (director, Ira F. Brilliant Center for Beethoven Studies) and Robin Wallace (associate professor of music history, Converse College), the musicological editors of the project.

My original intention had been to provide as comprehensive a spectrum of early-nineteenth-century perceptions of Beethoven's works as possible by including letters, memoirs, notes, essays, and sections of larger critical and biographical works, in addition to concert reports and reviews in periodical literature (including a large number of newspapers). By proceeding from a broad base, it was hoped to provide a collection that would be useful to literary historians and scholars in reception aesthetics as well as musicologists. Nevertheless, the materials collected soon became overwhelming, and it was obvious that the principle of selection had to be narrowed. Without notes, commentary and annotations, the introductory essays, and the name and work indexes, the final German-language manuscript still amounted to more than 1,000 single-spaced pages and contained 520 documents. It was then decided to limit the collection to periodical documents, including newspaper sources. It was also decided that because of the large number of sources of biographical materials (*Thayer's Life of Beethoven,* H. C. Robbins Landon, *Beethoven: A Documentary Study,* Maynard Solomon, *Beethoven,* etc.), biographical accounts and anecdotes should be limited as much as the texts allowed. The focus was to be on contemporary perceptions of Beethoven's music, including matters such as audience, setting, facilities, orchestra, instruments, and performers as well as the relationship of Beethoven's music to theoretical and critical ideas of the eighteenth and nineteenth centuries. This principle of selection was not always easy to carry out, given the frequent preoccupation with Beethoven the man *and* composer, and in some passages the biographical information is so closely intertwined with musical analysis that excision would have distorted the document. Even with the more restrictive selection process, the collection will appear in no less than four volumes of approximately 250 pages each.

The translation procedure was as follows. After the translation was completed, the manuscript was given to Professor Gertrud Schuback, a native German translator. Translation corrections were made, annotations added (all historical and literary annotations are my own), and then the manuscript was sent to Professors Meredith and Wallace, who added extensive musicological annotations and offered useful suggestions for improving the translations.

The format of all four volumes is the same, with slight exceptions: volumes 1–3 have introductory essays. Each volume will have name, periodical, subject, and work indexes; volume 4 will have complete name and opus indexes for all four volumes. Volume 1 begins with a general section, which includes documents that deal either with some general aspect of Beethoven's music or with so many different works that assigning the document to a specific opus number seemed fruitless. This section also contains documents that try to present general aesthetic ideas constituting the background of the reception of Beethoven's music or give expression to Beethoven's creativity and artistic powers. Here it was often difficult to excise biographical narrative. The general section is followed by documents on specific opus numbers up to op. 54; volume 2 will begin with op. 55; volume 4 will contain the works without opus numbers. Each document has an entry number, and all documents are numbered consecutively throughout all four volumes. The text of each document is preceded by bibliographic information: author (sometimes unknown, often indicated only by initials or code words, some of which defied identification), title (or the type of information needed from a title) in quotation marks, title of the periodical (in italics), date, and page or column number. Information within quotation marks often indicates the part of the journal the document was taken from (e.g., "News: Leipzig: Winter

Concerts"). Such information was considered to be of importance, for the very position a review, notice, report, or article is given in a publication may reveal something about the writer's or the editor's unexpressed attitude toward Beethoven's works. If the date is part of the document, it is within the quotation marks, if not, it remains outside the quotation marks.

Footnoting from the original document is distinguished from our annotations by quotation marks. The only intrusions into the text are note numbers and measure numbers, the latter indicated with brackets. The orthography of names in the originals was also retained. Cross-references are included at the beginning of each document and at the beginning of each opus number. More precisely, if a document deals with more than one opus number, the additional number is indicated at the beginning of the document. When documents deal with more than one opus number, the documents are placed according to the lowest opus number unless another, higher opus number overwhelmingly dominates the discussion. Documents that deal with a large number of works were placed in the general section.

In the notes stemming from the reviews, we have sought to identify individuals, terms, compositions, locations, and other details that would assist the reader. When formulating factual details for the short biographical notes, we have drawn (without further citation) from many standard reference works and tools: such works as the Kinsky-Halm thematic catalog, Dorfmüller, *Beitrage;* various editions of Thayer's biography; Johnson-Tyson-Winter, *Beethoven Sketchbooks; The New Grove Dictionary of Music and Musicians; Die Musik in Geschichte und Gegenwart;* Frimmel, *Beethoven-Handbuch;* Fétis, *Biographie universelle des musiciens et bibliographie generale de la musique;* Eitner, *Biographisch-bibliographisches Quellen-Lexikon der Musiker und Musikgelehrten;* Anderson, *The Letters of Beethoven;* Sieghard Brandenburg, *Ludwig van Beethoven: Briefwechsel Gesamtausgabe;* Barry Cooper, *The Beethoven Compendium; The Dictionary of Literary Biography;* Imogen Fellinger, *Verzeichnis der Musikzeitschriften des 19. Jahrhunderts;* Joachim Kirchner, *Die Zeitschriften des deutschen Sprachgebiets von den Anfaengen bis 1830, Neue deutsche Biographie, Biographisches Archiv,* and Wilhelm Kosch, *Deutsches Literatur-Lexikon.*

We intended to reproduce the music examples from the original periodicals (in this volume, all of the examples appeared in AMZ and BAMZ). The music examples in BAMZ were not printed originally in a clear enough fashion to be directly reproduced here (the copy of BAMZ in the Library of Congress was used for this volume). Accordingly, the music examples have been reset in modern typography following the originals as closely as possible (including distinctions between staccato dots and strokes). In those cases where the original examples contained mistakes, the corrections have been made here and indicated with brackets. However, the text to the song that is included in the music example for entry no. 138 has been reproduced here from the original example and not the first edition. The indexes were prepared by William Meredith and Patricia Elliott Stroh with assistance from Bonnie Elizabeth Fleming.

Although the original goal was to provide as complete a collection as possible, it is obvious that such a goal cannot be achieved. Nevertheless, these documents, the majority of which appear in English for the first time, should present readers with new insights into the perceptions that Beethoven's contemporaries had of his monumental music.

W. M. Senner

Abbreviations

A	*Abendzeitung nebst Intelligenzblatt für Literatur und Kunst*, Dresden, 1805–06 and 1817–27.
AMA (F)	*Allgemeiner musikalischer Anzeiger nebst einem kritischen Beiblatt Minerva*, Frankfurt, 1826–27.
AMA (V)	*Allgemeiner musikalischer Anzeiger*, Vienna, 1829–40.
AMBT	*Allgemeine Musikzeitung zur Beförderung der theoretischen und praktischen Tonkunst für Musiker und für Freunde der Musik überhaupt*, Frankfurt, 1827–28.
AMZ	*Allgemeine musikalische Zeitung*, Leipzig, 1798–1848.
AMZÖK	*Allgemeine musikalische Zeitung mit besonderer Rücksicht auf den österreichischen Kaiserstaat*, Vienna, 1817–24.
BAMZ	*Berliner allgemeine musikalische Zeitung*, 1824–30.
BMZ	*Berlinische musikalische Zeitung*, 1805–06.
C	*Cäcilia, eine Zeitschrift für die musikalische Welt herausgegeben von einem Vereine von Gelehrten, Kunstverständigen und Künstlern*, Mainz, 1824–48.
F	*Der Freymüthige oder Berlinische Zeitung für gebildete und unbefangene Leser*, Berlin, 1803–30.
HT	*Historisches Taschenbuch: Mit besonder Rücksicht auf die Österreichischen Staaten*, Vienna, 1802, 1807.
I	*Iris im Gebiete der Tonkunst*, Berlin, 1830–41.
JLM	*Journal des Luxus und der Moden*, Weimar, 1785–1814 (continued as *Journal für Literatur, Kunst, Luxus und Mode*, Weimar, 1814–26).
JR	*Journal de la Roer*, 1811–14.
JT	*Jahrbuch der Tonkunst von Wien und Prag*, 1796.
KZ	*Kölnische Zeitung*, 1801–08.
L	*Libussa*, Jahrbuch für 1845, Prague.
MAM	*Münchener allgemeine Musikzeitung*, 1827–29.
MC	*Musikalische Correspondenz der teutschen filharmonischen Gesellschaft für das Jahr 1791*, Speier.
ME	*Musikalische Eilpost*, Weimar, 1826.
MGS	*Morgenblatt für gebildete Stände*, Stuttgart, 1807–30.
MM	*Magazin der Musik*, Hamburg, 1783–86.
MT	*Musikalisches Taschenbuch*, Penig, 1803–05.

MZ   *Musikalische Zeitung für die österreichischen Staaten*, Linz, 1812–13.

T   *Thalia: Ein Abendblatt, den Freunden der dramatischen Muse geweiht*, Vienna and Trieste, 1810–11.

WAMZ   *Wiener allgemeine musikalische Zeitung*, Vienna, 1813.

WJ   *Wiener Journal für Theater, Musik und Mode*, Vienna, 1813.

WZ   *Wiener Zeitung*, Vienna, 1780–

ZEW   *Zeitung für die elegante Welt*, Leipzig, 1801–30.

ZTM   *Zeitung für Theater und Musik zur Unterhaltung gebildeter, unbefangener Leser: Eine Begleiterin des Freymüthigen*, Berlin, 1821–1827 (after 1822 *Zeitung für Theater, Musik und bildende Künste, Beilage zum Freymüthigen*).

Viennese and European Currencies, 1792–1827

Because of changes in types of money used, the introduction of paper money, inflationary pressures, and the 1811 devaluation of Austrian currency, it is not possible to present a simple, single chart illustrating the values of currency from 1792 to 1827. The following discussion is heavily indebted to the work of Julia Moore.

1792–1811

When Beethoven arrived in Vienna in 1792, the standard currency was the Conventionsmünze (CM) florin, which was issued as a silver coin also called a silver gulden. One CM florin was divided into 60 kreuzer. The gold coin in circulation was called the ducat and was worth 4.5 CM florins:

$$1 \text{ ducat} = 4.5 \text{ CM florins}$$
$$1 \text{ CM florin} = 60 \text{ kreuzer}$$

In 1795 the Austrian government issued its first paper currency, Bankozettel (BZ) florins. Initially, one BZ florin equaled one CM florin. However, due to inflationary pressures arising from the requirement to finance the wars against Napoleon, the BZ florin constantly lost value from 1796 through 1811. The following chart lists these values:

Value of CM florin compared to BZ florin, 1795–1811

Year	CM florins (silver guldens)	BZ florins (annual average)
1795	100	100.00
1796	100	100.13
1797	100	101.61

Year	CM florins (silver guldens)	BZ florins (annual average)
1798	100	101.06
1799	100	107.83
1800	100	114.91
1801	100	115.75
1802	100	121.67
1803	100	130.75
1804	100	134.24
1805	100	135.25
1806	100	173.01
1807	100	209.43
1808	100	228.15
1809	100	296.03
1810	100	492.12
1811	100	500.00

Source: Moore, *Beethoven and Musical Economics*, p. 123.

1811–19

In July 1810 Emperor Franz II appointed Count Joseph Wallis as his finance minister. The BZ florin suffered continuing devaluation until February 1811. The devaluation continued because (1) the Austrian government focused almost exclusively on the problem of the declining value of the BZ florin and failed to take into account the relation of consumer prices to the amount of paper money in circulation and because (2) Count Wallis had "no recorded expertise in finance." In February 1811 a state bankruptcy was declared. The terms of the bankruptcy were laid out in a *Finanzpatent* with the following terms:

1. All currency, including BZ florins, were called in and replaced with a new paper florin, the Wiener Währung (WW).
2. The exchange rate was 1 WW florin for 5 BZ florins.
3. BZ florins remained legal tender until 1 January 1812.
4. All prices were to be divided by five.

During the next few years, inflation and currency devaluation wreaked havoc on those who held cash assets and on salaried employees, since they effectively lost four-fifths of the value of their income's purchasing power. The new WW florin failed to maintain a stable value against a theoretical silver gulden (which had last been produced in 1809). Another state bankruptcy was narrowly averted in 1816. Instead of prosperity, the conclusion of the Napoleonic Wars brought a recession to the Austrian economy.

Value of CM florin compared to WW florin, 1811–19

Year	CM florins	WW florins (annual average)
1811	100	218.75
1812	100	201.83
1813	100	159.16
1814	100	228.79
1815	100	351.06
1816	100	327.04
1817	100	332.82
1818	100	255.39
1819	100	249.19

Source: Moore, *Beethoven and Musical Economics*, p. 124.

1817–27

In 1817 Count Stadion founded the Privileged Austrian National Bank, an institution funded in part with private capital but serving as the government banker. The CM silver gulden was gradually reintroduced through the new bank and its value stabilized by May 1818 at 2.5 WW florins. Thereafter during Beethoven's lifetime, CM and WW florins remained in circulation at the relatively stable value of 1 CM florin for 2.5 WW florins. (See Moore, *Beethoven and Musical Economics*, pp. 128–30).

Viennese Currency Abbreviations

fl	gulden (florin)
BZ	Bankozettel
ww	Wiener Währung
CM	Conventionsmünze
d	ducat
k	kreuzer

Paper gulden: BZ (in circulation until 1811)
                   ww (in circulation from 1811)
Silver gulden: CM (out of circulation 1809–18)

OTHER EUROPEAN CURRENCIES (1800–18)

To calculate exchange rates during Beethoven's lifetime, it is necessary to adjust for inflation as outlined above.

1. English pound (before 1800 and after 1818)
1 pound equals 11 CM florins, 2.4 ducats, or 20 shillings.
2. German Reichsthaler (before 1800 and after 1818)
3 Reichsthaler equals 1 ducat or 4.5 florins.
3. French Louis d'or
1 Louis d'or equals 2 ducats or 9 florins.
4. Italian zecchinos
1 zecchino equals 1.2 ducats or 5.5 florins.

BIBLIOGRAPHY ON CURRENCY RATES DURING BEETHOVEN'S LIFETIME

Cooper, Barry. "Economics and Logistics," in *Beethoven's Folksong Settings.* Oxford: Clarendon Press, 1994.

Hanson, Alice M. "Incomes and Outgoings in the Vienna of Beethoven and Schubert." *Music and Letters* 64 (1983): 173–83.

———. *Musical Life in Biedermeier Vienna.* Cambridge: Cambridge University Press, 1985.

Moore, Julia. "Beethoven and Inflation." *Beethoven Forum*, vol. 1. Lincoln: University of Nebraska Press, 1992.

———. *Beethoven and Musical Economics.* Ph.D. diss., University of Illinois, Urbana-Champaign, 1987.

Morrow, Mary Sue. *Concert Life in Haydn's Vienna: Aspects of a Developing Musical and Social Institution.* Stuyvesant NY: Pendragon Press, 1989.

Pribram, Alfred Frances. *Materialen zur Geschichte der Preise und Löhne in Österreich.* Vienna: Carl Ueberreuter, 1938.

The Critical Reception of Beethoven's Compositions
by His German Contemporaries, VOLUME I

Introduction

Beethoven's Critics and the Evolution of Music and Literary Aesthetics in Eighteenth- and Early-Nineteenth-Century Germany

This essay surveys the philosophic, aesthetic, and cultural backgrounds that form the historical basis for the reception of Beethoven's music in German periodical literature. After a sketch of the growth of this literature and public concerts and the introduction of some basic concepts underlying the writings of nineteenth-century music critics, the development of music criticism is traced from the philosophical systems of Descartes and Leibniz through the beginnings of aesthetics in Baumgarten's work to the music criticism of the Enlightenment as represented in the writings of Gottsched, Krause, Scheibe, and Mattheson. The final section of the essay deals with the yielding of the Enlightenment doctrine of affects to new aesthetic values offered by Herder, Schiller, and Kant and with the emergence of Romantic criticism.

BASIC CONCEPTS IN THE RECEPTION OF BEETHOVEN'S MUSIC AND THE EMERGENCE OF JOURNALS AND PUBLIC CONCERTS

The critical reception of Beethoven's compositions by his contemporaries embodies a broad spectrum of aesthetic categories that range from Enlightenment ideas such as "clarity," "simplicity," "nature," and "unity" to early-nineteenth-century ideas such as "romantic," "hieroglyphic," "dark," "infinite yearning," and so on, to cite just a few examples offered on the following pages. Even Beethoven's earliest critics were concerned with this spectrum of ideas and attempted to sort out and categorize the disparity of judgments of Beethoven's art during the composer's lifetime. In an article written for the *Berliner allgemeine musikalische Zeitung*, A. B. Marx offered one general account of the reasons why Beethoven's contemporaries passed so many judgments about his music that Marx considered to be *distorted*: "Actually the leaders in affairs of music were trained during the Mozart period and not just a few of them remained at this level. The works that these leaders inculcated in their pupils in every sense of the word as the guiding principle, law, and measure of all later achievement were those that they had embraced with youthful vigor and sensitivity. . . . They served as the foundation for their systems, or older systems had adjusted to them."[1] Although Marx does not cite examples of "distorted judgments," contemporary periodicals are filled with almost endless advice, condemnation, and praise of an immense diversity, unlimited to any period in Beethoven's life.

From the very beginning, correspondents were eager to advise Beethoven and inform the public on a number of principles they deemed necessary for good composition. Take, for example, one of their more common concerns about music composition, the qualities of simplicity, clarity, and unity: "His abundance of ideas . . . still causes him to pile up ideas without restraint and to arrange them by means of a bizarre manner so as to bring about an obscure artificiality or an artificial obscurity, which is disadvantageous rather than advantageous to the effect of the entire piece."[2] Also in 1799, a reviewer for the same periodical, the *Allgemeine musikalische Zeitung,* seethed about the lack of traditional concepts such as melody and nature and condemned Beethoven's work for its difficult, learned style: "But what a bizarre, laborious way! Studied, studied, and perpetually studied, and no nature, no song."[3] Even after Beethoven's death, similar complaints were offered to the public: "Unlike *Mozart* and *Haydn,* he does not know how to give his works that beautiful proportion in the individual sections. All too often he strays into areas from which he can only return with cold and chilling effects."[4]

Nevertheless, while some critics believed Beethoven had abandoned well-tested ideas such as unity, simplicity, beauty, clarity, melody, and nature when he ceased to follow the path of Mozart, others saw his discoveries not as a departure from Mozart but as an "artistic deed" that "opened the romantic world, in which Mozart's dramatic music moves, for instrumental music too."[5] Instead of judging music as mimesis of abstract, universal nature,[6] they envisioned nature as an organic metaphor in the service of hermeneutic criticism: "Beethoven ascended like youth decorated with all the colors of spring. He seats himself upon mountains. Wildly his steeds rush forth: brooding, he holds the reins firmly so that they rear at the precipice. He, however, peers into the abyss as if he had buried something down there. Then he bounds across the gaping crevices and proceeds home, playing as if in mockery or blustering as if in a storm. And that something in the depths strangely gazes after him—that is also life."[7] Turning away from traditional views such as neoclassical mimesis, some proclaimed a new-found philosophy of transcendental music: "He knows all the depths and secrets of art, and perhaps he has gone far beyond that which constitutes actual art. . . . His holy music will long be studied as exemplary."[8] Others tried to portray Beethoven's music as an appeaser of advocates of both old and new aesthetic systems: "However, that a glowing fantasy, a high flight of powerful and ingenious harmonies prevails in it throughout, is admitted even by those who hold clarity and songfulness to be the highest degree of art."[9] And some infused former negative values such as *dunkel* (obscure, dark) with a new sense of imagination and added them to a growing lexicon of new critical ciphers such as "romantic," "novel-like," and "hieroglyphic."[10] Finally, there were even those who saw in Beethoven's music such a total transformation of aesthetic values that they came to regard his music as a pedagogical model for the next generation of composers, as seen in this evaluation of Hector Berlioz: "Here, all the rules were trampled on, and only the unbridled fantasy of the composer dominated throughout. . . . It is just too bad that it is without any education. If he had this, perhaps he would become a Beethoven."[11]

As Marx intimated, the great disparity of opinions of Beethoven's music has its roots in the sporadic and fragmented development of the philosophy of aesthetics in the eighteenth century. Before 1750, sources containing aesthetic thought were dispersed among a variety of materials. They ranged from pedagogical and religious texts to books on composition and performance such as Johann Mattheson's *Das neue eröffnete Orchester* (1713) and Johann Kühnau's satirical novel *Der musikalische Quacksalber* (1700), which offers early insights into German views of the mathematical basis of music aesthetics, the doctrine of affects, and the new Italian vocal music. No homogenous philosophy of music appears until the middle of the century, when the philosophical ideas of Descartes, Leibniz, and Baumgarten had become established at German universities and periodical literature bearing the fruits of their ideas had begun to appear in rapidly increasing numbers, signaling a sudden, vast growth in the institutions of public knowledge.

The sudden ballooning of music criticism in music periodicals after the middle of the eighteenth century is all the more astonishing if one considers the fact that the first German scholarly periodical did not appear until late in the seventeenth century (Christian Thomasius's *Monatsgespräche,* 1688) and that the first German periodical devoted to music criticism was Mattheson's *Critica Musica* (1722–25, rpt. 1964), which appeared just seventy-six years before the primogenitor of modern music criticism, *Allgemeine musikalische Zeitung* (1798–1850).

A number of early critics and writers attempted to establish music periodicals to deal with increasing compositional activity and the growing interest in public concerts. Such attempts, however, remained sporadic and short-lived throughout the century, victims of financial failures, the lack of a network of skilled correspondents, and, particularly at the end of the century, the frequent interruptions of wars. Following the lead of Mattheson's *Critica Musica,* Lorenz Christoph Mizler (1711–78), a professor of music and mathematics at the University of Leipzig, offered reports and news about concerts in his *Neu eröffnete musikalische Bibliothek* (1736–54), as did Friedrich W. Marpurg (1718–95) with his *Historische-kritische Beiträge zur Aufnahme der Musik* (1754–62, 1778) and Johann A. Hiller (1728–1804) in his *Wöchentliche Nachrichten und Anmerkungen, die Musik betreffend* (1766–70). Heinrich Christoph Koch's short-lived venture with *Journal der Tonkunst* (1795; one issue only) at the beginning of the French invasions of Germany serves as an important example of how political and military events of the time could not only influence the content of journals (as well as public music life) but quickly weaken and bring an end to publishing enterprises, as was also the case with Friedrich Reichardt's *Berlinische musikalische Zeitung* (1805–1806) during the Napoleonic invasion of 1806. Much music criticism in the early journals was quite different from the musicological analyses found in many of the periodicals of the Beethoven era because of the early journal's primary concern with the evaluation of musical works according to normative, binding principles. That is to say, up to the age of Beethoven, music critics investigated works of music according to rules of music composition and reported the pros and cons of the composer's success in avoiding errors of theory.

The titles of the periodicals containing music criticism both before and during the Beethoven era also raise an important question as to whether we are dealing with journals or newspapers. The most frequent word used in titles is *Zeitung* (newspaper), and a handful of editors used titles such as *Journal* (*Journal des Luxus und der Moden,* Weimar, 1800–14), *-blatt* (*Morgenblatt für gebildete Stände,* Stuttgart, 1807–30), *Taschenbuch* (*Musikalisches Taschenbuch,* Penig, 1803–05), *Anzeiger* (*Allgemeiner musikalischer Anzeiger* 1826–27), and *Nachrichten* (Hiller's *Wöchentliche Nachrichten,* 1766–70), and so on. Only one music periodical, *Cäcilia* (1824–), uses the term *Zeitschrift* (journal) in its title. By reducing the coverage of actual music happenings and focusing on critical elements, *Cäcilia,* the namesake of the patroness of church music, fits more in line with literary theoretical periodicals of the eighteenth century and the scholarly journals of present times.

Why the popularity of the term *Zeitung?* Although the first European newspaper did not appear until 1702 in London, the reporting of news already had a long tradition in various written forms (broadsheets, almanacs, church notices, etc.). By the end of the eighteenth century, reporting the news of events, including concerts, had become a very popular way of attracting a broad public. This may explain why major journals such as the *Allgemeine musikalische Zeitung, Berliner allgemeine musikalische Zeitung* (1824–30), and *Wiener allgemeine musikalische Zeitung* (1813) not only preferred *Zeitung* to *Zeitschrift* but also included the word *allgemein,* used to mean *general,* whereas in reality there was little to distinguish their philosophical contributions from those in *Cäcilia.*

After the many short-lived music periodical ventures of the eighteenth century, Leipzig's *Allgemeine musikalische Zeitung* represents an astonishing accomplishment in the history of music criticism.[12] In appearance alone, the AMZ, with its double columns typical of newspapers and large quarto format, twice the size of many eighteenth-century periodicals, is a signal product of the fast-growing and highly educated middle class with its increasing thirst for reading materials of more specialized, challenging, and detailed content.[13] The times were ripe for the appearance of AMZ, for not only did the founding of the periodical come at the beginning of Beethoven's meteoric career, it also received its support from one of the most established families in the publishing business, the Breitkopfs. With a long-standing interest in German literature and music, the Breitkopfs had also published one of Germany's earliest music criticism journals, *Der critische Musicus* (1737), edited by the Gottsched protégé Johann A. Scheibe (1708–76).

An avid student of the German Enlightenment and the young new executive of the Breitkopf publishing company, Gottfried Christoph Härtel first tried to enlist the services of the Enlightenment music scholar Johann Hiller as editor of AMZ. Hiller was a composer of *Singspiele* and editor of one of the Enlightenment's music periodicals, *Wöchentliche Nachrichten und Anmerkungen, die Musik betreffend* (1766–70). At age seventy and facing a much more competitive market than during the middle decades of the German Enlightenment, Hiller proposed a young, upcoming author, Johann Friedrich Rochlitz (1769–1842), as editor. A librettist for Weber, Spohr, and Schubert and author of the four-volume work *Für Freunde der Tonkunst* (1824–32), which contains a wealth of information on the music scenes of the Beethoven era, Rochlitz played a major role not only in introducing Beethoven's works to the reading public but also in keeping J. S. Bach before the public and supporting the young Wagner. Although Rochlitz was a great advocate of Mozart, his university studies of Kantian aesthetics, which broke with the audience-oriented doctrine of affects of the Enlightenment, provided him with the insights necessary to appreciate the revolutionary aspects of Beethoven's music. They made him the ideal mediator for Beethoven's music, while still maintaining an understanding for older schools of music aesthetics. As editor and critic, Rochlitz is symbolic of the new direction of music criticism. Like him, many major critics of the age of Beethoven, for example, E. T. A. Hoffmann, Gottfried Weber (both of whom Rochlitz engaged as reviewers for AMZ), Friedrich Reichardt (editor of BMZ), Amadeus Wendt (professor of philosophy in Leipzig and Göttingen), and A. B. Marx (editor of BAMZ), were not only skilled musicians or composers but also authors with a thorough knowledge of German philosophy and literary theory and criticism. The educational background of these primary critics of Beethoven's music strongly speaks for the necessity of a combined study of literary and music criticism and theory to arrive at a balanced understanding of the basic concepts of music criticism as they appear in the documents of this period.

Like the music periodicals of the eighteenth century, AMZ also felt the severe consequences of war. On the one hand, the impact of the Napoleonic wars is reflected in the reactions to a resurgence of and reviews of patriotic music. On the other, the political reactions to the war, combined with censorship and the crackdown on liberal ideas, forced precarious decisions on the editorial staff in order to deal with the circumstances of its continued existence. Finally, the failing health of Rochlitz, the departure of major critics such as E. T. A. Hoffmann and Gottfried Weber, the founding of several competitive journals, and changes in editorial policy led to a weakening of the AMZ and eventually to Rochlitz's replacement by Härtel. Although Härtel had been an important publisher of Beethoven's works during the Rochlitz years, his break with the composer and the loss of good critics weakened the AMZ and subsequently reduced the journal's interest in Beethoven's music.[14] After 1820, few reviews of Beethoven's works appeared, most being of minor works. Following his death, scathing attacks on his late works demonstrate how significantly the relationship between the greatest composer and the most influential music periodical of the early nineteenth century had changed.

The AMZ is important because its editors and critics worked in close conjunction with the music scene in Vienna and because of its cleverly developed network of correspondents. To assure a broad readership, the AMZ not only assumed the format of a popular newspaper but enlisted the reporting skills of music patrons in 224 German communities from all corners of the world. The AMZ thus presents us with a vivid picture of music performances around Germany as well as insights into the critical reception of major and minor German and foreign composers. In addition, it offers lists of new works and essays on topics ranging from music history and the construction of instruments to music theory and aesthetics.

The success of the AMZ is also mirrored in distinct changes in public performances that had taken place by the end of the eighteenth century and in the relationship of public concerts to music reviewing and criticism. Any attempt to find the eighteenth-century predecessors of music reviews and reports of the frequency and kind that filled the pages of the AMZ, BAMZ, or WAMZ is frustrated by the lack of a clear picture of the evolution of public concerts.[15] To be sure, one can trace music reviews back to Johann Mattheson, but for the most part Mattheson, like many critics of the middle decades of the eighteenth century, focused on how works of art agreed with theoretical prescriptions and possibilities rather than serving as a chronicler of public music life. Obtaining an accurate picture of public concerts is even more complicated by eighteenth-century differences of opinion on the actual existence of public concerts. As late as 1775, Charles Burney hardly mentions public concerts in his *Present State of Music in Germany, the Netherlands, and the United Provinces*. Yet Friedrich Nicolai (1733–1811) reports heavy attendance of concerts in Berlin in his *Briefe über den itzigen Zustand der schönen Wissenschaften in Deutschland* (1755).

The lack of public concerts before the earliest ventures by Telemann (Frankfurt, 1713–) also precluded the necessity of critical reviewing. For that reason, much music criticism is embedded in various textbooks and theoretical treatises until the latter part of the century when the growth of public concerts and journalistic writing increased rapidly, particularly in Berlin, Leipzig, and Vienna. During the last decades of the eighteenth century, earlier forms of music performance such as the Concerts Spirituels, Collegia Musica, and theater interlude music yielded to the growing popularity of a large variety of public performances. These included free concerts, subscription concerts (such as those offered by Mozart), garden and café concerts, benefit and dilettante concerts, and music festivals such as the earliest large open-air concert at Frankenhausen (1810) and the Rhineland festivals of the 1820s, in addition to the traditional *Hausmusik* of the nobility. In response to the growth of public interest in music performance, cities began to provide concert halls like the Gewandhaus in Leipzig and the Kärntnerth or theater and Burgtheater in Vienna or regular amateur concerts in the open such as the Augarten series in Vienna (1787–   ) and established professional orchestras (Leipzig) and academies like the Berlin *Singakademie* (1790, by Karl Fasch)[16] and the Leipzig Singverein. Public art events were so successful that by 1784 the University of Göttingen music director Johann Forkel (1749–1818) was able to boast of nearly 400 living composers in German-speaking Europe. Writers were quick to seize on the importance of public events and the rapidly increasing thirst for information and knowledge. By the last decade of the century the number of literary periodicals alone in Germany had increased from 1 (1688) to 323 (1790).

As stated earlier, the wide divergence of ideas describing Beethoven's music derives from the collision of a long and slow maturation of aesthetic ideas in a few scattered sources during the eighteenth century with the appearance of new views that were held by only a small group of men of letters but that were telescoped by the explosion of periodical literature. The development of criticism and theory preceding the Beethoven era took place in a manner that directly mirrors German cultural history. The circumstances that shaped the intellectual climate of Germany in the eighteenth century can be attributed in part to the fact that for much of German history there had been two cultures: the courtly culture of governing society and the popular culture of the peasantry. With the emergence of the middle class in the eighteenth century and its gradual dominance of the financial and educational world, the other two cultures were driven into smaller and smaller enclaves and came to be regarded as morally and culturally inferior.

Without a standing cultural tradition and in opposition to the two existing cultures, men of letters developed a lack of trust in the public taste. In fact, the concept of "public" was nearly nonexistent. In his famous *Versuch einer critischen Dichtkunst,* Johann Christoph Gottsched (1700–66), Germany's most well-known scholar of the first half of the century, seems unaware of the concept of a public and arrogantly snubs the taste of the general populace as unschooled and primitive: "All of this leads to the conclusion that a poet must not turn to the taste of his times and places but must follow the rules of the ancients and the examples of great poets."[17] While this seems somewhat incomprehensible today, a look at Germany in the early eighteenth century reveals an almost barren wasteland of culture. Ravaged by the destruction of the Thirty Years' War, Germany had almost no cultural institutions for the public. At the beginning of the century there was essentially only one scholarly journal, no newspapers, no public libraries, no theaters, no picture galleries, no museums, no botanical gardens, no travel (unless one was rich), and no public concerts until Telemann offered the first one in Frankfurt in 1713. Even this early example illustrates that the idea of self-supporting concerts was so foreign to composers such as Telemann that tickets had to be sold under the guise of purchasing a booklet, the proceeds of which were promised to the poor. The picture we have of Germany less than a century before the flood of Beethoven criticism was widespread cultural impoverishment with the masses ignorant of much of the world and consuming all of their earnings for food, shelter, and clothing.

The typical daily life of the middle class was very orderly and conservative. Days were set apart at regular intervals for formal calls for bloodlettings, family celebrations, weddings, christenings, funerals, and the many festivals such as Christmas, Mayday, Midsummerday, Martinmas, and so on. The festivals did, however, contribute to the development of *Hausmusik* and in some way were conducive to the evolution of public and private concerts. On religious holidays, music was prohibited in many churches, which led to the performance of religious music for the public outside the church. Generally, however, such concerts had a local or congregational character.

PHILOSOPHY AND THE EMERGENCE OF AESTHETICS

Given the social and political circumstances described above, there were serious obstacles in the way of the emergence of a systematic philosophy of music criticism as the product of public music experience. The merging of two important academic traditions at German universities, however, one ancient, and one a modern change in philosophical direction, opened a new avenue of innovation within an antiquated educational system.

The first tradition is rooted in the nature of the academic curriculum, which had remained essentially the same since the Reformation. The subjects of instruction at German universities were strictly prescribed: Latin, Greek, dialectics, rhetoric, mathematics and Aristotelian philosophy, and theology. Lectures at the universities were held in Latin until the eighteenth century, and professional research was conditioned by the well-established principle of rhetoric and grammarian philology, which during the Renaissance became the *terminus technicus critica*. This highly respected tradition did bring about the widespread practice of the discipline called *critica*. One of the earliest uses of the word is found in a work by the Dutch scholar Jan Wower, who in 1602 applied the term *critica* to two tasks: *iudicium,* which ascertained the authenticity of classical writings through grammatical and rhetorical analysis, and *emendatio,* which improved misreadings.[18] During the next 150 years this literary practice was gradually separated from its philological past through the debate on taste and the introduction of the philosophical systems of Descartes, Leibniz, and Alexander Baumgarten to university curricula, which initiated the decisive philosophical turn toward aesthetics, the second part of the educational equation.

René Descartes (1596–1650) exercised perhaps the most important influence on German thinking before Immanuel Kant.[19] Descartes sought to bring systematic order to philosophical inquiry by rejecting dogmatic authority and making reason the primary judge of truth. He advocated a common scientific method for all philosophical disciplines, a fact that was to have important consequences for the branching out of the philosophy of aesthetics into music and literary criticism during the eighteenth century. Descartes believed that the scientific mind could avoid error if man applied the natural rules of intuition and deduction. Certain routes to knowledge could be obtained with the use of innate ideas, which he called "clear" and "distinct" and which he believed were implanted in the mind by nature or God and could not be derived from sense-experience. Descartes, however, had a great distrust for empirical experience and external stimuli: "Yet I have found that these senses sometimes deceive me, and it is a matter of prudence never to confide completely in those who have deceived us once."[20] For Descartes, sense perceptions are related to external stimuli, which arouse "obscure" and indefinable emotions. These in turn agitate and disturb the soul and thus disrupt the logical processing of clear and distinct ideas. He abhorred imagination, and even though he wrote a treatise on music, he refused to admit music into his rationalistic system of logical reasoning.[21]

Nevertheless, when Descartes discusses the feelings and emotions of the soul as being caused by some movement of the spirits in reaction to external stimuli in his *Passions of the Soul,* he is laying the modern philosophical foundation for one of the most important theories of eighteenth-century music aesthetics: the so-called doctrine of affects.[22] In fact, his *Compendium musicae* contains one of the earliest modern statements of this doctrine: "As regards the various emotions which music can arouse by employing various meters, I will say that in general a slower pace arouses in us quieter feelings such as languor, sadness, fear, pride etc. A faster pace arouses faster emotions such as joy."[23]

Cartesian reasoning found its most renowned German advocate in the philosophy of Gottfried Leibniz (1646–1716). A man of universal genius with encyclopedic knowledge, Leibniz is the first great German philosopher of modern Europe. His importance for aesthetics lies in his *Monadology,* which appeared in 1714 and became popular at German universities, particularly at eastern universities such as the University of Halle, a center of the German Enlightenment.[24] For Leibniz, the basis of metaphysics was the individual consciousness, which he referred to as the "soul." Leibniz chose the unusual name "monad" for this spiritual substance, which he viewed as universal, ranging from simple elements of things to human souls with consciousness. Monads are active and develop from one degree of clarity to another in a process directed toward achieving perfection or absolute clarity.[25] All monads (like nature in neoclassical aesthetics) mirror the preestablished harmony of the universe, but in differing degrees of perception. Some creatures have confused perceptions such as the sense of smell, color, and sound, and others, namely human beings, have distinct perceptions and can perceive abstractions by means of reason. Only human beings possess both degrees of perception, obscure and distinct.

The next step in the development of aesthetics in Germany was the advancement of Cartesian philosophy to include the concepts of pre-established harmony and continuity of the universe, which theoretically allowed not only for a science of logic (distinct perceptions) but also for a science of what were referred to, in scholastic terms, as obscure perceptions: sound, color, and shape, later to be recognized as the most basic elements of the major forms of art.

In the history of German philosophy and criticism, Alexander Baumgarten (1714–62) is regarded as the founder of the science of aesthetics. In his *Meditationes philosophicae de nonnullis poema pertinentibus* (1735), Baumgarten, for the first time in Western European civilization, used the term "aesthetics" to refer to the arts in general, including poetry, music, sculpture, architecture, and painting. With his concept of "aesthetica," he established the scientific basis for one of the most enduring principles of art in the eighteenth and nineteenth centuries: mimesis of nature as the mirror of a perfect and well-ordered universe. This concept also provides a philosophical foundation for the frequent references to the words "nature" and "natural" in much music criticism. For Baumgarten, aesthetics was a subordinate form of the science of logic. Although subordinate, it was equally valid as a science of sense perceptions, or the "confused" and "obscure" ideas of Cartesian philosophy: "Therefore, *things known* are to be known by the superior faculty as the object of logic; *things perceived* [are to be known by the inferior faculty, as the object] of the science of perception, or aesthetic."[26]

Baumgarten hierarchically divided "confused" ideas into "obscure" and "clear," "clear" approximating uniform and harmonious order (e.g., normal everyday speech, without an apparent, self-contained order, might be categorized as "obscure" whereas a poem would be defined as "perfect, sensate speech"). Following the Cartesian principle of a single method of investigation, Baumgarten founded his science on the basis of the Beautiful. The Beautiful differentiates art from philosophy (the science of abstract knowledge) and is defined as the perfection of sense perceptions. Basic to this method of analogous thinking is the belief held by Baumgarten and other scholars of the Enlightenment that if metaphysics and logic had systematic and normative concepts, the arts belonging to aesthetics were also in need of a scientifically founded system of laws. Accordingly, and in the framework of Enlightenment ideology, philosophy should attempt to reduce all aesthetic phenomena to a single principle, a principle that was to have profound consequences for eighteenth-century views of vocal and instrumental music and was to form the foundation for many observations on Beethoven's early instrumental music. With the emergence of music and literary criticism during the Enlightenment, the philosophical concepts of "clarity," "nature," "perfection," and "the Beautiful" became major building blocks in music aesthetics and basic lexical terms of criticism in the reception of Beethoven's compositions.[27]

FROM PHILOSOPHICAL AESTHETICS TO LITERATURE AND MUSIC AESTHETICS

The philosophical ideas that led to the founding of aesthetics as a field of inquiry soon appeared in lectures at German universities (Baumgarten at Frankfurt an der Oder and Christian Wolff [1679–1754] at Halle) and in practical criticism in the works of Johann Christoph Gottsched. As a professor at the University of Leipzig, he became the mentor of the Enlightenment music critic Johann Scheibe and copublisher with a second nearly as well-known music critic, Lorenz Christoph Mizler. Gottsched also worked with the leading composers of his times, including J. S. Bach, writing librettos for church music and operettas for the theater in Leipzig (the birthplace, seventy years later, of the most significant music journal of the Beethoven era: AMZ).[28] His major work appeared in 1730 under the title *Versuch einer critischen Dichtkunst*. *Versuch* provided the model for critical treatises on poetry and music throughout the first half of the century. The title itself suggests Gottsched's desire to make criticism a systematic science and the critic a philosopher with a knowledge of poetry and music. It also reflects the general belief in the concept of the artist-scholar.[29] Gottsched bases his understanding on the premise that if metaphysics, ethics, and theology are sciences with universal laws, then poetry and music too must have similar universal laws; Gottsched did not hesitate to apply his laws to his discussions of literary and musical works as well.

Without going into Gottsched's intricate descriptions for poetic and music genres, I shall simply state here that primary to all forms of artistic expression were rhetorical principles such as clarity, probability, uniformity, regularity, and above all, beauty. In Gottsched's eyes, the test for beauty was clarity:

the lack of clarity and uniformity distorted beauty and led to what was commonly referred to as "Bizarrerie," a term frequently applied to Beethoven's music.[30] The goal of all artistic expression was to stir the audience to a deeper understanding of moral and community betterment. To substantiate their aesthetic principles, Gottsched and other philosopher-critics relied on the authority of classical rhetoric (Gottsched on Horace, Krause on Quintilian, and Johann Mattheson on Cicero) and claimed that music, like its "superior sister," must communicate ideas (Krause: "Each tone is a thought").[31] Armed with the authority of classical antiquity, Gottsched proclaimed vocal music to be superior to instrumental music: the primal human instrument was the human voice.

ENLIGHTENMENT MUSIC AESTHETICS AND CRITICISM

The terminology used and principles basic to the music treatises of the Enlightenment show a remarkable continuity of major ideas from Descartes, Leibniz, Baumgarten, and Gottsched, which is not surprising since Baumgarten and Gottsched either worked with or mentored the major figures of the period. Christian Gottfried Krause (1719–70), a student of Baumgarten, reiterates the central position of mimesis in his treatise *Von der musikalischen Poesie,* in which he argues that clarity and harmony in the imitation of natural order through music instruct and communicate to man in a way that goes beyond science: "The admiration and love of order and proportion, be it where it may, naturally improves the character, is productive of social inclination, and offers a very great aid to virtue, which last is itself nothing other than love of order and beauty in society. . . . In none of the fine arts is there so much order and excellent relationship as in music." When Krause claims that all the aesthetic disciplines have a precise connection with one another, he reaffirms the Cartesian method, and in his assertion that music awakens "obscure" (dark) ideas he is using precisely the terms Baumgarten set aside for the science of aesthetics. In fact, reaffirming Baumgarten's differentiation between distinct ideas of logic and clear ideas of aesthetic perception, Krause warns against artful devices, excessive elaboration, ornamentation, and repetition, which can cause clarity to "increase to the point of distinctness" (a concept restricted by aestheticians to logic), resulting in "learned" music, which must be played out many times before it is understood.[32] As such, it will fail to move the heart to virtue and speak only to the intellect, objections often applied to Beethoven's music by his contemporaries.[33]

Scheibe, a student of Gottsched, who had arranged to have J. S. Bach write the music for one of Gottsched's funeral odes and later became a vociferous opponent of Bach, offers a lexical catalog of objections to Bach's music in his own periodical *Der critische Musicus,* objections that are repeated by Beethoven's critics:

This great man would be admired by the whole nation, had he more agreeableness and did he not keep naturalness away from his compositions by employing bombastic and intricate devices and darkening beauty with over-elaborate art. He judges the difficulties of his music according to his fingers. His compositions, therefore, are difficult to perform, as he demands that singers and instrumentalists perform with their throats and instruments the same feats he can perform on the clavier. This, of course, is impossible. All the ornaments, all the little grace notes, and all that are known as *agréments* are written out in full. Therefore his compositions are deprived of beauty, of harmony, and of clarity of melody, since the song is unrecognizable. All voices must work with each other, all with the same weight, so that it is impossible to recognize the principal voice. In short, Bach is to music what Lohenstein is to poetry.[34] Their inclination toward bombast led them both from naturalness to artificiality, from sublimity to want of clearness. With both one admires the laborious effort and the exceptional work expended in vain because they are not conformable to reason.[35]

The principles in Scheibe's treatise mentioned above are perfected in the work of perhaps the most influential critic and theorist of the Enlightenment: Johann Mattheson. Mattheson was a musician of extraordinary talent, having learned almost all the instruments of the eighteenth-century orchestra. He sang and directed opera in Hamburg but was forced to retire to writing and composing when he lost his hearing. He published two important music journals, *Critica musica* (1722–25) and *Der musikalische Patriot* (1728). His most important work, however, was *Der vollkommene Capellmeister* (1739), in which Mattheson includes several of the concepts of Enlightenment criticism already mentioned and adds a few others, which will help put many of the objections to Beethoven's music into clearer focus. Taking up one of the most accepted principles of aesthetics, mimesis, he writes that "Art is a servant of nature and serves to imitate it." Then he discusses a topic that was beginning to occupy the minds of scholars throughout Europe and that became the hallmark of German *Sturm und Drang* literary theory and formed the Enlightenment's focal point of the debate on vocal versus instrumental music: the origins of language and poetry in the songs of primitive man. Mattheson argues that "natural singing by man (I say by man) existed earlier than playing and the beautiful innate instrument of the throat yields only a single sound at a time. Normally [sic]." For Mattheson and most critics of the eighteenth century, melody was the basis of polyphonic texture and harmony, to which it was superior: "Melody is the chief component and the highest peak of musical *perfection*. . . . *Melody alone moves hearts with its noble simplicity, clarity and distinctness in such a way that it often surpasses all harmonic artifices*." As the basic building block of all music, melody bears the characteristics that we have already witnessed as criteria for good art in Enlightenment criticism: good melody is "facile, clear, flowing, and lovely."[36]

Matteson's analysis of the four principles of melody provides a clear understanding of a number of lexical terms that appear in many reviews of Beethoven's works. For example, to obtain "simplicity," composers should restrict themselves to the familiar and avoid "all that is forced, far-fetched, and difficult in nature." Also, artifice (particularly complicated counterpoint) should be set aside and "brevity preferred to length." "Clarity" demands that the composer avoid abrupt changes in rhythm and excessive embellishment. "Flowing quality" requires regularity of rhythms, a predictable sequence of phrases, no unexpected changes or interruption of melody. Finally, "loveliness" demands even and small intervals over large leaps and wild runs and the avoidance of too much repetition. With these principles of Enlightenment music aesthetics, Matteson provided Beethoven's contemporaries with a well-stocked and well-tested arsenal of critical weapons, which were frequently employed to expose his failure to live up to the normative doctrines of his predecessors, a test that placed his critics in the framework of mid-eighteenth-century music criticism. Finally, Matteson not only places the human voice at the center of music, but he also bases his concepts of criticism and theory on classical literary rhetoric, insisting on "proper *Commata, Cola,* periods etc."[37]

POST-ENLIGHTENMENT AESTHETICS AND CRITICISM

Indications that the Enlightenment doctrine of affects was beginning to lose ground to the growing doubts about the traditional views of the role of human emotions in art are particularly apparent in the work of Johann Gottfried Herder (1744–1803). The name Herder has now become a household word inseparable from the aesthetics of the *Sturm und Drang* period. He believed that the acerbic, negative criticism of Enlightenment reviewing, which sought to discover the conformity of works to theory, was alienating the public and discouraging writers. In Herder's view, the critic should play the hermeneutic role, serve as an advocate for the artist, and interpret for the audience. Criticism should be creative and even revelatory and recognize that taste is temporal and subject to historical change and traditional practices. For that reason, Herder advocated a better understanding of national consciousness and the creative continuity of national art in the form of folk art. His advocacy of the primacy of imagination in the original expressions of human speech and folk poetry caught on quickly with many German poets, particularly during the Romantic period, but as can be seen in some reviews, it fell short of the concept of ideal beauty in Enlightenment aesthetics.[38]

The philosophical *coup de grâce* to the Enlightenment doctrine of affects came with the publication of Immanuel Kant's work, particularly in his *Critique of Judgment* (1790). There he asserts that taste is always subjective and individual and can only become universal in the public forum when the critic thinks as a human being and not just as an individual with private interests. Therefore, aesthetic taste becomes the capacity to judge the beautiful with disinterest, without regard for the pleasurable or the good, which are bound to private and social interest. Judgment of the beautiful, the function of criticism, becomes entirely contemplative and is no longer didactic, since it no longer has the aim of educating the public. In spite of Kant's intent to promote the public use of reason and his exclusion of music from his philosophy, his advocacy of the aesthetics of productive imagination and the autonomy of art provided the foundation for a view of art that Beethoven's contemporaries could use to attack his Enlightenment opponents.[39]

That the tide was turning against some basic tenets of Enlightenment aesthetics is particularly evident in the work of Friedrich Schiller (1759–1805), a student of Kant's work. Schiller's place in eighteenth-century aesthetics is generally associated with his *Briefe über die ästhetische Erziehung des Menschen* and *Über naive und sentimentalische Dichtung*. In the latter, Schiller points out that modern man is no longer in unity with Nature. The modern or sentimental poet, in contrast to the ancient or naive poet, is "subjective" and more interested in the impressions that objects make on him than in the objects themselves. The sentimental poet creates the impression of nature by means of reflective fantasy but is basically alienated from nature. The naive poet creates nature spontaneously without reflection. Whereas the naive poet is limited to his direct experiences, the sentimental poet has access to a world of the infinite through imaginative speculation in a philosophical sense. On the negative side, Schiller saw the critic and the poet as alienated from their own society. The aims of art in the eighteenth century had become so divergent from the interests of the masses that it appeared no longer possible for the critic to speak on behalf of the general public.

What had happened in less than a century to bring about such a gap between art and society, the unification of which was the goal of the Enlightenment? The Enlightenment's own success provides one explanation. In regard to music, Forkel, as indicated above, revealed the success of the Enlightenment in the increase of composers and public concerts by the beginning of the last decade of the century. The success was even greater in literature. By the end of the century the number of readers, journals, books, and writers had become so great that the very group that had thought it could educate the public saw itself losing its grip on the medium for educating the public.[40]

With the emergence of mass entertainment, Enlightenment critics found it increasingly difficult to steer education by means of the literary medium. By the turn of the century, there was a definite feeling that public reason had become instrumentalized under the control of commercial and state interests, a danger that Mattheson had perceived with totally different eyes earlier in the eighteenth century.[41] Many men of letters regarded this growing situation with great alarm, while others of a younger generation saw it as the birth of a new age, in which Beethoven was quickly becoming its hallmark.

Clemens Brentano, one of the great poets of the Romantic era and an ardent admirer of Beethoven's music (see his "Nachklänge Beethovenscher Musik"), places the dilemma of Enlightenment aesthetics into historical perspective: "Furthermore, wanting to use public, sensible criticism to improve theaters and actors would be an extremely incomprehensible project. . . . Since the Hamburger Pastor Goeze's condemnation of the theater (an opinion we almost completely subscribe to), since Lessing's vital dramaturgy . . . not a single theater critic . . . has produced even the slightest change in European theater, any more than the voices of publicly political writers will ever be able to exert an active, effective influence on the course of history."[42] Brentano regards the contemporary artistic scene as not only a sign of the failure of the Enlightenment but also an indication that artists are no longer purveyors of ideas for the betterment of society but, to the contrary, have become isolated from society and appreciated only by an elite few, a condition that underscores a unique endorsement of what was perceived as the isolated, creative genius of Beethoven.[43]

Similar ideas are expressed in another work that is often regarded as one of the major sources of Romantic aesthetics: *Herzensergießungen eines kunstliebenden Klosterbruders* (1797) by Wilhelm Wackenroder (1773–98), a close friend and colleague of the Romantic poet Ludwig Tieck. Wackenroder was married to the sister of the wife of Friedrich Reichardt (editor of BMZ 1805–06). Wackenroder describes the protagonist of *Herzensergießungen*, Joseph Berglinger, as "an artist" who "must be an artist only for himself, for the exaltation of his own heart and for one or a few people who understand him." The reason for his isolation is given early on: "As long as you live, he thought, you must hold fast, unwavering, to this beautiful poetic ecstasy, and your whole life must be a piece of music."[44]

Soon after the premature death of Wackenroder, Friedrich Schlegel (1772–1829), the theoretical leader of the Romantic movement, established the new direction of aesthetic criticism: "Poetry can only be criticized by poetry. A judgment on art which is not itself a work of art, either in its subject matter as the representation of a necessary impression in its genesis, or in its beautiful form and liberal tone in the spirit of old Roman satire, has no citizen's rights in the realm of art."[45] The Romantic critic perceives a work of art as a medium, as an inspiration to free subjectivity, and the ego that is able to utilize a work of art in this sense becomes itself a work of art. Art does not serve society, as Mattheson and his contemporaries had claimed; it serves art itself and becomes the impetus to artistic creativity. For similar reasons, Romantics opposed rules and judgments based on correctness of details, or so-called atomistic criticism, without relation to the whole. Friedrich's brother, August Wilhelm Schlegel, as well as E. T. A. Hoffmann, believed that in a true work of art there is no individual beauty; only the whole is beautiful. Hoffmann even advocated the study of all the works of an artist before attempting to render any kind of judgment.[46]

Perhaps the most frequently cited statement on the meaning of the word "Romantic" comes from Friedrich Schlegel's *Gespräch über die Poesie,* which appeared in the journal *Athenäum* in 1800. One particular idea that Schlegel makes characteristic for the novel, for which the German word forms the linguistic source of "Romantic," is the openness of form and the delight in insoluble mixtures of anything antithetical: nature and art, poetry and prose, gravity and jest, one of the highest taboos of Enlightenment aesthetics. Thus novel-like works were often viewed as "Romantic," whose "differentiating characteristic consists in the fact that they [i.e., several works by Beethoven] belong completely to a poetic, primarily novel-like, fantastic world"[47] able to express what they often regarded as the goal and essence of art: the infinite, religious experience. In an article published in 1810 in AMZ, Hoffmann writes, in a now famous formulation, that "Beethoven's music . . . awakens that interminable longing which is the essence of Romanticism."[48] The medium of art and of criticism serves in a sense to deconstruct the reality that stands between the fantasy and the infinite religious experience. For that reason we often see terms like "hieroglyphics," "dark," or "obscure" that in Enlightenment aesthetics were negative terms, referring to the medium of Romantic art. It is the function of the critic to decipher the hieroglyphic medium and thereby remove the barrier between the reader or the listener and the art itself.

A statistical survey of the proportion of vocal to instrumental music in the reviews of musical works in AMZ reveals how certain basic music tenets of German Romanticism are mirrored in the journal's editorial policies. On the basis of the entire life of the journal, 42 percent of the reviews are on vocal music, whereas 58 percent of the reviews deal with instrumental music, 44 percent of which are on piano music. This squares directly with the views of the Beethoven critic, E. T. A. Hoffmann, who in the same AMZ article (1810) explains his view of the unqualified rank of instrumental music: "When we speak of music as an independent art, we should have in mind only instrumental music, which scorning every aid, every admixture of another art, expresses the pure essence of this particular art alone. This is the most romantic of all the arts—one might say, the only purely Romantic art."[49]

Aside from the obvious underpinnings of the stereotypical, Romantic view of Beethoven's music as the symbol of infinite longing and the liberation from banal reality through creative imagination, the relationship between the actual reviewing and Romantic theory presents, at the least, a dichotomy of theory and practice. Along with other Romantics, Hoffmann can extol the superiority of instrumental over vocal music with a declaration that turns an Enlightenment doctrine on its head: "Beethoven is a purely Romantic (and precisely for that reason truly musical) composer, and this may be the reason that he has been less successful with vocal music, which does not allow for unspecified yearning, but only represents those affects that are indicated by words" (see op. 67 in vol. 2 of this work).[50] In apparent contradiction to these words, Hoffmann and other Romantic authors wrote major works that are almost exclusively dedicated to vocal music. Take, for example, Ludwig Tieck's *Musikalische Leiden und Freuden* and, most importantly, Hoffmann's *Rat Krespl*, a novella about a female singer whose voice symbolizes the highest realm of musical experience but that at the same time threatens her life with tragic death. These examples seem to suggest that Romantic theories gave expression to ideas on music on two different levels: creative writing as hermeneutic criticism and the specific, pragmatic analysis of individual works (often couched in the lexicon of Romantic poetics), which became a philosophically successful form of criticism once the Enlightenment view of the moral function of music lost its predominance.

In the documents of Beethoven criticism that follow, the reader will find a wide spectrum of ideas that can be traced to the perceived conflicts between the Enlightenment concepts of prescriptive, normative aesthetics and the Romantic view of the transcendental nature of the isolated, creative genius. In many cases, however, the views expressed by critics are the product of a dialectical process in which these two major philosophies of aesthetics are not always at odds with each other but rather condition one another and produce a vigorous and multifaceted palette of ideas that form the foundation of many contemporary opinions of Beethoven's music.

Wayne M. Senner

NOTES

1. See entry no. 29, BAMZ (12 May 1824). Throughout this introductory essay and in the notes of the translated documents in volume 1, periodical titles not listed in the abbreviations will be given in full the first time they are referred to; thereafter they will be abbreviated. Within the documents themselves, titles will always be given in full.

2. See entry no. 63, AMZ (9 October 1799).

3. See entry no. 65, AMZ (5 June 1799).

4. See entry no. 50, MAMZ (7 June 1828).

5. See entry no. 39, BAMZ (4, 11, and 15 October 1826).

6. *Mimesis* is a Greek term meaning "imitation" in a very broad, aesthetic sense and could refer to processes, gestures, spiritual conditions, and entities as well as objects, human or inanimate. Mimesis was accepted as the goal and method of the arts in general until the last quarter of the eighteenth century.

7. See entry no. 36, Gottfried Wilhelm Fink, AMZ (25 January 1826).

8. See entry no. 49, Gottfried Wilhelm Fink AMZ (12 and 19 March 1828).

9. See entry no. 122, AMZ (19 February 1812).

10. The appearance of the term "hieroglyphic" in Beethoven criticism reveals how contemporary issues often informed the lexical foundations of criticism. After the discovery of the Rosetta Stone in 1799 in Egypt, scholars in Europe became embroiled in the

controversy over the phonetic vs. symbolic nature of ancient Egyptian hieroglyphics, which for centuries had been thought to be simply mysterious images with occult meanings. The controversy gave new life to the traditional understanding of the hieroglyphics, which continued long after Jean-François Champollion (1790–1832) discovered that the characters were phonetic rather than mysterious pictures. For usage of the terms "romantic" and "novel-like," see E. T. A. Hoffmann's review of the Fifth Symphony, op. 67 (in vol. 2 of this work) AMZ, 4 and 11 July 1810, and entry no. 23, AMZÖK (18 January 1820).

11. See entry no. 54, AMZ (30 December 1829).

12. For a detailed, historical discussion of the AMZ, see Reinhold Schmitt-Thomas, *Die Entwicklung der deutschen Konzertkritik im Spiegel der Leipziger Allgemeinen musikalischen Zeitung (1798–1848)* (Frankfurt/Main: Kettenhof, 1969). For a critical examination of the music aesthetics of critics publishing on Beethoven in the AMZ and other contemporary periodicals, see Robin Wallace, *Beethoven's Critics: Aesthetic Dilemmas and Resolutions during the Composer's Lifetime* (Cambridge: Cambridge University Press, 1986).

13. See Richard van Dülmen, *The Society of the Enlightenment: The Rise of the Middle Class and Enlightenment Culture in Germany,* trans. A. Williams (New York: St. Martin's, 1992), for an account of the roles of academies, reading societies, publishing houses, and of general reading habits in eighteenth-century Germany.

14. In a letter dated 22 April 1801, Beethoven asked Breitkopf & Härtel to "advise your reviewers to be more circumspect and intelligent, particularly in regard to the productions of younger composers. For many a one, who perhaps might go far, may take fright. As for myself, far be it from me to think that I have achieved a perfection which suffers no adverse criticism. But your reviewer's outcry against me was at first very mortifying" (Emily Anderson, ed. *The Letters of Beethoven,* 3 vols. [London: Macmillan, 1961], letter no. 48; henceforth cited as Anderson).

15. Walter Salmen offers an entertaining, historical overview of public concerts in *Das Konzert: Eine Kulturgeschichte* (Munich: C. H. Beck, 1988). See also Mary Sue Morrow, *Concert Life in Haydn's Vienna: Aspects of a Developing Musical and Social Institution* (Stuyvesant NY: Pendragon, 1989); Julia Moore, "Beethoven and Musical Economics" (Ph.D. diss., University of Illinois, Champaign-Urbana, 1987); and Tia DeNora, *Beethoven and the Cultural Construction of Genius* (Berkeley and Los Angeles: University of California Press, 1995).

16. Karl Fasch (1758–1800) was a close associate of Friedrich Reichardt, a student of Kant and Schiller and editor of the BMZ. He was also the music instructor of one of the philosophical fathers of music criticism of German Romanticism, Wilhelm Heinrich Wackenroder.

17. Johann Christoph Gottsched, *Versuch einer critischen Dichtkunst* (Leipzig, 1751; rpt. Darmstadt: Wissenschaftliche Buchgesellschaft, 1962), 139, para. 26.

18. For a good account of the origins and development of the term *criticism,* see René Wellek, "The Term and Concept of Literary Criticism," in his *Concepts of Criticism* (New Haven: Yale University Press, 1963), 26–36.

19. In regard to some basic psychological tenets of the doctrine of affects, Johann Mattheson also recommends that composers read Descartes (*Der vollkommene Capellmeister,* trans. Ernest Heinz [Ann Arbor MI: UMI Research, 1981], 107). For a study on Descartes's influence on Mattheson and the latter's view of the doctrine of affects, see George J. Buelow, "Johann Mattheson and the Invention of the *Affektenlehre,*" in *New Mattheson Studies* (Cambridge: Cambridge University Press, 1983), 393–409.

20. René Descartes, *Meditationes de prima Philosophia,* trans. George Heffernan (Notre Dame: University of Notre Dame Press, 1990), 89.

21. For very similar reasons, both Schiller and Kant excluded music from their philosophy of aesthetics more than a century later. If one does regard Descartes as the father of rationalism, as do many, then it would be difficult logically or historically to derive

eighteenth-century philosophies of music (e.g., the doctrine of affects) from the genesis of rationalism without a reification of Alexander Baumgarten's aesthetics as a coordinate system of thought.

22. In general, eighteenth-century aestheticians argued that music moved the emotions of the listener according to rules relating musical devices (rhythms, figures, etc.) to particular emotional states. Some argued with Krause and Mattheson that imitation should be utilized to express a specific passion in harmony with the totality of the work: "One must always aim at one specific passion" (Mattheson, *Capellmeister,* 111). There is, however, much disagreement about the nature of causality and the scope of causes and affects. See Joel Lester, *Compositional Theory in the Eighteenth Century* (Cambridge MA: Harvard University Press, 1992); and Bellamy Hosler, *Changing Aesthetic Values of Instrumental Music in 18th-Century Germany,* Studies in Musicology, ed. George Buelow (Ann Arbor MI.: UMI Research, 1981).

23. René Descartes, *Compendium of Music* (*Compendium musicae*), trans. Walter Robert (Rome[?]: American Institute of Musicology, 1961), 15.

24. Both Thomasius, founder of the first German periodical (1688), and Baumgarten, founder of aesthetics, had academic careers in Halle.

25. The philosophical claim of a "natural" development toward "perfection" marks a sharp break from the static world view of Lutheranism and is reflected in the numerous references to this latter term in philosophical and critical works of the eighteenth century. Note, for example, the adjectival modifier in *Der vollkommene Capellmeister* by Johann Mattheson.

26. *Reflections on Poetry: Alexander Baumgarten's Meditationis philsophicae de non-nullis poema pertinebus,* trans. Karl Aschenbrenner and William Holther (Berkeley and Los Angeles: University of California Press, 1954), 78.

27. The following remarks made in entry no. 57 could easily derive from Baumgarten's theory of aesthetics: "Because of an obvious desire to be completely novel, B. is not infrequently incomprehensible, disconnected, and obscure, and much of his work is extremely difficult without compensating with distinguished beauty" (WJ 1 [1806], 53).

28. For Gottsched's music relation with Mattheson, see Siegfried Kross, "Mattheson und Gottsched," in *New Mattheson Studies* (Cambridge: Cambridge University Press, 1983), 327–45.

29. "A composer will never be prominent in his art if he is not a scholar" (Mattheson, *Capellmeister,* 248).

30. In his *Tonkunst* (Bern, 1777), p. 63, Karl Ludwig Junker refers to "Bizarrerie" as an oddity, an unexpected surprise that "is only interesting by means of a kind of novelty." In AMZ (7 December 1825), a reviewer writes: "However, it is often the case with him that in his intention to create something even more original he becomes incomprehensible to the listener and degenerates into bizarrerie." See entry no. 35. Many of the documents in this volume make use of various grammatical forms of this word to characterize Beethoven's music.

31. Christian Gottfried Krause, "Von der Musikalischen Poesie 1752," *Music Aesthetics: A Historical Reader,* vol. 1: *From Antiquity to the Eighteenth Century,* ed. Edward A. Lippman (New York: Pendragon, 1986), 164.

32. Lippman, *Antiquity,* 171, 165.

33. See, for example, entry no. 129 (ZEW 1 [April 1801]): "However, that he wrote *too learnedly* for a ballet, and with too little regard for the dance, is certainly not subject to doubt."

34. Daniel Caspar von Lohenstein (1635–83) was one of the better-known Baroque poets, whose bombastic, inflated, rhetorical style made him the target of much Enlightenment criticism, particularly in Gottsched's works.

35. Johann Adolf Scheibe, *Der critische Musicus* 6 (1737). Compare the examples at the beginning of the introduction along with entry no. 65 (AMZ 5 June 1799), where

the following objections to Beethoven's music are found: "There is obstinacy for which we feel little interest, a striving for rare modulations, a repugnance against customary associations, a piling on of difficulty upon difficulty so that one loses all patience and enjoyment."

36. Mattheson, *Capellmeister,* 303–04, 305–06. The concept of "noble simplicity" became a major concept of German classical literature (Goethe and Schiller) during the last decades of the eighteenth century through the work of Johann Joachim Winckelmann's *Reflections on the Imitation of Greek Works in Painting and Sculpture,* published sixteen years after Mattheson's *Capellmeister.* Winckelmann's usage established the term as the secular expression of classical harmony, proportion, and perfection. There is good reason to believe that Mattheson's usage derives from the sixteenth-century "edle musica" (Martin Luther) and the seventeenth-century "simplicitate" in *Disputatio musica* (Johannes Lippius), lending the expression a definite religious connotation. As late as 1827, this idea is still applied to Beethoven's music: "After all it is the fashion of the new school to replace the natural and simply noble with extreme artificiality and floridity and to suppress poor melody beneath a very heavy harmony" (see entry no. 42, AMA, 24 January 1827).

37. Mattheson, *Capellmeister,* 307–13, 317–18.

38. In his *Ideen zu einer Ästhetik der Tonkunst,* Daniel Schubart (1739–91) gave the term *simplicity* new meaning by calling for a replacement of courtly melodies with songs of common man. For one critic's view of Beethoven's musical treatment of this type of poetry, see entry no. 138 (AMZ 28 August 1805).

39. Although Kant had little understanding for music, his lectures and particularly his *Critique of Judgment* were highly regarded and vigorously promoted by his student Johann Friedrich Reichardt (1752–1814), the editor of the BMZ, which contains several pieces on Beethoven. The article "On Naive and Sentimental Music" offers a good example of how his close acquaintanceship with another student of Kant, Friedrich Schiller ("Über naive und sentimentalische Dichtung," 1795–96), strongly influenced music criticism and views of Beethoven at the turn of the century. See entry no. 6. For a detailed account of Reichardt's life and works, see Walter Salmen, *Johann Friedrich Reichardt: Komponist, Schriftsteller, Kapellmeister und Verwaltungsbeamter der Goethezeit* (Freiburg: Atlantis, 1963).

40. Friedrich Nicolai's attempt to educate the public by reviewing all published books in Germany serves as a case in point. In the course of about forty years (1765–1806), he published reviews on more than 80,000 books and eventually gave up after failing to cover even half of the books published each year.

41. Although Mattheson, like most composers and critics of the Enlightenment, strongly believed in the social function of music, he saw the necessity of institutional control to achieve the goals of the Enlightenment. He writes that secular music "requires much official supervision if it is to produce good citizens and virtuous inhabitants rather than give cause for all sorts of scandal, sensuality, impious gallantry and wastefulness. Our pens are insufficient, the long arm of the law must do this" (Mattheson, *Capellmeister,* 128).

42. Clemens Brentano, "Über Anforderungen an die moderne Bühne: Theaterkritik und die Art, eine Oper zu behandeln," *Werke* (Darmstadt, 1963), 1135.

43. In a piece entitled "Letter to Johann Wolfgang von Goethe" (28 May 1810), Bettina Brentano, Clemens's sister, expresses a common Romantic view of the isolated artist: "What should contact with the world mean to him [Beethoven] who even before sunrise is at the holy work of day and after sunset hardly looks around, who forgets the nourishing of his body and is carried in flight past the shores of insipid pedestrian life by the stream of inspiration." See *Goethes Briefwechsel mit einem Kind: Werke und Briefe,* vol. 2 (Darmstadt, 1959), 246.

44. Wilhelm Heinrich Wackenroder, *Sämtliche Werke und Briefe,* vol. 1 (Heidelberg: Carl Winter, 1991), 142, 133. It is indicative of the formative processes of early Romantic

music aesthetics that many ideas later used in relation to Beethoven's "Romantic" music derive from music experiences much closer to the aesthetic principles of Mattheson. Wackenroder is a case in point. He studied with Karl Fasch (1736–1800, Berliner Singakademie) and admired his music and the music of his student Karl Friedrich Zelter (1758–1832), who condemned Beethoven's music to Goethe.

45. Friedrich Schlegel, "Kritische Fragmente," *Kritische Schriften* (Munich: C. Hanser, 1964), 22.

46. See Hoffmann's review of the Fifth Symphony, op. 67 (AMZ, 4 and 11 July 1810): 630–42, 652–59.

47. Schlegel, *Kritische Schriften,* 473.

48. Hoffmann, review in AMZ 12 (1810): 633.

49. Hoffmann, review in AMZ 12 (1810): 631.

50. Hoffmann, review in AMZ 12 (1810): 633.

General Section

~

1.
Karl Friedrich Cramer, ed.,[1] "Louis van Betthoven,"
Magazin der Musik 1 (Hamburg, 2 March 1783; rpt. Hildesheim, 1971):
394–95.

Louis van Betthoven, son of the above-mentioned tenor, a boy of eleven years and of very promising talent.[2] He plays keyboard skillfully and powerfully, sight-reads very well, and to sum it up, he mostly plays *The Well-Tempered Clavier* of Sebastian Bach, which Mr. Neefe placed in his hands.[3] Whoever knows this collection of preludes and fugues in all keys (which one could call the *non plus ultra*) will know what that means. Insofar as his other duties allow, Mr. Neefe has also given him some instruction in thoroughbass. Now he is training him in composition and to give him encouragement has had his variations on a march for keyboard engraved in Mannheim.[4] This young genius deserves the support to enable him to travel. He would certainly become a second Wolfgang Amadeus Mozart if he were to continue to progress as he has begun.[5]

NOTES

1. Alexander Wheelock Thayer notes (*Thayer's Life of Beethoven*, rev. and ed. Elliot Forbes, 2 vols. [Princeton: Princeton University Press, 1964], pp. 65–66; henceforth cited as Thayer-Forbes) that this announcement was prepared from information supplied by C. G. Neefe, one of Beethoven's first teachers in Bonn. Karl Friedrich Cramer (1752–1807) was a writer, book dealer, and professor of Oriental languages in Kiel. His *Magazin der Musik* was published for only five years (1783–88) but contains important information on new publications, concert life, and music theory. Christian Gottlob Neefe (1748–98) was a composer who moved to Bonn in 1779 as the music director for Grossmann-Hellmut's theater troupe. In 1782 he was appointed to the position of chief organist in the chapel of the elector of Cologne; the young Beethoven worked under him first as "Adjunct" and then after 1784 as second organist. Beethoven's instruction with Neefe must have begun before 1783, the date of this notice. In 1796 Neefe left Bonn to take the position of music director in Dessau. Beethoven credited Neefe for any future success in a fragment of a letter to his teacher, perhaps written in 1792–93: "Should I ever become a great man, you will have had a part in it, that will bring you joy all the more, since you could be convinced [letter breaks off]" (Anderson, letter no. 6; *Ludwig van Beethoven: Briefwechsel Gesamtausgabe*, ed. Sieghard Brandenburg, 8 vols. [Munich: G. Henle, 1996], letter no. 6; henceforth cited as Brandenburg).

2. The author is mistaken about Beethoven's age. Beethoven was actually twelve in March 1783 but probably thought he was ten. There was considerable confusion about the year and day of Beethoven's birth during his lifetime. For example, on 2 May 1810

Beethoven wrote, "Unfortunately I lived for a while without knowing how old I was" (see Anderson, letter no. 256, and Brandenburg, letter no. 438). For a summary of the confusion over the birth year, see Maynard Solomon, "Beethoven's Birth Year," *Beethoven Essays* (Cambridge, MA: Harvard University Press, 1988), 35–42. Note that the original spellings of Beethoven's name are maintained throughout this volume.

3. Christian Gottlob Neefe; see also n. 1, this entry. According to Nicolaus Simrock, he gave Beethoven the preludes mentioned in the next sentence in 1780 (if Simrock knew Beethoven's correct age). In a letter from Simrock to Gottfried Weber, dated 28 March 1828, Simrock declared, "I made young Beethoven a present of the preludes and fugues in his ninth year, on condition that he soon play some of them for me, which indeed did not take long. He studied them daily with heart and soul" (see Wilhelm Altmann, "Aus Gottfried Webers brieflichem Nachlaß," *Sammelbände der Internationalen Musikgesellschaft* 10 [1908/09]: 477–504). Because the *Well-Tempered Clavier* was first published in 1801 by Simrock in Bonn and Nägeli in Zurich, Beethoven must have studied the works in one of the many manuscript copies in circulation. Beethoven's own copy of the 1801 Nägeli printing of volume 1 is now in the Staatsbibliothek zu Berlin, Preussischer Kulturbesitz (Autogr. 41). For information on Beethoven's knowledge of Bach's music, see Donald MacArdle, "Beethoven and the Bach Family," *Music & Letters* 38 (1957): 353–58; and Warren Kirkendale, *Fugue and Fugato in Rococo and Classical Chamber Music,* trans. Margaret Bent and Warren Kirkendale (Durham NC: Duke University Press, 1979), 212–14.

4. The Nine Variations in C Minor on a March by Ernst Christoph Dressler, WoO 63, were published by Götz in Mannheim in 1782. The title page also contains the wrong birth date: it states that the set was composed "by a young amateur Louis van Beethoven, ten years old" (see Georg Kinsky, *Das Werk Beethovens: Thematisch-bibliographisches Verzeichnis seiner sämtlichen vollendeten Kompositionen,* ed. Hans Halm [Munich: G. Henle, 1955], 509–10; henceforth cited as Kinsky-Halm).

5. This comparison of Beethoven to Mozart establishes this as the earliest printed document to support Beethoven and to urge him to travel to Vienna, the music capital of western Europe. As a public statement, it may have been made to encourage the elector (Maximilian Friedrich) in Bonn to send Beethoven to Vienna. His successor, Maximilian Franz, did send Beethoven to Vienna in 1787 for an ill-fated stay during which he may have played for Mozart. In 1792, on the eve of Beethoven's final departure for Vienna from Bonn, Count Waldstein wrote that Beethoven was going to Vienna to receive the "spirit of Mozart from Haydn's hands." There is extensive literature on Beethoven's debt to Mozart. For a summary and new information, see Lewis Lockwood, "Beethoven before 1800: The Mozart Legacy," *Beethoven Forum,* vol. 3 (Lincoln: University of Nebraska Press, 1994), 39–52.

❧

2.

C. L. Junker,[1] "Something More from the Electoral Orchestra of Cologne," *Musikalische Korrespondenz der teutschen filharmonischen Gesellschaft für das Jahr, 1791* no. 48 (Speyer, 23 November 1791): 380–81.

Mentioned: Three Sonatas for Piano, WoO 47

Yet I heard one of the greatest fortepianists,[2] the dear, good Bethofen, some of whose compositions appeared in the Speyer *Blumenlese* of 1783, composed already in his eleventh year.[3] To be sure, he couldn't be heard in a public concert, perhaps because the instrument didn't comply with his wishes. It was a Spath fortepiano, and in Bonn he is accustomed to playing only on a Stein fortepiano.⁴ Nevertheless, what was infinitely preferable to me, I heard him improvise: indeed, I was even asked to propose a theme for [him to use as the basis for a set of] variations. In my opinion, the greatness of this dear tenderhearted virtuoso can be estimated from his nearly inexhaustible wealth of ideas, from the entirely unique manner of expression of his playing, and from the skill with which he plays. I would not know what he might be lacking to achieve greatness as an artist. I have heard Vogler on the fortepiano (I make no judgment of Bethofen's organ playing because I haven't heard him on the organ),⁵ have heard him often, have heard him for hours, and have always admired his extraordinary skill. However, in addition to being extraordinarily skilled, Bethofen is more eloquent, more significant, and more expressive; in short, he is more for the heart: therefore, a good Adagio as well as Allegro player. Even the excellent players of this orchestra are without exception his admirers and are all ears when he plays. Yet he is the epitome of modesty, without any pretensions. Nevertheless, he has admitted that on the journeys that the elector made him take he seldom found in the most well-known, good fortepianists what he believed himself entitled to expect. His playing is also so different from the usual way of treating the fortepiano that it seems as if he intended to pave his own way entirely in order to achieve the goal of perfection before which he now stands. If I had yielded to the urgent entreaties of my friend Bethofen, whom Mr. Winneberg also supported, and remained another day in Mergentheim,⁶ I believe Mr. Bethofen would have played for me for hours, and in the company of these two great artists the day would have been transformed for me into a day of the sweetest ecstasy.

NOTES

1. Carl Ludwig Junker (1748–97) was a chaplain at Kirchberg in Hohenlohe, amateur composer, and dilettante music critic (see Ludwig Nohl, *Beethoven nach den Schilderungen seiner Zeitgenossen* [Stuttgart: J. G. Cotta, 1877], 9–10). In a letter of 29 December 1824, Beethoven apparently referred to this article by Junker: "I see from your periodical [*Cäcilia*] that Junker is still alive. He was one of the first who noticed me 'when I was young and innocent' [a quotation from the poem *Phidile* by Matthias Claudius]. Give him my warm regards"; see Anderson, letter no. 1358, and Brandenburg, letter no. 1917.

Heinrich Philipp Carl Bossler (1744–1812) was a well-known music publisher and writer; he published the journal cited here as well as Beethoven's Three Sonatas, WoO 47, and other titles.

2. From this point on, Junker and others use the terms "Flügel" and "Fortepiano" interchangeably. In the English translations, "fortepiano," the term generally reserved for the piano of the late eighteenth and early nineteenth centuries, will be used. To illuminate historical usage, however, the term "pianoforte" is retained as it appears in the German originals.

3. "Also, three sonatas for keyboard were published by him at this time in the Bossler publishing house."

4. Junker undoubtedly mentions that Beethoven was used to the Stein pianos because of important differences between the two types. For a summary of Beethoven's pianos and

their construction, see William S. Newman, *Beethoven on Beethoven* (New York: Norton, 1988), 50–54; and Josef Mertin, "Über die Klaviere Beethovens," *Beethoven Almanach 1970*: 91–100. The Stein pianos were known for their lighter touch because of individually hinged and springloaded escapement levers to keep the hammers from jamming against the strings. On Beethoven's preferences regarding different piano builders, see William S. Newman, "Beethoven's Pianos versus His Piano Ideals," *Journal of the American Musicological Society* 23 (1970): 484–504.

5. Abbé Georg Joseph Vogler (1749–1814), an influential music theorist, was better known for his skill in improvisation than for his compositions. At this time, Vogler was involved in trying to reform and simplify the structure of the organ. Thus the implied comparison of his and Beethoven's organ playing is quite topical. He was also famous for the storm effects he created in his organ recitals. Margaret H. Grave's article in *The New Grove Dictionary of Music and Musicians* (ed. Stanley Sadie, 20 vols. [London: Macmillan, 1980], 20: 59–63; henceforth cited as *New Grove*) quotes Joseph Gänsbacher, who also heard both men play, as judging Vogler's improvisations superior to Beethoven's.

6. In the fall of 1791, Elector Maximilian Franz presided over a grand meeting of the Teutonic Order, for which theatrical and musical activities were provided. See Thayer-Forbes, 101–02.

≈

3.
"Virtuosi and Dilettanti from Vienna,"
Jahrbuch der Tonkunst von Wien und Prag (1796): 7–8.

Bethofen, a musical genius who has made his residence in Vienna for the last two years [*sic*].[1] He is universally admired for his speed of playing and the extraordinary difficulties that he executes with such great ease. For some time he seems to have penetrated more than usual the inner sanctuary of art that is distinguished by precision, feeling, and taste, and by this means he has increased his fame considerably. Convincing proof of his real love for art is that he has placed himself in the charge of Haydn in order to become initiated in the holy secrets of composition. During his absence, this great master has placed him in the charge of the great Albrechtsberger.[2] What is then beyond all expectation when such a great genius yields to the instruction of such excellent masters? We already have several beautiful sonatas by him, among which his latest are particularly distinguished.

NOTES

1. Beethoven had actually been in Vienna since November of 1792.

2. Johann Georg Albrechtsberger (1736–1809), Austrian composer and theoretician, was one of Beethoven's composition teachers. His composition treatise, *Gründliche Anweisung zur Composition* (1790) was one of the most popular of the times. For information on Albrechtsberger's importance as a teacher to Beethoven, see Thayer-Forbes, 146–50.

In the final sentence of the article the author is referring to the three Piano Sonatas, op. 2, which were published in March 1796 by Artaria and Company in Vienna. The Sonatas in op. 2 were the latest because Beethoven had published the Kurfürsten Piano Sonatas, WoO 47, in 1783.

~

4.
"The Most Famous Female and Male Keyboard Players in Vienna, Vienna, the 22nd of April, 1799," *Allgemeine musikalische Zeitung* 1 (15 May 1799): 523–25.

From this imperial city, I will keep my word and continue my news about its music.[1] But in return you must allow me to follow my whim, postpone for today my observations on the latest operas, and tell you about the fortepiano virtuosi here. I will only speak of those whom I myself know; I can, however, boast of knowing the most excellent ones. Also, here as everywhere, I will give you my opinion in the truest sense of the word without heeding the gossip of the great masses.

A few weeks ago I heard Demoiselle Auernhammer, who is probably known to you through her reputation and her published compositions (various parts of variations).[2] She gave a concert in the Imperial Court Theater for her benefit. She offers such proof of her livelihood and diligence every year. The latter, her diligence, is, however, all that one can in actual truth praise her for. Her entire endeavor is concerned with overcoming almost insuperable difficulties. In the process, she neglects what one calls performance in a more noble sense of the word. Under these circumstances she will never really play beautifully and with expression. I don't want to decide whether it is a lack of refined feeling or the desire to shine (two common causes for this in general), that is responsible for this virtuoso's situation. It is too bad that so many skillful virtuosos, and particularly keyboard players, still do not want to realize that clarity, taste, and beautiful performance have incomparably more value than the endless rushing of unclear passages and skipping about, whereby every third note is almost always missed, which spoils the entire piece for the serious connoisseur as well as for the educated man who himself is not exactly a virtuoso. At any rate, I gladly concede to Dem. A. that according to the manner already indicated she did play quite nicely and struggled nobly with her difficulties. She particularly pleased all of us with the variations she composed on the duet: "La stessa, la stessissima," from Salieri's opera.

Quite in contrast to the playing of this virtuoso is that of Miss von Kurzbeck, whom I recently had the pleasure of hearing. She is completely occupied with expressive and agreeable performance and thinks her way into the meaning of the compositions that she performs. Thus I heard her play a sonata by J. Haydn, which performed in this manner had to create, and did indeed create, the most exquisite effect because she also possesses the skill to play all passages with rare precision. She completely deserves the fame of being the most splendid and especially the most agreeable female pianist in Vienna.

After having granted the ladies precedence, as is proper, let us now turn to the gentlemen. Among the latter, Beethoven and Wölffl cause the most sensation.[3] Opinions about preferences for one over the other are divided. Nevertheless, it seems as if the majority is inclined toward the side of the latter. I shall endeavor to indicate the characteristics of both without taking part in the controversy over their rank. Beethoven's playing is extremely brilliant but less delicate, and it occasionally crosses over into the obscure. He demonstrates his greatest advantage in improvisation. And here it is really quite extraordinary with what ease and yet steadiness in the succession of ideas B. does not just vary the figurations of any given theme on the spot (by means of which many a virtuoso makes his fortune and—"fame") but really performs it. Since the death of Mozart, who for me still remains the *non plus ultra,* I have never found this kind of pleasure anywhere to the degree provided to me in Beethoven. Here, Wölffl is inferior to him. However, Wölffl has advantages over him in that he, possessing fundamental musical learning and true dignity in composition, plays passages that seem impossible to execute with astonishing ease, precision, and clarity. Of course he is aided by the large structure of his hands, and his playing is always so appropriate and, especially in Adagio passages, so pleasing and ingratiating, equally removed from sterility and excess, that one not only admires him but also can enjoy him. As you know, he is now on tour. That Wölffl gains a special advantage because of his unassuming, pleasant bearing over Beethoven's somewhat haughty manners is very natural. (Joh. Nep.) Hummel is also a distinguished fortepianist who went on long tours and won much approbation as a boy.[4] However, he seldom plays in public now (he dedicates himself completely to composition), and I have not had the opportunity to hear him privately. Thus I can only offer you the opinion of impartial connoisseurs from here who call his playing brilliant and yet very clear.

NOTES

1. "Compare the 28th number of this newspaper, pp. 446ff."

2. Josepha Au[er]nhammer (married name, Bösenhönig) gave yearly concerts for several decades. In 1781 she studied with Mozart, who thought she played delightfully but held a professional opinion of her similar to that expressed in the review: "She totally lacks a true, fine, singing taste in cantabile style, she plucks everything to pieces" (*Deutsches biographisches Archiv* [New York: K. G. Saur, 1982–   ], microfilm; henceforth *DbA*).

Magdelene Kurzbeck was a favorite of Joseph Haydn, who dedicated a grand piano sonata to her (*Oeuvre* 92me). See also entry no. 70. The conclusion of the article was omitted because in general it merely chats about Mozart's reception in Paris.

3. Joseph Wölffl (also Wölfl; 1772–1812) was a famous piano virtuoso and composer. A student of Michael Haydn and Leopold Mozart, Wölffl began his career with dazzling brilliance, but soon drifted into poverty and obscurity. See also Thayer-Forbes, 204–07.

4. Johann Nepomuk Hummel (1778–1837) was an Austrian pianist and a prolific composer of orchestral, choral, and chamber works; he was a student of Mozart, Anton Salieri (1776–1841), and Johann Albrechtsberger (under whom Beethoven also studied).

~

5.

"Overview of the Individual Products of Art: 1. Music as Independent Art.
2. Pure Instrumental Music," *Musikalisches Taschenbuch* 1 (Penig, 1803):
78–81.

Symphonies are the triumph of this art. Unlimited and free, the artist can conjure up an entire world of feelings in them. Dancing merriment, exultant joy, the sweet yearning of love and profound pain, gentle peace and mischievous caprice, playful jest and frightful gravity pour forth and touch the sympathetic strings of the heart, feeling, and fantasy; the complete multitude of instruments is at his command. However, this freedom is not lawlessness; also, these gigantic works of art are subject to the necessary conditions of the mutual determination of content and form and of unity in diversity, not to mention the other conditions. These conditions in particular must be recalled to mind because they are precisely the ones that most, indeed the greatest, symphony composers frequently neglect.—*Mozart* and *Haydn* have produced works of art in this genre of instrumental music that deserve great admiration. Their great, inexhaustible genius, their profundity and universality, their free, bold, vigorous spirits are expressed most purely therein. Mozart's symphonies are colossal masses of rock, wild and abundant, surrounding a gentle, laughing valley; Haydn's are Chinese gardens, created by cheerful humor and mischievous caprice. Both have in common a brisk, full, romantic life, boldness and strength. Mozart's convey reassurance and satisfaction, while Haydn's lack essential unity; their individual passages are isolated and do not form a whole. *Beethoven,* a novice in art who is, however, already approaching the great masters, has in particular made the great field of instrumental music his own. He unites Mozart's universality and wild, abundant boldness and Haydn's humoristic caprice; all his compositions have abundance and unity. The symphonies by *Clementi, Viotti, Winter, Pichl, [and] Kraus,*[1] are full of power and pomp; those by *Boccherini, Hoffmeister, André,* [and] *Gleisner* are interesting and tasteful.[2]

In regard to similar works of other composers, *Pleyel's* belong to the mediocre;[3] in regard to his other compositions they are the best products he has delivered although his one-sidedness and limitations cannot be mistaken in them. In his symphonies, as in his other works, *Gyrowetz* has a certain manner;[4] one cannot deny him liveliness and characteristic modulations, but his false rhythmic successions and his errors against the purity of phrasing make him unworthy of being called an artist. *Dittersdorf's* and *Rosetti's* characteristic symphonies are a limited genre that do not live up to even their own limitations.[5] On the symphonies by Vanhall, Reichardt, Stamitz, Wranitzky, Devienne, Neubauer, Sterkel, Kospoth, Abel, Kirmair, Lachnith, Teyber, and others there is nothing to say.

NOTES

1. Muzio Clementi (1752–1832), Italian piano composer and pedagogue, stopped performing in 1786 and became a highly regarded publisher and piano teacher. He participated in the founding of the Philharmonic Society in London, and his *Gradus ad parnassum* remained one of the most popular textbooks for pianists for nearly a century. Although he is best known today as a rival of Mozart, his piano works in many ways foreshadow developments in Romantic composition for that instrument. He was also a leader in the manufacture of pianos and other musical paraphernalia. For more information on Clementi, see Leon Plantinga, *Muzio Clementi: His Life and Music* (London: Oxford University Press, 1977).

Giovanni Battista Viotti (1755–1824), Italian violin virtuoso and composer, made important contributions to the founding of the Italian opera school. In "Beethoven and the French Violin School" (*Musical Quarterly* 44 [1958]: 431–47), Boris Schwarz argues that Beethoven, especially in his violin works, was heavily influenced by Viotti and other contemporary French violinists.

Peter Winter (1754–1825), composer and conductor, was a student of Abbé Georg Joseph Vogler. Winter was one of the most sought after opera conductors of his time, and his operas paved the way to early Romanticism. He wrote the music for Goethe's second part of *Die Zauberflöte* under the title *Das Labyrinth oder der Kampf mit den Elementen*.

Wenceslaus Pichl (1741–1805) was a violinist and composer from Bohemia; he translated Mozart's opera *Die Zauberflöte* into Czech. He also had some associations with Prince Nikolaus Esterházy that brought him into contact with Haydn, who performed some of his music at Esterháza.

Joseph Martin Kraus (1756–92), a German composer and student of Abbé Georg Joseph Vogler, was particularly active in Sweden, where he was considered to be the most noteworthy composer at the court of Gustavus III. His music was highly regarded by Gluck and Haydn for its rich harmonies and cosmopolitan sensitivities. See H. C. Robbins Landon, "Johann Martin Kraus" (*Musical Times* 103 [1962]: 25–26) for commentary on an edition of some of his quartets recently published by Novello, which Landon compares favorably to Haydn's works.

2. Luigi Boccherini (1743–1805), an Italian composer, was a court composer of Friedrich Wilhelm II, king of Prussia from 1786 to 1798. An accomplished cellist, Boccherini was also a prolific composer who became the chief representative of Italian instrumental music during the Classical period.

Franz Anton Hoffmeister (1754–1812), German composer and music dealer, transcribed much of Mozart's music and published some works by Beethoven, for example, Piano Concerto No. 1 in C Major, op. 19 (1801), and Piano Sonata, op. 22 (1802), through his firm Hoffmeister and Kühnel, Bureau de Musique in Leipzig, which became C. F. Peters Publishing in 1814.

Anton André (1775–1843) took over his father's important publishing business in Offenbach in 1799. André was also a performer, composer, and arranger. He is well known for having acquired the rights to Senefelder's and Gleissner's lithographic processes in 1799 and for his purchase of the Mozart-*Nachlaß* that same year. During his tenure as director, the firm published several reprints and arrangements of Beethoven's music; a partial list is found in Kinsky-Halm. See the entry for the family in *Music Printing and Publishing,* ed. D. W. Krummel and Stanley Sadie (New York: Norton, 1990), 140–42.

Franz Gleissner (1759–1818) was a German composer and, with Alois Senefelder, invented note lithography. He also wrote a thematic index to Mozart's music.

3. From 1795 through 1831, the major business of Ignaz Pleyel (1757–1831) was music publishing in Paris, where he reprinted many of Beethoven's works. He also established a piano factory. See Rita Benton, *Pleyel as Music Publisher: A Documentary Sourcebook of Early Nineteenth-Century Music* (Stuyvesant NY: Pendragon, 1990). The book includes a useful composer index.

4. Adalbert Gyrowetz (1763–1850), a Bohemian composer and opera conductor in Vienna, was known for his association with Haydn, whose style he continued to cultivate long after it went out of fashion. He took an active part in the arrangements for Beethoven's funeral.

5. Karl Ditters von Dittersdorf (1739–99) was an Austrian composer known especially for his comic operas. Among his best-known works are a series of program symphonies based on Ovid's *Metamorphoses,* which have names like "The Four Ages of the World," "The Fall of Phaeton," and "The Peasants Changed into Frogs." He also wrote a symphony that describes "The Combat of the Human Passions," and one describing the musical tastes of five nations, the "Italian" section of which is one of the most drastic examples of musical humor to be found anywhere. These works are catalogued in Barry Brook, ed., *The Symphony: 1720–1840,* series B, vol. 1, ed. Eva Badura-Skoda and Kenneth E. Rudolf (New York: Garland, 1985), xli–lxviii. They are compared pejoratively to Beethoven's symphonies by E. T. A. Hoffmann in his review of the Fifth Symphony (see vol. 2 of this work).

Franz Anton Rössler (Rosetti) (1750–92) was both a composer and choral conductor in Ludwigslust, whose symphonies are catalogued in *The Symphony: 1720–1840,* ed. Barry Brook (New York: Garland, 1986), 486–95. His "characteristic symphonies" might include the Symphony in D Major, Kaul 1/18, titled "La Chasse." *New Grove,* 16: 206–07, also mentions a "Telemaque" symphony. The *New Grove* article also clarifies some confusions concerning the composer's identity that are reflected in Robert Eitner, *Biographisch-bibliographisches Quellenlexikon der Musiker und Musikgelehrten der christlichen Zeitrechnung bis zur Mitte des 19. Jahrhunderts* 2nd edn. (Graz: Akademische Druck- und Verlagsanstalt, 1959–60), and other sources.

∾

6.
C. F. "Something on Sentimental and Naive Music,"[1]
Berlinische musikalische Zeitung 1 (1805): 149–50.

It seems to me that one can assume three basic types of musical composition, although music is seldom found that in itself contains one of these types in an unmixed fashion. First, the composer can represent in his music something objective, an ideal world of tones, an organic structure of tones that pleases through its free regularity and delights as free beauty without expressing something definite beyond itself. This kind of composition is pure-epic, pure representation, its prevailing characteristic is objectivity. It pleases because of its mere form. Here belong many fugues and other harmonically artistic works that excite our admiration, and that we declare to be great or beautiful, like their artful, visible organizations in nature, without being able to find a definite meaning in them or without feeling our sympathy moved by them. Second, the composer can represent the subjective: the expression of sensations and emotions, affects and passions. This music pleases partially through inner beauty (according to its form), partly through truth (because of its content). It not only delights, it also interests and is moving as a true, expressive portrait of the soul. This kind one can call lyrical. It is the expression of feeling, full of dominating subjectivity. It is not just beautiful, it is also moving. Third, music can unite feelings and their underlying causes in a representation that illustrates, in connection with an affect, objects through which it is aroused and demonstrates stirrings of the soul and that which motivates them in one and the same piece of music. This kind is lyrical-epic, a representation of feelings and its objects or causes. It pleases not just directly by means of beautiful form and stirring expression, but also indirectly in the reflection of the relationship of feeling to its object. Here the struggle of affect with its opposition, or its victory, or the overcoming of affect and passion is often interesting.

Thus lyrical music is either naive or sentimental. In the greatest simplicity and calm, naive music expresses the gentle emotions of a soul in harmony with itself, of a heart free from the unrest of violent affects and passions and contented with itself. Its melody is gently flowing, artless, its harmony simple and natural in its chords and passages, its motion uniform and mild, its modulations without bold skips and striking changes. The nuances of its expression are gentle, and it is free from strong contrasts. Everything that makes music piquant and humoristic, for example, by means of strange harmonic modulations, shattering dissonances, unexpected dynamic changes, rhythmic illusions and the like, is distant from this genre.

More frequently encountered than naive music is sentimental music, which reveals not so much an unclouded clarity and calm simplicity of the soul in a harmonic play of feelings but expresses more a longing and striving for that condition. Here the naive appears only in isolated traces, amiable innocence only in refracted rays. The melody winds its way, as it were, through art and struggle toward that simplicity. In this music the soul seeks in many different ways to visualize its beautiful goal and to approach it. Longing is expressed as a mixed, melancholic sweet feeling. The restrained heart suspects approaching liberation and expands more and more. It is difficult to describe how this mixture of grief and joy, the sublime and the beautiful, melancholy and cheerfulness, is represented in music through melody struggling for clarity, through the resolution of gently blended dissonances, through the gradual elevation or calming of expression, etc. Most of our more recent and best music is sentimental and examples for it are provided by Jos. Haydn,

Mozart, Eman. Bach, Reichardt, Zumsteeg, Beethoven, Cherubini, among other masters.[2]

Sentimental poetry has been divided into the satirical and the elegiac. By contrasting reality to the ideal, the satirist treats the ideal with aversion and proceeds against reality either bitterly with punitive gravity or jocularly with cheerful caprice. Shouldn't music also be capable of satirical traits? I believe it can express mockery of a serious and playful manner and that one finds in operas and symphonies, for example, by Mozart and Haydn, many things written in this mood. Serious satire will contain something sublime and incline more toward a gloomy nature. In jocular mockery there appears more beauty, charm, and cheerfulness. However, it is often difficult in musical representation to draw the lines sharply between mockery and defiance: in the former there is more ease, dexterity, and change; in the latter more gravity, solidity, and tenacity.

No one doubts that the gentle melancholy and sweet sadness of the elegy can overflow into melodic tones of lament; this is proven by a large number of the most beautiful and moving Largos, Adagios, Cantabiles and Andantes of our best composers.

NOTES

1. The basic concepts sketched in this article derive from Friedrich Schiller's *Über naive und sentimentalische Dichtung.* Published in 1795, this work represents one of the cornerstones of classical literary theory in Germany. It has often been applied to define the differences between Goethe, the "naive" poet, who proceeds intuitively from the variety of experiences, and Schiller, the "sentimental" poet, who proceeds speculatively from the unity of ideas. The author's usage of these two concepts makes it clear that the terms "naive" and "sentimental" are profoundly different from modern usage. In spite of the author's attempt to apply a contemporary literary theory to music, the transposition of Schiller's concepts is not free of ideas from the doctrine of affections.

2. Carl Phillip Emanuel Bach (1714–88) was the second surviving son of J. S. Bach. He was the most prolific of the Bach sons and held positions of great importance in Hamburg and Berlin. His music is the clearest example of the "sensitive style" (*empfindsamer stil*) of the early Classical period.

Johann Friedrich Reichardt (1752–1814) was a composer, writer, and editor of the *Berlinische musikalische Zeitung,* with which he helped pioneer music journalism and advocated classical German aesthetics. The BMZ is also one of the first periodicals in northern Germany to publish music criticism on Beethoven. Because of his unorthodox life style, Reichardt was frequently at odds with political authorities and often moved about from post to post. His opposition to Napoleon is largely responsible for the abrupt end of the BMZ. In Germany he is known for his *Lieder,* particularly his musical compositions of Goethe's poetry.

Johann Rudolf Zumsteeg (1760–1802), composer of operas, ballads, and songs, attended school with the poet Friedrich Schiller and composed the stage music for the latter's first *Sturm und Drang* play, *Die Räuber.* His *Lieder* were often more advanced than those of Reichardt, and they significantly influenced the young Schubert.

Luigi Cherubini (1760–1842), born in Florence, began his career as a composer of church music. Later he turned to opera (*Lodoiska, Anacreon*) and gained international fame for his music in Paris. Beethoven regarded him as one of the greatest composers of his time (see Thayer-Forbes, 683). His style ranged from Classical opera in the manner of Gluck to the colorful music of early Romantic opera.

∼

7.

Michaelis,[1] "A Few Remarks on the Sublime in Music," *Berlinische musikalische Zeitung* 1 (1805): 180–81.

In many great symphonies by Haydn, Mozart, Beethoven, among others, one finds an order, a spirit similar to the grand plan and character of a heroic epic. A simple introduction prepares the listener for the rich presentation that follows in a slow meaningful section in which an exuberant melody is not dominant; ordinary chords slowly appear and are almost more common than modulations. The imagination is attuned only to gentle presentiments of what is to come. This section is short and suggests only in general what is to follow; it prepares and builds up expectation, which only gradually is to be fulfilled or exceeded. Then other sections are added in which a great rich theme is developed. Its content becomes clearer and clearer in all its depth and opulence. This theme expresses a heroic character by asserting itself in a struggle with many opposing motions. Here contrasts are appropriate, here the accompaniment and the polyphonic, figured treatment of the music are allowed to appear powerfully and place the principal subject in a brilliant light. Now the most effective expression is revealed in the most diverse stirrings. How very much the composer proves here his genius and his taste in the order of the movements of the symphony, in the development of its content, in the clear, correct design of its characteristic themes, in their statement and execution, in the wise application of contrasts and episodes, in the expression of pathos, in the original invention and treatment of melody, in the dignity and charm of modulation and harmony, and in the true, vivacious depiction of affects and passions! Its melody is flowing without being weak, often sublime without being bombastic. The individual features of its musical portrait intermesh marvelously, make one another necessary, and form a large, effective, magnificently organized whole.

NOTE

1. Christian Friedrich Michaelis (1770–1834) was a frequent contributor of articles on music and archeology in AMZ, BMZ, and ZEW. He studied Kant's and Fichte's philosophy and as a professor lectured on the philosophy of law. His reference to Beethoven's "great [=large] symphonies" here is to Symphonies No. 1 (published in 1801) and/or 2 (published in 1804), both of which contain the kind of slow introductions described by Michaelis. Although the *Eroica* had been composed in 1803, it was not published until 1806 and does not have the kind of introduction Michaelis describes.

8.

Johann Friedrich Reichardt,[1] "Obituary,"
Berlinische musikalische Zeitung 1 (1805): 252.

Noble, fault-finding quibblers in art might indeed like to act as if Haydn's original and naive works would have to yield to the more difficult, more artistic quartets by Mozart, which they so seldom know how to make sound even tolerably genuine and comprehensible. They claim that at best they could still only be heard alongside the Mozartian quartets of Romberg and Beethoven's most recent works.[2] The real connoisseur and impartial judge is happy to see these new, real talents and artists associated with those heroes of art without dislodging them from their high position, gained by genius and industry, even by a hair. It is and will remain the highest triumph of real genius and true art that their genuine, perfected works will remain valid whatever thousand upon thousand merriments time and fashion and their slaves revel in, deified and deuced, according to the measure of sunshine and the sky's gently passing clouds of today and yesterday.

NOTES

1. Reichardt's next important work containing some of his views and observations of Beethoven's music appeared under the title *Vertraute Briefe, geschrieben auf einer Reise nach Wien und den Oesterreichischen Staaten zu Ende des Jahres 1808 und zu Anfang 1809*. A review of the book appeared in AMZ (12 [31 January 1810]: 274–79) and offers the following by Reichardt on Beethoven. The reviewer points out how delighted Reichardt was that his own compositions of Goethe's poems pleased Beethoven. Also, he describes the conflict between Beethoven's external, rough appearance and behavior and his reception by the Viennese. Reichardt was convinced, continues the review, that "his best,(?) most original works could only be brought forth within such an obstinate, profoundly discontented mood. People who are in the position to delight in his works should never lose sight of this and not take offence at any of his external peculiarities and rough edges. Only then will they be his true admirers." For more information on Reichardt, see Alfred Kalischer, "Hofkapellmeister Joh. Friedr. Reichardt und Beethoven," *Beethoven und Berlin* (Berlin: Schuster & Loeffler, 1908–10), 39–66.

2. The two Romberg cousins, Andreas (1767–1821) and Bernhard (1767–1841), played in the Bonn electoral court orchestra (1790–93), where Beethoven began his career. Both were composers, and both toured widely in Europe. The reference here is probably to Andreas, who was particularly well known for his string quartets. Various members of this illustrious family of musicians are mentioned throughout these reviews. *New Grove*, 16: 144–46, details their identities, relationship, and instrumental specialties.

~

9.
J. F. R.[1] "Reviews,"
Berlinische musikalische Zeitung 1 (1805): 275.

Seldom does a reviewer have the pleasure to be able to recommend with the happiest heart and most complete conviction new works as genuine, without any consideration for the personal life of the composer and publisher, as is not only possible but obligatory for the above-mentioned works.[2] This pleasure is enhanced by the fact that they are the works of two virtuoso brothers[3] who captivate all friends of the beautiful and the good through their beautiful, noble union in life. Their works also quite clearly prove how they together, on the twofold path of industrious and purposeful practice and basic study, have reached a rare degree of virtuosity and mastery in composition. So few others have achieved this because most neglect the twofold interlocking study, which only becomes fruitful in true union and leads to the perfection that we admired in earlier times in Handel, the Bachs, the Bendas,[4] later in Mozart and Clementi, still admire and must always admire, most recently in Beethoven and Dussek.[5] In this noble pair of brothers we must recognize and value this perfection to a quite superior degree and with true devotion.

NOTES

1. Johann Friedrich Reichardt.
2. The reference is to four works by Bernhard and Andreas Romberg.
3. By calling the composers brothers, the reviewer seems to believe he is dealing with the Romberg brothers (Anton [1771–1842] and Bernhard [1767–1841]). Here, however, the reviewer seems to have been misled by the French descriptions. Andreas Romberg (1767–1821) was a cousin (not brother) to Bernhard Romberg. Most of his operas, orchestral, chamber, and choral works are largely forgotten, except for his setting of one of Friedrich Schiller's most famous poems, *Das Lied von der Glocke*.
4. This probably refers to the brothers Franz Benda (1709–86), Johann Georg Benda (1713–52), Georg Anton Benda (1722–95), and Joseph Benda (1724–1804), Franz's successor as concertmaster in Berlin. Though Bohemian, they are usually known by the German forms of their names. For details on these and other members of the large Benda family, see *New Grove,* 2: 462–66.
5. Johann Ladislaus Dussek (Czech Dussik or Dusik; 1760–1812) was a piano virtuoso and composer from Bohemia. He wrote some innovative music that anticipated the Romantic approach to his instrument and, through his connection with the Broadwood firm in London, contributed to the expansion of its range.

~

10.

"From Leipzig," *Abendzeitung nebst Intelligenzblatt für
Literatur und Kunst* 1 (22 February 1806): 64.

In the fourteenth concert in the Hall of the Woolen Merchants' Exchange, a solid amateur, the notary Hoffmann, could be heard with much skill on the bassoon. In the fifteenth the organist Voigt on the viola, and in the sixteenth Mr. Barth in a concerto for the clarinet by Krommer. The sound and skill of both on their instruments deserve to be praised, and the compositions that they performed were very agreeable. We thus also heard some of the most beautiful symphonies and overtures by Haydn, Mozart, and especially a more recent work by Beethoven whose profoundly serious fantasy and imaginative artistic depth transported us, full of enchantment, beyond the time of the performance.[1] The artist seems to have exhausted his strength with complete love.

NOTE

1. As Werner Felix notes, the Leipzig Gewandhaus often performed Beethoven's symphonies and other orchestral works "only a few months after their first performance in Vienna." See his "Zur Tradition der Beethoven-Pflege des Gewandhaus-orchesters," in *Bericht über den Internationalen Beethoven-Kongress, 10.–12. Dezember 1970 in Berlin* (Berlin: Neue Musik, 1971), 141–46. Because of the Gewandhaus tradition, the work included on this concert could have been one of the first two symphonies or any of the overtures performed or published by 1806.

~

11.

"On the Purposeful Use of the Elements of Music,"
Allgemeine musikalische Zeitung 8 (25 December 1805): 198–99.[1]

With distinguished talent and a great knowledge of art, Cherubini and Beethoven follow this master[2] in similar ways, where greatness is concerned, but not without their own distinct manner. However, until now neither, unlike Mozart, has been able to subdue his nature and guard against excesses everywhere: for Cherubini, excesses of harshness and repugnance that insult the meaning; for Beethoven, excesses of bombast and exhaustion to the point of disgust. Nevertheless, whoever doesn't recognize—as even now some try not to—the exquisite artist, born particularly for this genre, in several of Beethoven's instrumental pieces, particularly in his symphonies and fortepiano concertos, and also in various of his quartets and sonatas, regardless of the abuses (not glossed over here) and many irregularities of details: such a person can only be pitied, not disputed. The same is true in regard to many major scenes in Cherubini's operas. To such people this old saying applies:

> For years we draw water with a sieve and
>   Incubate the stone;
> But the stone doesn't get warm,
>   And the sieve doesn't get full.

NOTES

1. The entire article comprises cols. 193–201.
2. Mozart.

~

12.
"Beethoven's Most Recent Works in Vienna (Excerpt from a Letter)," *Journal des Luxus und der Moden* 24 (January 1808): 29.

Mentioned: Three Quartets for Strings ["Razumovsky"], op. 59; Symphony No. 4, op. 60; Violin Concerto, op. 61; Overture to *Coriolanus,* op. 62; *Fidelio,* op. 72; and Mass in C Major, op. 86

With great pleasure I offer you the news that our Beethoven has just completed an extraordinarily beautiful mass, which is quite worthy of him and is supposed to be performed at the Maria festival at Prince Esterházy's.[1] Beethoven's opera *Fidelio,* which in spite of all the protests contains extraordinary qualities of beauty, is supposed to be performed in Prague in the near future with a new overture.[2] His Fourth Symphony is being engraved, also a very beautiful overture to *Coriolan,* and a big Violin Concerto. At the same time, he is also beginning a new mass; in addition, three quartets are being engraved.[3] From that you see how ceaselessly active the brilliant artist is!

NOTES

1. The Mass (op. 86) was performed at Eisenstadt on Sunday, 13 September 1807 instead of on the name day of Princess Esterházy (8 September 1807) as requested by Prince Esterházy. The Mass was criticized by the Prince and laughed at by his concertmaster, which may explain why the Prince received neither the manuscript nor its dedication. The Mass, although eagerly anticipated by the Prince, was not well rehearsed even by the standards of the day and received an unsatisfactory performance. In a letter written shortly after the premiere to Countess Henriette von Zielinska, the Prince described the Mass as "unbearably ridiculous and detestable, and I am not convinced that it can ever be performed properly." For the history of the premiere, see *Letters to Beethoven and Other Correspondence,* ed. and trans. Theodore Albrecht, 3 vols. (Lincoln: University of

Nebraska Press, 1996), 1:192–95; and J. Merrill Knapp, "Beethoven's Mass in C, op. 86," in *Beethoven Essays: Studies in Honor of Elliot Forbes,* ed. Lewis Lockwood and Phyllis Benjamin (Cambridge MA: Harvard University Dept. of Music, 1984), 199–216.

2. See Helga Luhning, "Fidelio in Prague," in *Beethoven und Böhmen* (Bonn: Beethoven-Haus, 1988), 349–91.

3. All four publications appeared from the Viennese publisher Bureau des Arts et d'Industrie in 1808; the String Quartets and the Overture to *Coriolan* in January, the Violin Concerto in August, and the Fourth Symphony later in the year. See Kinsky-Halm, 144.

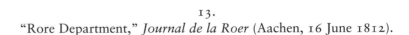

13.
"Rore Department," *Journal de la Roer* (Aachen, 16 June 1812).

The concert Madame Becker gave yesterday attracted a splendid social group and many amateurs in music. It was regrettable that Haydn did not assume his place at this music performance as usual.[1] They began with a symphony by Romberg, which was listened to with pleasure. Mademoiselle Varnhagen[2] performed a concerto by Beethoven on the fortepiano. This young lady plays with much taste; she overcomes the greatest difficulties and was greatly applauded. It is simply too bad that such a beautiful talent was fruitlessly squandered on such an unsatisfactory instrument in such large premises. Its dry and monotonous tones competed to its great disadvantage with an entire orchestra, the combination of so many different instruments. Madame Becker still astonished with the breadth, purity, and strength of her voice. Often, it seems we are no longer hearing her voice but a real instrument from which she entices new tones that are like the purest silvery sounds of a flute. Above all, she gained general acclaim with the polonaise.

Nevertheless, why do great artists always select pieces in which only art rules when they want to make a show of themselves and seem to desire only the applause of the initiated? It seems to us that they don't understand what would be in their real interest. Perhaps it would be a refinement of art if they would apply only a few of the abundant means at their disposal. The greatest effects are always produced by the simplest means. At any rate we must not forget that art is merely the means and not the purpose. The purpose of the fine arts is to stir the heart and ignite the soul.

The orchestra played with fire and consonance, particularly the beautiful overture by the young Heinrich.

NOTES

1. Because Joseph Haydn had died in 1809, the reference is obviously to his music.

2. The article does not provide enough information to determine whether this is a reference to Rahel Varnhagen (née Levin, 1771–1833), who married Karl August

Varnhagen von Ense in 1814. Both were acquainted with Beethoven briefly, and in later years Karl Varnhagen compared the public's reception of Wagner's works with those of Beethoven: "In regard to the peculiarities of this music, I have this to remark, that fifty years ago I heard exactly the same reproaches expressed against Beethoven as are now being expressed against Wagner. The peculiarities in Beethoven are now recognized as the highest level of excellence. Whether the same fate can be predicted for the Wagnerian peculiarities, I certainly cannot say" (Karl August Varnhagen, "Wiesbaden, Sonntag, 11 August 1853," in *Tagebücher,* vol. 10 [Hamburg, 1868], 226).

∾

14.
K. B. "Miscellaneous," *Allgemeine musikalische Zeitung*
15 (8 December 1813): 806–07.

Mentioned: Overture to *Coriolanus,* op. 62, and
Music to Goethe's *Egmont,* op. 84

As is well known, there is a collection of copper engravings fashioned after the great Shakespeare gallery in England, which thereby, however, certainly should not be praised as works of art as such. If only, on the other hand, the greatest Romanticist of music, L. v. Beethoven, would enrich us with a musical Shakespeare gallery! No poet ever penetrated and perceived the innermost being of music so clearly and profoundly as Shakespeare himself. Indeed, in many of his splendid creations he attributed a unique, wonderfully significant effect to music. Here I call to mind in particular his *Merchant of Venice,* the *Tempest,* and others. Who has ever attended a good performance of his works without feeling stirred and moved in his innermost being? How much more would the effect of these works of the highest poetry be facilitated and increased if overtures, conceived entirely in Shakespeare's spirit, were to introduce them, to anticipate our feelings in between acts, and to prepare them for what was to come; and if suitable melodies accompanied splendid songs inserted here and there, as well as in the scenes in which the poet himself expressly prescribed music! With what gigantic power would Beethoven let us look into the depths of the realm of darkness in an overture to *Macbeth,* for example![1] How he would intertwine love and pain, death and transfiguration into a heavenly wreath in a composition for *Romeo and Juliet,*[2] or as in the *Tempest* transport us to a magic land full of charming melodies, strange airy sounds, and fantastic illusions.[3] Whatever we would be justified in expecting from this ingenious master in this area, he has demonstrated in his overture to *Coriolanus* and, above all, in his music to Goethe's *Egmont,* a work in which the artist appears in all his greatness and splendor.

NOTES

1. In 1808 Beethoven collaborated briefly with the librettist Heinrich von Collin on an opera on *Macbeth*. Preliminary sketches are found on p. 133 of the sketch miscellany

Landsberg 10. The project was abandoned "because it threatened to become too gloomy" (see Thayer-Forbes, 441). Beethoven remained fascinated with the play, however, and in 1822 discussed it with Heinrich Anschütz (see his *Erinnerungen* [Leipzig: Reclam, 1886]). For an extended general essay, see Caldwell Titcomb, "Beethoven and Shakespeare," in *Critica musica: Essays in Honor of Paul Brainard* (Amsterdam: Gordon and Breach, 1996), 429–60.

2. The coda of the slow movement of the String Quartet in F Major, op. 18, no. 1, depicts the funeral scene from *Romeo and Juliet*, as is clear from Beethoven's own testimony as recounted by Karl Amenda and by written annotations on the sketches (see *Beethoven: Ein Skizzenbuch zu Streichquartetten aus Opus 18* [Bonn: Beethoven-Haus, 1972–74], 1:8–9 [sketchbook known as Grasnick 2]). For a transcription and discussion of these notations, see Myron Schwager, "Beethoven's Programs: What is Provable?" *Beethoven Newsletter* 4 (1989): 49–55.

3. Beethoven's Piano Sonata in D Minor, op. 31, no. 2, is nicknamed the "Tempest." For a discussion of the history and significance of the nickname, see Theodore Albrecht, "Beethoven and Shakespeare's *Tempest:* New Light on an Old Allusion," *Beethoven Forum*, vol. 1 (1992), 81–92.

~

15.

K. B. "Miscellaneous," *Allgemeine musikalische Zeitung* 16 (8 June 1814): 395.

Originality is such a rare advantage, even with artists, that it might well be attributed to only a few chosen ones, geniuses of first rank. Which contemporary artist would indeed possess this divine gift to a higher degree than Beethoven? Perhaps the originality of his *completed* works can be compared only with the originality of Shakespeare. The most profound humor and most tender romantic feeling are completely united in them.

~

16.

K. B. "Miscellaneous," *Allgemeine musikalische Zeitung* 16 (27 July 1814): 506.

Many lovers of music—and it is certainly not to be held entirely against them—are not just a little astonished at many of the scherzos in Beethoven. They think they just don't seem to be quite *playful* at all.[1] Well, they are right, in their way! But is there not a *jest*,[2] which according to its innermost nature as well as in its sound is related to *pain?*[3] If you have never become aware of this, then certainly these scherzos will have to remain eternally incomprehensible hieroglyphics for you![4]

1. "Scherzhaft."
2. "Scherz." The author is trying to satirize with a play on the words "scherzo," "Scherz," and "Schmerz."
3. "Schmerz."
4. On the complicated evolution of the scherzo in the Classical period, see Tilden Russell, "Minuet, Scherzando, and Scherzo: The Dance Movement in Transition, 1781–1825" (Ph.D. diss., University of North Carolina, Chapel Hill, 1983); and Michael David Luxner, "The Evolution of the Minuet/Scherzo in the Music of Beethoven" (Ph.D. diss., Eastman School of Music, 1978). An older but still valuable classic is Gustav Becking, *Studien zu Beethovens Personalstil: Das Scherzothema* (Leipzig: Breitkopf & Härtel, 1921).

≈

17.

K. B. "Miscellaneous," *Allgemeine musikalische Zeitung* 16 (27 July 1814): 505–06.

In the works of great poets there is an irony that gently hovers over the entire piece, but also frequently breaks forth incisively, making itself easily noticeable to the judiciously attentive. I recall here, in place of all others, only Shakespeare, Cervantes, and Goethe. For a long time, Beethoven's compositions have not been considered enough from this point of view. But precisely from just this vantage many things that *appear* to be harsh and strange in him are recognized as exquisite and necessary. This true, poetic irony, gentle, but often also piercing and terrible, hovers over many of his most splendid productions. Indeed, frequently a deep, repressed rage speaks to us from his music, but let us not forget that it is a pure, holy rage.[1]

NOTE

1. There is a substantial literature on irony in Beethoven's music. See, for example, Rey Longyear, "Beethoven and Romantic Irony," in *The Creative World of Beethoven* (New York: Norton, 1971), 145–62; and Sylvia Imeson, *"The Time Gives It Proofe": Paradox in the Late Music of Beethoven* (New York: Peter Lang, 1996).

≈

18.

K. B. "Miscellaneous," *Allgemeine musikalische Zeitung* 16 (23, 30 November 1814): 795, 810–11.

Beethoven's great instrumental compositions, seen from one point of view, are to a certain degree like volcanos that pour out their rivers of fire in all directions. Like the former they are destructive, but, and that is the difference, they destroy only impermanent, common, and conventional things. Like volcanos, they fructify, only faster, more richly even, and more magnificently.

Now and then it has been stated that in Beethoven's music melody is often subordinated to the power of harmony. *Often*—hardly! Occasionally—certainly. However, this might well be the case for every master with an abundantly rich fantasy. But what other living composer is capable of the opposite, as he is, of making the deepest, most intimate feeling resound from harmony? His soul is like the sea: when it is peaceful, the sky with all its constellations is mirrored in its tides. If, however, the almighty breath of nature passes across it, it too billows and breaks upon the shore, foaming and surging. So too with *him*. If his soul is peaceful and quiet, then an endless abundance of friendly, illuminating beams break forth from him in all directions and a world of wonders is opened up to us with its magic glow. However, if the innermost source of his being is stirred by hostile powers, then to be sure, only waves of harmony rush turbulently forth, thundering and surging. But even into this hurricane there penetrates a gentle, heavenly sound that points to peace, to a lulling of the storm. There opens to the mind's eye a view, as if of boundless distances across a broad mirror surface, which no storm will again disturb.

19.

K. B. "Miscellaneous," *Allgemeine musikalische Zeitung*
17 (11 October 1815): 694.

Beethoven is unquestionably the boldest sailor on the tides of harmony. Every one of his journeys on this sea is a voyage of discovery. If it occasionally seems as if he is off-course, the fixed star of the North Pole always shines for him, and at last he always lands in a new world. But to settle down there calmly is certainly not his way!

20.

"The Music Festival in Edinburgh," *Allgemeine musikalische Zeitung*
18 (11 September 1816): 635.[1]

However, on page 121 he [F. Graham] makes a comparison of Haydn, Mozart, and Beethoven that I don't want to omit. "On the preceding pages we have had the opportunity to note the admirable qualities of each of these three distinguished, most recent composers, Haydn, Mozart, and Beethoven.

These three famous men are so utterly different in their style and manner, however, that perhaps an exact comparison of their particular merits can take place without appearing improper. One can, indeed, go so far as to say that Haydn and Mozart are equally noteworthy because of the purity and clarity of their style and the select arrangement of their musical sentences. The first appeared to be more distinguished because of his broad manner and knowledge of effect; the second because of his noble feeling and cultured expression. With an imagination less ordered and mature than Haydn's and Mozart's, Beethoven seems to possess just as much fire and vigor as both. There is a certain wildness and Herculean capturing of imagination that is characteristic of this excellent musician. It is his pleasure to wander about in the regions of darkness and magic and to make the heart shudder with sounds that appear to resound from the inhabitants of an undiscovered land and from whose borders no traveler returns. Nevertheless, in his search for novelty he strays into desolate and untraveled fields, which yield nothing to him but a few raw, shapeless results that are difficult to obtain, and which could have deceased without being lamented."

NOTE

1. This entry is part of a large article comprising cols. 629–36. The author translates passages from *An Account of the First Edinburgh Music Festival,* by F. Graham Esq., and adds comments of his own.

❧

21.
Friederike Susan,[1] "Ludwig van Beethoven: Sonnet," *Allgemeine musikalische Zeitung mit besonderer Rücksicht auf den österreichischen Kaiserstaat* 1 (18 September 1817): 340.

A new life stirs in my breast,
The sparks shoot upward from great depths,
Which burn through my breast like a ray of sun,
And lift my spirit upward to the blue heaven.

I see heavenly forces intertwine with the world,
See beautiful Eden of the first creation blossom,
When like Apollo's magic harmonies
The wonderful strings of the master of tones quiver.

Here below the power has been given him
To break the tight prison bonds,
And penetrate the sanctuary.

There his inimitable striving rules freely,
Where all spirits themselves must serve him,
And the fame of the mighty magician will blossom forever.

Ried, 15 August 1817

NOTE

1. "Born Salzer." Friederike Susan (1784–?) published poetry (over 600 poems) in numerous periodicals, including AMZ and WAMZ (1817). She lived most of her life in Salzburg and ceased publishing around 1824 (*DbA*).

∿

22.

Ely, "Cursory Remarks on the Present Situation of Music in Vienna,"
Allgemeine musikalische Zeitung mit besonderer Rücksicht auf den österreichischen Kaiserstaat 2 (26 December 1818): 473–76.

"There is an exception to every rule" is my favorite saying, and it must be the same for every mortal being who cannot see everything and know everything. I am speaking in general, and whoever believes he is being referred to should always remember that in good company those present are the exception to every rule stated. Since the reader and the writer face one another, so to speak, every person who reads these pages will immediately become aware that I did not mean or allude to him under any circumstances. Enough of this introduction and on avoiding misunderstandings!

The first observation that becomes apparent to any foreign friend of music who comes to Vienna and is introduced into several music circles is the disparity between vocal and instrumental music, which is more noticeable here than anywhere else.[1] In the latter, one finds artists of first rank everywhere and hears enchanting productions. In the former, one could hardly be entirely satisfied by one entire piece, and the best productions of this kind offer quite monstrous weaknesses in spite of their great costs.

This situation is not very pleasant for the present and much less so for the future, and if no remedy is forthcoming, after several years it might look bad not only for the art of singing in the Imperial City but also for the art of music in general. One can very easily provide the evidence for this hypothesis. For the last thirty years every instrument has made gigantic progress. Whatever was once a task for a master, is no longer so for students. Now only an exerted effort of several years can prepare one for the latest works, and a single piece often demands many weeks. For that reason there have arisen many great disadvantages. The first and the greatest is the victory of mechanics over feeling, understanding, and even genius. Not just artists, no, amateurs too, who do not wish to descend to become a mere nothing, must sacrifice everything to the tiresome dexterity of the hands, and rather than give character and suitable expression to the total piece, they must take pains to perform all passages and fingerings clearly and precisely. Now, to be sure, someone will object that precisely the latter is hardly so completely indispensable any more, for, thanks to our most recent composers, the latest pieces (*le suprême bon ton*)[2] are hardly anything other than good or bad combinations of passages in which melody plays the least and often no role at all. I must also admit the validity of this objection in its entirety and at the same time not let it go unnoticed that this is the source of the entire malady. Where is all this mechanical dexterity supposed to lead, when all the runs, trills, *Salti mortali* that amaze leave one cold and in the end are simply boring?[3] Oversatiation will breed disgust, music will become more and more difficult but less satisfying, the joy of music will decrease, and people will retreat.

Being unfamiliar with the goings-on here and imagining things differently than they are, I did not understand for a long time how *Tancredi* could please Vienna,[4] the city of art lovers and connoisseurs. The reason is clear to me now: the people were delighted to hear *singing* once again. Melody and performance enchanted their ears, penetrated their hearts. There was nature, feeling, pure rhythm. But, alas, how much emotionless, unrhythmic nature did they not have to swallow in instrumental and, to a degree, in theatrical productions. How much of that did they not have to tolerate every day!

The worst aspect of this apex(?) [*sic*], to which instrumental music has ascended, is the fact that song cannot strike a balance with it. By no means do I fail to recognize what is being done for this branch in many ways and that the most noble efforts are often rewarded the least with proper recognition. On the whole, however, there is a need for a powerful emphasis, and the establishment of a conservatory might be indispensable if art, that most divine art, is not to decline. The how and when should be left up to those who are qualified. However, it is quite certain that the Imperial City would gain new splendor from a conservatory, the Empire itself would be glorified, and the entire matter certainly deserves to be regarded as a universal effort; nothing is to be gained by individual efforts.

Until this wishful thinking becomes something more than a beautiful dream, I must point out a new and certainly significant source of the malady. For some time, people have let a good old custom die out completely. According to this custom, every person who dedicated himself to the art of music above all else studied singing for a year until he applied the principles he learned to an instrument. The following will demonstrate how useful, even necessary, this is. Song alone educates the ear and makes it reliable and accurate. Song alone gives one a sense of true, enchanting melody. Echoing from boyhood, like the idea of a paradise of innocence, it works its way into the memory of a youth, breathes into him an abundance of lyrical tones, and never allows the realm of Polyhymnia[5] to become degraded into a playground of mechanical dexterity. If one also takes into consideration that this preparation in song can and will win many an excellent talent for singing, that the human voice is not always just the most beautiful but also the most productive instrument for its practitioner, then certainly no one will disregard this ancient principle and will always begin the education of initiates with singing.

Only then can one hope that a new day for the art of music will dawn. For now, this goddess is only the object of pomp and superficial splendor for her confidantes and even many of her admirers. She blinds without satisfying the soul. Then, like Mozart's chords, she will completely fulfill her sacred destiny on the wings of melody and penetrate the soul in sweet anticipation of the inexpressible.

I didn't find *Beethoven's* splendid keyboard compositions as well known here as I had imagined. In the beginning this struck me as odd, but soon I became aware of the reasons. *Beethoven's* genius could not be limited by the narrow barriers of the instrument. He disdained to write for six-octave, key-action implements and ten trained fingers. To him the fortepiano was only the least imperfect expression of his overflowing feeling, of his glowing fantasy. He wrote for himself, like *Mozart,* unconcerned about the player, while most of the others, descending from Clementi's school, kept only the instrument and the player in mind. For that reason *Beethoven's* masterpieces delight the connoisseur, please more and more the more often they are listened to, and enchant the nonconnoisseur who has heard them a few times. They are difficult, but fortunately for the performer they don't blind and they don't overpower immediately. Therefore one rarely plays them because music, as stated, has become more a matter of pomp and frivolity than the object of feeling and judicious enjoyment.[6]

NOTES

1. For a detailed study of concert life in Vienna, see Mary Sue Morrow, *Concert Life in Haydn's Vienna* (Stuyvesant NY: Pendragon, 1989), which also contains much information about performances of Beethoven's music.

2. "The finest tone."

3. "Death leaps."

4. *Tancredi,* a melodramatic, heroic opera by Gioacchino Antonio Rossini (1792–1868) was written in 1813 to a libretto based on Torquato Tasso's epic *Gerusalemme liberata* (1575) and Voltaire's *Tancrède* (1760). The popularity of Rossini's operas in Vienna during Beethoven's last years is well known.

5. Polyhymnia, one of the nine muses in Greek mythology, presided over the creation of songs to the gods.

6. The final paragraph, which contains rhapsodic descriptions of generalized feelings and ideas on music unrelated to Beethoven, has been omitted.

23.

"Beethoven's Birthday, Celebrated by a Society of Friends of Music in Bremen,"[1] *Allgemeine musikalische Zeitung mit besonderer Rücksicht auf den österreichischen Kaiserstaat* 4 (18 January 1820): 14–15.

Mentioned: Septet, op. 20; *Fidelio*, op. 72; Overture to Goethe's *Egmont*, op. 84; and *Wellingtons Sieg oder die Schlacht zu Vittoria*, op. 91

Yesterday, 17 December (1819), a select if not large circle of friends of music celebrated with great interest the birthdays of two most intimately known and highly revered artists: *Ludwig van Beethoven*,[2] the greatest composer of our time, and then an active, solid artist from our vicinity who is close to him, also acknowledges being his admirer, and is therefore highly qualified to be counted among his followers. It was a rare coincidence that precisely on this day of precisely this month, the gift of life was allotted to both of them. A beautiful omen, a happy gathering that brought many a sublime pleasure to those who delight in heart-lifting song and playing, in whom the benevolent sense of golden harmony is planted, and to whom the blessed realm of tones was revealed! On the seventeenth of December of the year 1770 *Beethoven* was born in Bonn on the Rhine.[3] Previously the date of his birthday was not generally known and his birth year was likewise incorrectly indicated (as 1772).[4] Thus, on this day this famous artist of music entered his forty-ninth year and therefore in twelve months he will celebrate his fiftieth jubilee, certainly a significant epoch in the history of music that *Beethoven* has so entirely transformed and reformed, and advanced by so much. Who does not know his grand, sublime symphonies—a kind of musical poetry that he actually created for the first time—his music to *Egmont,* his opera *Fidelio oder Leonore,* his sacred music and great fortepiano concertos, particularly the Battle Symphony on *Wellingtons Sieg* and the famous Septet, not to speak of the many larger and smaller beloved keyboard compositions by means of which he has so endlessly expanded and enriched this area. In total, we already count over a hundred of his works and among them so many artful, new creations, rich in ideas, whose most highly original and differentiating characteristic consists in the fact that they belong completely to a poetic, primarily novel-like, fantastic world. What activity and restless efforts and how carefully each piece of music is worked out in every nuance! Let the gratitude and love of the present and future generations be bestowed upon him.

To give the ingenious poet of music a sign of the warmest reverence on this day, felicitations had been sent to him, accompanied by a few poems and other enclosures that contained attempts to express sentiments of devotion and the wish to see him among us being effective and spreading joy for yet a long, long time. A few pieces by the worthy master, performed by several participants of the party, glorified the beautiful celebration of the day. May untroubled cheerfulness and health stand at his side and shelter him henceforth! We hope that this is the vigorous desire of all true friends of music, in whom the memory of an artist (of whom the fatherland is proud), will thrive ceaselessly and who, even if later, will feel moved, inspired by the same interest to celebrate this festival with us in memory.

NOTES

1. "Also appeared in *Bonnerwochenblatt*, no. 479 (1820)." For further information on Beethoven and Bremen, see Bernhard Bartels, *Beethoven und Bonn* (Dinkelsbühl: Kronos E. C. Frohloff, 1954).

2. Beethoven was born on either 16 or 17 December 1770; his birthday was frequently celebrated on 16 December in Vienna. See Theodore Albrecht and Elaine Schwenson, "More Than Just *Peanuts:* Evidence for December 16 as Beethoven's Birthday," *Beethoven Newsletter* 3 (1988): 61.

3. The baptismal record is dated 17 December.

4. See Maynard Solomon, "Beethoven's Birth Year," in *Beethoven Essays*, 35–42.

≈

24.

G. C. Lobedanz,[1] "Comparisons of Great Poets with Great Composers," *Zeitung für die elegante Welt* 20 (24 July 1820): 1130–31, 1140–41.

In a circle of cultured friends, the popular party game was played whereby the similarities and differences between two things are indicated successively. Since there happened to be several friends of poetry and music at the party, parallels were drawn between poets and composers. First Pergolesi and Hölty.[2] "Both," said a charming and already universally esteemed artist who had hardly reached his fifth lustrum,[3] "both blossomed beautifully but briefly, modest like violets, almost in feminine tenderness and therefore particularly dear to the fair sex. With their elegiac charm they put forth more and more beautiful blossoms until a cold, icy wind made them wither away too early. They are different, however, in that Pergolesi did not attain the classical perfection of Hölty, who had excellent critical friends."

The first task was thought to be solved sufficiently, and now a comparison of Ramler and Sebastian Bach was posed.[4] It was the turn of a somewhat sought-after, curly headed conductor with expressive, black eyes. "Both," he began, "are distinguished by their profound knowledge of the mechanical aspects of their art. Their works will remain eternal models for developing artists and touchstones of their erudition. They are different in that Ramler emulated Horace.[5] Bach was his own model and original himself."

Now they moved to a comparison of Handel and Klopstock.[6] "The similarity is obvious in that both selected the composition of the most sublime object for their immortal works, the *Messiah*," replied a cheerful elderly gentleman with white hair. "But undoubtedly there are even more similarities. Both strive for the highest correctness without the slightest harm to the expression of feeling, and both know how to bring forth the most exquisite effects with a single stroke of the brush, it seems. They are different in that Klopstock's compact brevity is missing in Handel."

"Graun and Gellert,"[7] a young lady said, "are similar in their general intelligibility and a certain charming loquaciousness that expresses everything that comes to mind. They also have established excellent models for hymns. They are different since Graun lacks Gellert's jocular vein."

Another young lady compared Majo and Ernst Schulze (author of *The Enchanted Rose*)[8] with the exquisite hummingbird that hovers gently in the warm sunshine, but only for a brief moment, and is enchanting with its golden colors. "The difference," she began to stutter with the sweetest modesty, "I cannot indicate sufficiently since I only know a little about both. I can't tell you why but Schulze's verses sound wonderfully beautiful and in Majo's very beautiful songs there are often passages which seem to struggle with a reluctant theme."

Now Jommelli was to be compared with Thümmel, and it was a poet's turn.[9] "These two men," he began, "are both original geniuses, but otherwise very different. They are similar in that they belong to the most ingenious in their art. Just as Thümmel emulated the French without losing his Germanness, Jommelli also emulated the Germans during his stay in Stuttgart without disposing in the least of the Italian singing style. If I may say so, one often finds a summer lightning of genius in both. Thümmel is a master of humor and the naive, but at least as far as I know Jommelli has produced nothing of that nature."

Now, a dignified matron was to compare Gluck with Lessing.[10] In her golden years she charmed all circles with her exquisite voice, like Faustina Hasse,[11] and her poetry was written not just for poetic annuals. Even now she still attracted youth through her Attic humor and informative conversations, like Sevign and Ninon.[12] "Gluck," she said, "is the creator of a genre, like Lessing. Both swing the club of Aeschylus, but in regard to feeling Gluck stands far above Lessing, who often only works for reason but who also excels Gluck in correctness. One can deduce individual aspects of beauty in Lessing's *Emilia*,[13] but in Gluck's *Iphigenia in Tauris* anyone not poorly educated will feel them. As reformers, both men are pathbreakers in the history of art. A thorough study of antiquity led them to this high level of art." Everyone in the party agreed with this judgment and now entreated a silver-haired educator, who counted the most excellent poets among his former pupils, to make a comparison of J. Haydn and Voß.[14] "The idyllic character, as well as their naiveté," he began, "which inspires both is what particularly differentiates them from other masters. In this respect we find something similar only in Anacreon and Claudius.[15] Voß and Joseph Haydn have achieved the highest clarity and correctness, and like Homer and Virgil will serve posterity as models. Both please equally because of eurythmy and the self-contained solidity of their works. However, only a thorough study of their unique characteristics will make it possible to explain the marvelous effects they bring forth."

After Wieland was compared with Winter, and Heinse with the excellent singer Sacchini, a fiery brunette was to compare Hoffmann, the author of *Phantasiestücke in Callots Mannier,*[16] with Cherubini.[17] Nevertheless she assured us that this task was too difficult for her because a sublime spirit inspired both of them in their own spheres of activity, Hoffmann in the humorous and Cherubini in the sentimental and romantic. Both were unexcelled and left everything far behind them. Therefore someone suggested a comparison of Jean Paul with Beethoven, which she wanted to engage in even less.[18] Nevertheless she did allow these few words to be enticed from her rosy lips. "Jean Paul and Beethoven descend on a demonic bridge from the Elysian Fields into the Cocytus and manipulate the human heart like Arion did on the zither so that all the strings resounded.[19] Their works are charming lakes, with swans gliding gently between glaciers and rocks accessible only to chamois. Their entire difference exists only in the fact that each uses a different medium, the latter notes, the former words, in order to express the highest things that more consummate human beings feel within themselves."

Now it remained only for the hostess of the house to compare Mozart and Goethe. She too belonged to the highly educated of her sex and was soon ready with her answer. "Mozart and Goethe," she said,

are the greatest universal geniuses in their arts. All other artists have their area in which they are particularly at home. These two, however, are great in everything they undertake. If one imagines the spirit that is dominant in *Hermann und Dorothea*[20] or in *Faust,* and again in *Wilhelm Meister,*[21] and that in *Don Juan,* then in the *Requiem,* and then the spirit in the *Entführung aus dem Serail:* what diversity. One cannot believe that the mind of one human being can embrace so much! In the most complex tasks they do not even momentarily lose sight of aesthetic unity or clarity of representation. Even the smallest dance and the seemingly insignificant song bear the stamp of genius just as does the great symphony, the most sublime poem. Fantasy, reason, and feeling are captivated equally and completely, and there is hardly a weak-hearted person who would not be brought out of his apathy through something by these heroes.

Otherwise, ladies and gentlemen, I am sorry that you placed my favorite composer, Cherubini, together with Hoffmann (whom I otherwise value very highly) because I would have compared him with my favorite poet Schiller.

Everyone asked her to do it anyway and this ingenious lady was prevailed upon. She asserted,

Schiller and Cherubini have far surpassed their predecessors in tragedy, Shakespeare and Gluck. Schiller created unattainable ideals in his *Jungfrau von Orleans* and Cherubini in his *Medea*. Their characters are drawn firmly, and fortunately both avoid Shakespeare's superabundance of thoughts as well as Gluck's economy in the use of melodic figures and melismata that borders on scantiness. Both are different in that Schiller always has his sights fixed on the totality and doesn't easily get lost in pretty details. Cherubini, on the other hand, occasionally overrefines details, at least in his earlier and otherwise very excellent works, without, however, harming the unity of the whole.

"Fine and true," the conductor said, "but in regard to this overrefinement, that is to say, the many small notes in the accompaniment, much depends on the human voice (which presents such things) being powerful and the orchestra discrete. If you, honorable madam, want to provide the proof with your full voice, then here is Spontini's masterpiece *La Vestale*,[22] in which there are several of the small notes in the accompaniment." Everyone desired this pleasure, and our obliging hostess sang Julia's great scene in the second act, which the conductor accompanied masterfully on a fortepiano made by Schanz.

Meanwhile the time approached for dinner, where gracious, affable humor and real Hochheimer wine enlivened the gathering until late into the night, and everyone parted merrily.

NOTES

1. C. F. F. Lobedanz (1778–?) studied law and worked in the superior court system in Schleswig. He published some compositions for the piano (*DbA*).

2. Giovanni Battista Pergolesi (1710–36) was a composer from Naples who achieved posthumous fame in the development of Italian comic opera. Writing in both the *seria* and *buffo* styles, Pergolesi created spirited and lively characters with light touches of sentiment.

Ludwig Christoph Hölty (1748–76) was known primarily as a member of the student group the Göttinger Hain (e.g., Friedrich Klopstock, an early favorite of Beethoven), which fostered sentimentalism in lyrical poetry and ballads. Hölty's own poetry is written in a tender, melancholic style that shows elements of both Rococo and *Sturm und Drang* poetry. His poems were set to music by Mozart and Schubert, among others; he wrote the text of Beethoven's song *Klage,* WoO 113.

3. A Latin term meaning a period of five years; used here to help engender an atmosphere of cultivated discussion.

4. In addition to his long tenure as a professor of logic at Berlin's military academy, Karl Wilhelm Ramler (1725–98) gained his literary reputation as a poet of the German Enlightenment and as an imitator of the strict verse forms and rhetorical devices of the classical ode of Roman antiquity. He wrote the text of Carl Heinrich Graun's Passion *Der Tod Jesu* (1775), one of the most widely performed oratorios of the eighteenth century (see n. 7, this entry).

5. Horatius Flaccus, 65–8 B.C., was one of the greatest poets of the age of Augustus. In eighteenth-century Germany he was esteemed for his odes and epistles (e.g., *Ars poetica,* which was important to the development of neoclassical literary and music aesthetics). See Christoph Johann Gottsched, *Versuch einer critischen Dichtkunst,* and the introductory essay to this volume.

6. Friedrich Gottlieb Klopstock (1724–1803) brought to his contemporaries a new poetry of emotional experience and revelation through intensified poetic expression as well as a new concept of the poet as a religious seer and creator with a patriotic mission.

7. It is unclear whether the author is referring to Carl Heinrich Graun (1703/4–59) or his brother Johann Gottlieb Graun (1702/3–71). Both served in the musical establishment of Frederick the Great before and after he became king. C. H. Graun is remembered as one of the foremost German composers of Italian opera in the mid-eighteenth century; his Passion *Der Tod Jesu* continued to be performed for more than a century after his death.

Gellert was one of the most popular poets of his time and gained his reputation as a primary representative of the German Enlightenment with his moral fables and tales, which are written in a gracefully humorous style. His poetry embodies the Enlightenment aesthetic doctrine of *utile dulci* (pleasure and utility), a popular quotation from Horace's *Ars poetica.* See n. 5, this entry.

8. Gian Francesco de Majo (1732–70) was an Italian composer, some of whose works resemble Gluck's reformed opera with its strong emphasis on dramatic music and modified arias. His music was admired by Mozart.

Ernst Konrad Friedrich Schulze (1789–1817) was a minor poet, but his *Bezauberte Rose: Romantisches Gedicht in drei Gesängen* (The enchanted rose, a romantic poem in three cantos) received the prestigious Brockhaus prize one month before his early death.

9. Niccolò Jommelli (1714–74) conducted and wrote operas in Italy, Vienna, and Germany. Like Gluck, he worked to reform traditional *opera seria* by making it more effective dramatically.

Moritz August von Thümmel (1738–1817) wrote satirical and erotic verse epics in the graceful style of French Rococo. He was a close friend of Gellert.

10. Christoph Willibald Gluck (1714–87) was respected by his contemporaries for his opera reforms and the establishment of a new equilibrium between drama and music. It is ironic that even though the author believed that Gluck was limited in his technique, he seems unaware that Gluck's theory of the subordination of music to poetry places him closer to the rationalist music aesthetics of Johann Gottsched (1700–66) and Johann Mattheson (1681–1764) than the humanistic aesthetics in Lessing's *Hamburgische Dramaturgie* (1767–69), the latter's major work in theater criticism and Aristotelian based aesthetics. The author also places Lessing (1729–81) in the rationalist tradition, whereas historically Lessing is recognized as Gottsched's usurper in literary aesthetics.

11. Faustina Bordóni (1700–81), called Hasse-Bordóni after her marriage in 1730 to the composer Johann Adolf Hasse, was considered one of the great singers of the mid-eighteenth century. A biographical sketch appears in K. J. Kutsch and Leo Riemens, *Großes Sängerlexikon* (Bern: A. Francke, 1987), 319–20.

12. Marie de Sévigné (1626–96) portrayed the social life in Paris during the reign of Louis XIV in nearly 1500 letters addressed to her daughter, who maintained a rustic, aristocratic life in Provence.

Ninon de Lenclos (1620 or 1623–1705), was renowned for her beauty, intellect, freedom of spirit, and amorous adventures. She published her letters of artistic and aristocratic life as well as sketches of seventeenth-century Paris in *La Coquette vengée* (1659).

13. *Emilia Galotti* is a drama that exemplifies the new bourgeois tragedy of the eighteenth century. To preserve her virtue, Emilia begs her father to stab her and save her from corrupt seduction by the prince.

14. Johann Heinrich Voß (1751–1826) was valued by his contemporaries for the sober,

idyllic style of his early portrayals of contemporary life and his precise knowledge of classic verse forms of antiquity, which he exemplified in his model translations of Homer.

15. Anacreon of Teos (ca. 572–488 B.C.) was recognized in Germany as the progenitor of a lyrical poetry celebrating the joy of life, wine, and song.

Matthias Claudius (1740–1815) was a popular lyricist known for naive simplicity, modest piety, and naturalness in his verse.

16. See entry no. 29, note 21.

17. Christoph Martin Wieland (1733–1813), along with Lessing, was one of the primary poets of the Enlightenment. Although he had a large range of literary accomplishments, his sensitive elegance, playful spirit, and frivolous grace and irony were the characteristics appreciated by his contemporaries.

Wilhelm Heinse (1746–1803) was a *Sturm und Drang* writer who advocated a libertine, hellenistic epicureanism of beauty and sensuality.

Antonio Sacchini (1730–86) was an important opera composer, known primarily for his works in *seria* style. His operas contain themes from Greek antiquity and *Sturm und Drang*.

18. Johann Paul Friedrich Richter (1763–1825) spent much of his life in impoverished conditions, finding permanent roots only during the last two decades of his life. His work is difficult to define with its varying combinations of sentimentality, Rococo, and classical ideals of humanism on the one side and fantastic excursions into a dream world of subjectivism on the other. His characters often reveal a predilection for an inner world of grotesque but humorous strife that is resolved in a sentimental recognition of the limitations of man. His style reflects the thematic sway between sentimentality and satire in its free-wheeling play with extreme possibilities of linguistic expression.

Amadeus Wendt also makes the comparison between Jean Paul and Beethoven in his lengthy essay on *Fidelio* (see op. 72 in vol. 2 of this work). For a discussion of this tradition of linking Beethoven to Jean Paul (and other literary figures), see Elisabeth Bauer, "Beethoven, unser musikalischer Jean Paul: Anmerkungen zu einer Analoge," *Beethoven / analecta varia,* Musik-Konzepte, ed. Heinz-Klaus Metzger and Rainer Riehn (Munich: Edition Text Critic), 83–105.

19. Elysian Fields is a Greek mythological heaven of eternal blessedness where only the good were sent.

Cocytus is a Greek mythological river of lamentation.

Arion was a Corinthian poet from the eighth century B.C., who in a mythological story saved himself from murder with his enchanting harp music and singing.

20. A verse epic in hexameter written in 1796–97 dealing with the contemporary problem of German refugees during the French Revolution.

21. Most likely *Wilhelm Meisters Lehrjahre* (1795–96), a significant *Bildungsroman,* which portrays youth's discovery of the way to an active life of duty.

22. Gaspar Luigi Pacifico Spontini (1774–1851) was an Italian composer active in Paris and Berlin. At the time of this article, he was conducting the Berlin Court Opera where his rivalry with Carl Maria von Weber involved him in considerable controversy.

25.

"Miscellaneous," *Allgemeine musikalische Zeitung* 24 (8 May 1822): 310.

Our Beethoven seems to be becoming more receptive to music again, which he has shunned almost like a misogynist since his worsening hearing ailment. He has already improvised masterfully a few times in a social gathering to everyone's delight and proved that he still knows how to handle his instrument with power, joy, and love. Hopefully the world of art will see the most exquisite fruits spring forth from these desirable changes.[1]

NOTE

1. As this notice alludes, such improvisations, even in private circles, were rare in Beethoven's last decade. For another account of a twenty-minute improvisation on an eight-note theme from 1825, see Sir George Smart's anecdote in Thayer-Forbes, 963.

≈

26.
Amadeus Wendt,[1] "On the Condition of Music in Germany: A Sketch,"
Allgemeine musikalische Zeitung mit besonderer Rücksicht auf den österreichischen Kaiserstaat 6 (30 November 1822): 761–62.

The exalted organ even now has not yet been completely orphaned by the great artists, but in recent times it has been played less artistically. Also, first-rate organ players lack to some extent the opportunity to demonstrate autonomously the power and depth of their instrument. They also lack good organs since the *best* are also the work of *older* masters, and more recent organ builders of reputation find little work and encouragement.

The number of instruments has been increased in most recent times by many new inventions, but only a few (e.g., the terpodion) have met the general needs of music lovers. Fondness for the *guitar* has finally decreased very much, probably because the imperfect qualities of this instrument have been very much understood. On the other hand, the harp is unjustifiably still in decline and will remain so as long as the *better* instruments we obtain from Paris are too expensive.

I have been speaking first about instruments and their culture because they have the most significant influence on the highest genre of instrumental music: I mean the grand symphony. The symphony is a tone painting that is produced through the collaboration of orchestral instruments. The masters who have devoted themselves to this genre, and they are the greatest composers of our nation, have elevated German orchestras greatly by the demands that they made on instruments in their symphonies.

The expanding art of virtuosity supported these demands, and therefore those masters could require accomplishments from the orchestra that otherwise could be required only of virtuosos. They could engage the masses of sound that an orchestra made available to them as a master engages the sounds of a pianoforte on which he improvises in a free flight of fantasy.

And, in fact, this happened through *Beethoven* and others who in this regard have brought forth unexcelled original works. Occupied with these works, our orchestras have achieved a high degree of perfection; indeed, we see even our amateur orchestras overcoming difficulties now that otherwise would have been considered insurmountable. However, the gigantic works of *Beethoven* seem to frighten off his descendants in this area.

For approximately two years no new work in this genre has appeared. Traveling virtuosos who were concerned about pleasing with lightweight goods pushed aside the grand symphony and replaced it with generally nondescript overtures (mostly an introduction, or rather something to be introduced).

This malady can be counteracted with *well-established* concerts.[2]

NOTES

1. Amadeus Wendt (1783–1836) was a writer, critic, and professor of philosophy in Leipzig. Largely on the strength of his extensive treatment of *Fidelio* in AMZ (see vol. 2 of this work), he is considered one of the most important of Beethoven's contemporary critics. For more on Wendt and his contributions to AMZ, see Robin Wallace, *Beethoven's Critics* (Cambridge: Cambridge University Press, 1986), 26–35, 169 n. 57.

2. The last section of the article has been omitted as totally unrelated to Beethoven.

∽

27.
F. A. Kanne,[1] "On the Perceptible Lack of Great Oratorios,"
Allgemeine musikalische Zeitung mit besonderer Rücksicht auf den österreichischen Kaiserstaat 7 (1 January 1823): 1–3.

Mentioned: Various works, including *Christus am Ölberg,* op. 85

The great master shipbuilder Noah looked out of his cabin across the immeasurable flood to discover a solid point of land hidden beneath the waves, with exactly the longing with which we, as stouthearted seamen of a musical North Pole expedition, look through our acoustical Crazyland day-in and day-out in order to find a passage through the pole. In other words, to find a floating, truly great, new piece of music—an oratorio—in the great, wide Atlantic Ocean of music publications.

A few, like the bold Franklin,[2] decided to undertake such a great journey to discover a gateway with rare, almost adventurous courage. Even though they struggled with all the privation of living in horrible wastelands, nearly sacrificing their lives to certain starvation, which they almost were unable to escape in such a passage from the musical Atlantic Ocean through the North Pole of all artistic productivity to the higher regions of a new world, this has remained nothing more than an idle wish. And in spite of the fact that they rushed headlong toward an almost unavoidable starvation in their endeavor to create a new, great oratorio, it still remained an idle wish.

Many let themselves be frightened away by the large icebergs that the polar stream of counterpoint sets against general melodic rotation and turned back after a few successful bear hunts at which probably a few rare goats were shot too. And then again others gave up halfway through the magnificent project, preferring to catch a few stockfish near Newfoundland, and instead of a great oratorio preferred to produce a few quickly marketable works *pour le saison*. Many preferred to cast the pretty little products of their enthusiastic fantasy, as they call it, into the great monstrous pot from which now half of the music world sups—they call it potpourri. Still others forfeited their lives during the great preparations for their bold undertaking—and thus until this very day the wish of every true friend of music to see finally, once again, a new product of true great inventiveness remains unfulfilled.

Just as in the case of the business indicated in the allegory above, it is preeminently England, which, almost until now, has felt the necessary energy, and thus we are indebted to her alone for the gigantic works of former times, which rest immovably like solid continents in the universal musical deluge and which were able to defy the storms of time.

In more recent times, Vienna, in its golden age of music as we would like to say, has equaled England in this through the great productivity of its creative minds. Particularly *Haydn's* great genius created gigantic works of power that still gleam with radiant luster in the musical heavens. *Mozart's* self-created monument remains unshakable and protects the eternal peace of his burial place against the storms of time.

The power of the great *Beethoven* likewise has revealed itself in a few works of the above-mentioned genre, full of superb genius and sterling quality, which brightly and clearly proclaimed the future that we had yet to expect from him. His *Christus am Ölberg* stands out as an exquisite blossom of his great fantasy. The Abbé Maximilian Stadler,[3] who still remains the Nestor[4] of Viennese composers, ardent in his love of everything beautiful in music, is gloriously known for his former views and genuine products in the area of the oratorio. He also has been active in this music genre with great dedication and has left posterity many a lasting monument.

In Leipzig, the worthy and knowledgeable *Friedrich Schneider,* inspired by Apel's poetic spirit, has caused the trumpet of the final judgment to sound, and through his beautifully conceived and truly artfully worked out choruses he has earned the joyful gratitude of so many a true, sensitive friend of music.[5]

Many a work may, however, still be lying in some dusty corner, a pupa in a state of metamorphosis, awaiting the consummation of more favorable moments to dare its ascent with unfettered wings. We will indulge in this pleasant hope because minds have never been inhibited nor hindered by circumstances. Nevertheless, the present point in time, which is so rich in musical productivity and yet so poor in true great works of music, admonishes us to reflect on what is the actual reason for this paucity.

First of all, experience forces us to see that nowadays the eager culture of music in general is carried on entirely in the same spirit as the prevailing mechanical processing of sheep's wool, and the general proliferation of Merino sheep is progressing.[6]

Where are the mountain ridges and the stony soil supposed to get all the spicy herbs to nourish the immense number of longhaired silky sheep, which, you will note, are known as gourmands among creatures and eat only the freshly budding young leaves of meadow grass?

Just as all the farmers are thinking only of increasing and improving their sheep farms and in the end will painfully feel the noticeable lack of other useful domestic animals, in the same way the mania for music, the craze for composition in our time, has made such rapid progress that a calm, experienced observer almost shudders when he surveys the huge, universal flood of music in which the life of true art finally seems to be buried.

For many reasons that we intend to indicate below, it would almost be desirable that the ingenious means that an inventive farmer in Swabia applied against the current, ominous increase of field mice (he filled the numerous holes with smoke and plugged them up tight) could also be applied to this dangerous increase, although with a few changes and variations.[7]

NOTES

1. Friedrich August Kanne (1778–1833), a Viennese composer, writer, poet, and student of theology, is now remembered primarily as a music critic; he was one of the few who appreciated Beethoven's late works. He contributed scholarly articles on medieval music to WAMZ, served as its editor for a short period, and may also have written some of the early AMZ reviews of Beethoven's works. See Wallace, *Beethoven's Critics,* 16–17, 74–77. According to Fétis, he published a literary fantasy on Beethoven's death. See François-Joseph Fétis, *Biographie universelle des musiciens et bibliographie générale de la musique,* 2nd edn. (Paris, 1874), 4: 474.

2. Sir John Franklin (1786–1847) sought a passage through the Arctic islands of North America.

3. Maximilian Johann Karl Dominik Stadler (1748–1833) was active in Austrian musical life for several decades. An accomplished composer and pianist, he completed a number of works left in fragmentary form by Mozart and was involved in a lengthy dispute over the authenticity of his own copy of Mozart's Requiem. His activities as a music historian are mentioned in Beethoven's conversation books.

4. In the *Iliad,* Nestor is portrayed as the oldest and wisest of the Greek chieftains, whose counsel was held in the highest esteem.

5. Johann Christian Friedrich Schneider (1786–1853) was the foremost member of a family of musicians, a teacher, and a composer of a large number of oratorios. He is also credited with giving the first performance of Beethoven's "Emperor" Concerto, op. 73. A report on this performance appeared in AMZ 14 (1812): 8.

Johann August Apel (1771–1816), a scholar of metrics, wrote the text for Schneider's most well-known oratorio, *Das Weltgericht* (1819). Apel is also known for writing the ghost story (*Der schwarze Jäger*), which served as the basis of Weber's opera *Der Freischütz.*

6. A new type of sheep from Spain with very fine, soft, and curly wool, it was making strong inroads into the sheep farming industry and was ranked high as a mutton producer.

7. This marks the end of the first part of Kanne's essay on the oratorio in this issue. A later, second part makes reference to the rumor that Grillparzer had written the libretto (*Melusine*) for a new Beethoven opera and expresses Kanne's enthusiasm for the verse text *Der Sieg des Kreuzes,* by Karl Bernhard, which Beethoven was to set to music. Neither project came to fruition.

～

28.

"Correspondence: Berlin, 11 February," *Berliner allgemeine musikalische Zeitung* 1 (18 February 1824): 67.

Concertmaster Möser is also continuing this winter to entertain friends of classical chamber music with his ingenious performance of the choicest quartets by J. Haydn, Mozart, Beethoven, and Andreas Romberg.

One quartet in particular, by Beethoven, received distinguished applause because of the characteristic manner of the performance. For that reason it was performed repeatedly by demand at two sessions.

The humor with which Möser performs the Haydn model quartets, and the way in which wit and caprice sparkle, is well known. Mozart may suit the fiery temperament of the players less than Beethoven's bold, often bizarre fantasy. But the energy and romanticism that is expressed in most tone paintings of this genius, who has retreated into himself and carries within himself a world of musical notes, does excite feeling less than Mozart.

～

29.

A. B. Marx,[1] "A Few Words on the Symphony and Beethoven's Achievements in This Field," *Berliner allgemeine musikalische Zeitung* 1 (12 May 1824): 165–68, 173–76, and 181–84.

Mentioned: Symphony No. 1, op. 21; Symphony No. 2, op. 36; Symphony No. 3, op. 55; "Appassionata" Sonata, op. 57; Symphony No. 6, Pastoral, op. 68; *Wellingtons Sieg oder die Schlacht bei Vittoria,* op. 91; and Sonata in C Minor/Major, op. 111

As little as this author intends to put forth a history of the symphony, it nevertheless will be useful—particularly because of the numerous performances of Beethoven's symphonies in Berlin—to take a brief look at the genesis of these compositions in order to gain a more certain overview of how they have continued to develop and of what Beethoven in particular has accomplished.

No art has sprung forth from the head of a human being, like an armored Minerva, any more than it will follow the coffin of an individual into the grave.[2] Rather, the history of each individual demonstrates how an idea of art (and from it that which is called form, as if it were something different) develops more and more freely and abundantly in and with each cultural period until the intellectual strength of the people becomes exhausted and degeneration sets in. The fact and reasons why scientific culture always seems to outlive artistic culture—or rather why scientific culture doesn't seem to exist until later—are beyond the scope of our present consideration. In addition to the interest indicated above, however, this consideration does promise to lead us to a clear understanding of all individual accomplishments.

For a long time vocal music, with the aid of poetry, was already tailored enough to perfection, and this twin sister of language was nourished by all the latter's powers. Also, all the churches, and later the theater too, granted song an honorable position. The most extensive church, Catholicism, even entrusted it with the holiest part of the worship service. During this time, instrumental music was kept in a subordinate position and in the beginning, as it seems, was used only in support of song, for extrinsic purposes (dances and marches), and then to introduce and fill in the pauses in festive occasions (also in larger vocal works). And even here, the introductions were highly insignificant. A few blasts on the trumpet,[3] to capture the attention of the public, were the first overtures. Overtures and symphonies were essentially not differentiated except that the introductory symphony was given the name overture.[4] Here we believe we have found the origins of the symphony.

It seems as if overtures were developed earlier than symphonies. At first, the reason was perhaps that composers had to prove their mastery immediately in the first movement. Not until later did the reason become the higher intention of preparing the content of the work musically. For example, let us go back to the oldest of the composers to be discussed here, *Handel,* who is still more universally known in the present musical world. In some of his oratorios we find overtures well composed in the fugue form dominant at that time. There is no evidence of any special significance (e.g., in the overture to *Alexander's Feast*)[5] that is relevant to his subsequent work, apart from the general solemnity and liveliness required by the form. Only in his most profound and purest work, *The Messiah,* does the special meaning of the overture, so significant in relation to what follows, come to the fore.

Symphonies that served as instrumental interludes in the development of oratorios seem even more to be dedicated to extrinsic purposes. We meet them, for example, in *Saul* by Handel and can consider them entirely as unessential, interpolated interludes for the purpose of resting singers, for variation after a series of vocal pieces, or for diversion. Indeed, in older English scores symphony movements like that are not written, but are marked: here the organ plays,—an opportunity for the organist to demonstrate his art. Other symphony movements suitably adapted themselves to the total work (e.g., the movement before the song of triumph in the first part of *Saul*). Indeed, they became essential, marvelously interlocking parts of the whole, for example, the shepherd symphony in *The Messiah*. However, there are only a few cases like this, and from the predominant, inferior tendency of the symphony there arose an inferior, arbitrarily constructed form. Movements of various character, mostly with varying tempos, often dance forms, were grouped together under the name symphony in countless numbers, and when, in particular, there was a lack of ability or time to write a competent fugal overture,[6] a symphony was probably performed in its place.

In the meantime, however, the higher development of the symphony was being prepared from another direction. Musical training had advanced further, in Germany too, and one had learned to comprehend an idea, a melody, faster. Now there arose for composers the freedom and for listeners the need for a greater abundance of ideas and melodies.[7] The expanded influence of Italian and German composers schooled in the Italian style (Hasse[8] among others) made itself felt here too. Finally, the making and handling of individual instruments progressed, and later more of them were invented or made suitable for use in the orchestra. All of this not only made improved methods of composition possible but also demanded them as a necessity.

With the tendency toward fuller sequences of melody, the fugue form finally had to retreat more. In its place there appeared a new form, not structured and conditioned by polyphony but by the flow of melody. Melodies designed to establish the principal key with only temporary deviations formed a section at the conclusion of which one turned to the key of the dominant and here offered a second section. This was the first part. The second began either without or with an insignificant interlude and repeated the first part, but with the difference that it transposed its second section into the tonic in order to end satisfactorily in this key. This form became dominant in the first parts of arias, in solos for instruments, and in overtures, etc.[9] Alongside of this there appeared the rondo, of Italian origin, which always returns to the principal idea after it has inserted other melodic phrases, and variation: not the treatment of the theme according to various types of double counterpoint,[10] as frequently practiced until recently, but a simple ornamentation, melodic transformation, and working out of the principal theme.

Among these forms the sonata developed for one instrument or with the accompaniment of a few others. In particular, it was thoroughly developed in keyboard compositions since the keyboard seemed most suitable to present a complete piece of music, that is, one worked out melodically and harmonically. As a rule the sonata was given three movements (one fast, one slow, and another fast). At first this was probably to enable it to display a greater fullness and variety in which, of course, unified character was to be striven for. Moreover, the first movement always received the first of the above-mentioned melodic constructions,[11] the second sometimes a rondo form, sometimes a variation, the third generally the rondo form. One soon recognized the sonata as the most useful medium for putting together one's ideas in a rich, diverse, yet unified way. Thus it became the form that composers selected first and most frequently whenever they wanted to give life to their ideas free of extrinsic considerations and relieved of all external needs (an orchestra and the like). Even now they are usually valued not just as the first public attempts of some significance but also as the favorite form when it comes to communicating ideas that decisively belong to the mind of the composer alone, and that are too new and profound for one to expect to find more than *individuals* receptive to them.[12] Thus the sonata maintained the greatest influence on instrumental composition.

How the quartet and its related compositions, as well as the concerto, arose from the sonata can be passed over here. For now, the sonata shall be considered only as the preparation for the symphony in its more permanent and higher form, which the symphony above all also owes to it. The need to fill up the pauses in festivities with music had remained, and there was an obvious desire to use the prevailing and accepted form of the sonata to test the power of the orchestra, that is the power of pure instrumental music. And thus the symphony came about with three principal movements, with another movement of lighter character inserted between the second and third: the minuet, constructed and named after the familiar dance piece.

Here we have arrived at the point where we shall describe the symphony according to its situation under Haydn and Mozart and their imitators. In general we could say that at this stage the symphony was a sonata for orchestra. Even this general designation will yield many characteristics unique to the symphony. How could the refined miniature features (often the glory of a sonata) in a solo instrument have been transferred to the orchestra? How could suppleness, receptiveness, and the ability to follow a flight of ideas be expected from an orchestra (this immensely mixed assembly) as it was from an individual player of a sonata? How could the power and depth of an orchestra not inspire more magnificent ideas? How could its polyphonic nature and flexibility not inspire more profound and mature execution? Thus, on the whole, the symphony obtained a steadier, grander motion, and more profound content instead of the freer and extrinsically (in individual ideas) richer flow of the sonata. Its melodies unfolded more powerfully and more significantly, its harmony became richer and more artistic, its modulation bolder, and part-writing was not shackled by the inferior means of one or a few performers. Contrapuntal interlacing—indeed, the form of the true fugue—also comes more freely into play in the new form of instrumental composition. In instrumentation the strengths of various instruments were heeded above all, as were, to a greater or lesser degree, their peculiarities. Strings were considered to be the principal voices to which the winds were generally added to intensify and augment. However, often even Mozart himself (as an exception to the ideas asserted here) assigned solos to the wind instruments; these passages do not obscure the fact that the winds in general were granted only a secondary role.

If one asks about the intellectual meaning of these symphonies and the nature of the impressions they leave with us, we will have to ascribe a purely lyrical tendency to them. The same emotional impulse that becomes an ode when expressed by individuals and a hymn when expressed by a multitude takes the form of a sonata in the same way as the ode, and a symphony in the same way as the hymn. This is what Mozart put down in symphonies and what he perfected. And who would have been capable of this more than he whose spirit, whose entire nature was dissolved in musical feeling? Regardless of this not being the place to analyze one of his symphonies, let us nevertheless refer to his G-Minor Symphony,[13] which throughout demonstrates the expression of a restless, unsettled passion, of a struggling and fighting against a powerfully intruding agitation. Let us also recall his Symphony in E♭ Major (the so-called swan song),[14] which is dominated not by the language of tears, nor that of disconsolate longing, but rather by the language of a gentle longing illuminated by many a heavenly beam of hope.

Before we turn to Beethoven, however, and observe the shaping of the symphony in his hands, we need another look back at Mozart's predecessor, Haydn. However much in substance the above-mentioned characteristics of Haydn's symphonies resemble Mozart's, we nevertheless still find in them an impurity that is entirely absent in Mozart. It seems as if his feeling, especially his childlike, untroubled joy, which so often unexpectedly bursts forth from him, sometimes seizes upon certain extrinsic objects and blends their representation into the expression of the emotion itself. Whoever listens with sensitivity to the scherzo of the Symphony in C Minor by Haydn must visualize at the same time (if not even before) the general expression of gaiety, a rustic scene, a rustic, merry dance to the village melody of the cello. Even the boisterous "hurrah!" is not forgotten by the violins.[15]

These are the main features of Beethoven's accomplishments in the area of the symphony. In the areas of the sonata and the symphony, Beethoven began at Mozart's level, and his first outpourings can be called lyrical, even though the feeling in them was expressed more definitely and more intimately. Even if many a moment shone forth more freshly and brightly than in the more gentle Mozart and echoed the Haydn school, and even if a greater, more deeply founded unity became manifest in Beethoven's compositions, the basic idea was, nevertheless, the same as stated above. His more advanced development led to a higher cultivation of the sonata form, in which Dussek[16] and the ingenious Prince Louis[17] also took part. The newer the principal idea was and the more powerfully it usually was formed in the first Allegro, the more richly the second modulating section[18] had to proceed from it.

Its novelty was expressed, as it were, in various directions (keys) and configurations (fragmentations and so forth) until it assumed its most appropriate position again in the principal key. To this more richly developed section was added as further confirmation a concluding section, repeating the principal idea. Above all, however, the minuet—usually under the name *scherzo*—was elevated to an essential part of the entire piece. To this period belong Beethoven's Symphonies in C Major and D Major.[19] The first can be called Mozartian without hesitation: the second is written in a similar spirit, but is expanded more and therefore goes beyond Mozartian symphonies in size.

This period above all seems to have established Beethoven's fame and, strangely enough, also the distorted judgments that were passed down about him later. Actually the leaders in affairs of music were trained during the Mozart period and not just a few of them remained at this level. The works that these leaders inculcated in their pupils in every sense of the word as the guiding principle, law, and measure of all later achievement were those that they had embraced with youthful vigor and sensitivity. Their inspiring impression remained in their memories in later years when they were no longer capable of being sensitive to such impressions. They were the works that captivated all their attention, reverence, and admiration at the very time when they began to develop their faculty of judgment. They served as the foundation for their systems, or older systems had adjusted to them. As long as Beethoven followed Mozart he received their applause. But in that period whenever they suspected the distinctive qualities of his music that later became pronounced, it was considered to be an aberration or some kind of excess, and they hoped he would return to the Mozartian way. Those arbiters stayed where they were, but art didn't, nor did Beethoven, in whose works the greatest progress in music after Mozart has become evident (mostly in his sonatas and symphonies).

In the area of the latter, Beethoven experimented in three directions, characteristically in each. Beethoven's Symphony in C Minor[20] emerged from the indefinite lyricism that we believed to find in Mozart's earlier symphonies, although still remaining a part of that lyricism. However, it does not exhibit a single feeling but rather a series of spiritual conditions, with deep psychological truth. It is the struggle of a strong being against an almost overwhelming fate. A hard battle in the disconnected beats of the first Allegro:

OP. 67
Allegro con brio, mm. 1–4

the painful lament of a deeply wounded and yet unweakened soul in the second subject:

OP. 67
Allegro con brio, mm. 63–66

then in the *Andante* the yearning, barely hopeful entreaty:

OP. 67
Andante con moto, mm. 1–4

then the menacing night echoing from the first subject and powerfully encouraging proclamation in C major—

OP. 67
Andante con moto, mm. 31–35

finally elevated by the sublimely peaceful lingering

OP. 67
Andante con moto, mm. 147–53

to the highest majesty of self-confidence and courage—now in the Allegro the struggle against dark fate—gloomy but not violent, as in the first theme,

OP. 67
Allegro (III), mm. 1–4

casting broader and broader shadows and yet retreating more and more—and now finally the most sublime hymn

OP. 67
Allegro (IV), mm. 1–4

which, with triumphant flight, with exalted jubilation,

OP. 67
Allegro (IV), mm. 12–14

and with sure, solid, proud progression,

OP. 67
Allegro (IV), mm. 253–57

in brief, with every note, celebrates the most exquisite victory of the spirit. Even for someone who doesn't know the symphony, it is unnecessary to explain the further development of its contents and the idea dominating the entire piece. Moreover, *Hoffmann* has written about it splendidly in his *Fantasiestücke*.[21]

If we could regard this symphony as the first to advance beyond the Mozartian point of view, then we must now follow Beethoven in a second, entirely heterogeneous direction in which he developed the symphony. Here it wasn't just the more elevated soaring of ideas that led him to new avenues, but also a deeper penetration into the abundance and immense capacity of instrumentation. To portray extrinsic conditions through the orchestra without explanatory words, without the support of pantomime (as in ballet), became his task in the Pastoral Symphony, which presents rustic scenes. The same is true of the Battle Symphony,[22] which has given occasion to so many misinterpretations and unsuccessful imitations. Why should not music try its might in other regions too since it has been applied first and foremost to the representation of spiritual conditions? Humanity exists in nature just as it does in man; it is simply elevated in the latter. Light and night, strength and weakness, desire and flight, satisfaction and abstinence are not exclusively human relationships, they belong to nature too. This in itself allows us to suppose a more general significance in music as well. Furthermore, is not the area of musical allegory productive and is not many an enduring musical form in its generally recognized meaning useful in making completely comprehensible extrinsic references that are not grounded in nature or in music? The regular folk songs (e.g., in Beethoven's *Schlacht:* "Rule Britannia" and "Malborough s'en va-t-en guerre") leave no one with any doubts which nations are opposed to one another. And, after the battle is fought, when the French march "Malborough" etc. returns in a quite strange F♯ minor (before, it was in the bright fresh C major), *piano,* with faltering motion, in disarray as it were, interrupted by the feverish tremolo of the strings and the hollow and very exhausted, lamenting E of the horn: no one can be uncertain about the outcome of the battle.

In this way the unique meaning, the character, and capability of the various instruments may have become clearer and clearer to this indefatigably progressive master. Soon they were no longer a dead artifice for expressing one's subjectivity and feeling by means of expedient selection and arrangement and that at best ought to replace human speech and song (musical speech). They appeared before him in their complete, solidly delineated individuality, and the orchestra became for him an animated chorus engaged in dramatic action. It is certain that this structuring process did not come about suddenly, but rather that it could be detected even in the works of his predecessors and began to take shape in Beethoven's earlier works, for example, those mentioned above. It is just as certain that those earlier tendencies were not abandoned, but that everything now was united: *psychological development,* connected to a series of *extrinsic* circumstances, represented in a thoroughly *dramatic action* of those *instruments* that form the orchestra. And this is the third direction in which Beethoven developed the symphony—the highest point it has achieved.

The first achievement that we have to touch upon here is the *Eroica* Symphony, which was recently performed at Mr. Möser's concert.[23] There is no need for the reference in the title to know that a hero is being celebrated here. Right away the first movement with its bold principal idea, so accessible to the brass instruments,

OP. 55
Allegro con brio, mm. 3–6
(transposed up one octave)

which is passed on to all the parts and right away in the beginning victoriously counters a ferocious conflict of the entire orchestra

OP. 55
Allegro con brio, mm. 29–34

with the sound of trumpets and horns (p. 4 [mm. 30–40] of the [1822 Simrock] score), which after an even harder struggle (pp. 33ff. [mm. 247–55]) is extended overwhelmingly

OP. 55
Allegro con brio, mm. 300–307

and still further through fifteen measures (p. 40 [mm. 308–22]), where, countering the incessant pressure of the basses (p. 43 [mm. 337–47]) it resounds turbulently

OP. 56
Allegro con brio, mm. 338–43

from all the parts like the encouraging calls of comrades-in-arms, and in the end is celebrated by the joyful flight of the violins (p. 73 [mm. 627–32]) and the jubilation of the trumpets and drums (p. 76 [mm. 664–50]). This entire movement shows the successful image of heroic life, and also the painful lament over much loss

OP. 55
Allegro con brio, mm. 83–86,
322–23

is lacking as little as is the lively tempo of bellicosity

to complete the portrait of the hero and the war.

Notwithstanding the utmost precision of the individual ideas and the complete lack of ambiguity through which the meaning of the entire first movement is revealed to those who immerse themselves in it with all the power of their minds, a gratifying comprehension and clear understanding of the meaning is not easy. The themes are so short that they seem to develop right before our very eyes (this has already been suggested in reference to the principal subject), and the instruments occasionally struggle to take possession of the subject and snatch it away before it is completed. Thus the orchestration is divided (p. 5 [mm. 41–50])

among the oboe (1, 5, and 9), clarinet (2, 6, and 10), flute (3 and 7), violin (4 and 8). Not until 10 do the clarinet and bassoon join in, and not until then do all instruments come together in unison (in octaves). The orchestration gains somewhat more stability in the beginning of the second part (p. 20 [mm. 161–71]) in this manner,

where it is executed by the oboe in 1, by the bassoon in 2, but in 3 and 4 by the flute. In contrast to this, at least in the second half the entrance by the bassoon, one octave lower in 2, causes an even greater interruption than the distribution among instruments of the same pitch as indicated above. Not until p. 29 [mm. 218–26] does the subject remain undivided to the end. There is no need for an additional reminder that these are only indications of the distinctive characteristics of the masterpiece. They would only be necessary for the information of those who, being insufficiently familiar with the language of music, could doubt the significance of the composition in general because of the difficulty of comprehending it. Therefore we return to general observations.

The Adagio, entitled Funeral March, is too grand for it to accompany us to the gravesite of a single individual. After having heard the war song of the first Allegro, who doesn't visualize in this Adagio the picture of a bloody battlefield, who doesn't understand the dark thoughts that here must press upon the victor too,

OP. 55
Marcia funebre, mm. 23–29

and who isn't invigorated by the soft voices that seek to console in the change to C major until the heroically bold cry rises above mourning and solace as if reminding us of immortality? After the return of the Funeral March, individual voices of lament and sympathy rise. When feeling becomes intensified almost overwhelmingly, the voice of sacred solace enters (p. 118 [mm. 207–14]) in Db major, and the subject expires in terrible darkness and silence—as it were, the last stirring of life in this field of death.[24]

We need only these suggestions about the first two movements to find successfully the meaning of the last two and of the entire piece.

If in the principal subject of the *Eroica* we discovered the struggle of melodies and instruments to attain definite form, then everything in the Symphony in A Major appears definite, formed, and unambiguously designed:[25] the development of the ideas and the dialogue of the instruments in the most successful harmony. Without any externally derived designation (as e.g., that of the nations in the battle at Vittoria), the meaning of this symphony develops with such victorious precision that one need simply surrender oneself to the effect of the notes in order to visualize such an individual portrait—or perhaps it is better to call it a drama—as never before has been produced in music.

The introduction is composed thoroughly in the sense of the kind of invocation with which we are particularly familiar in epic poets.

"Listen to the wondrous tale," the wind instruments seem to be calling to us, one after the other, with the powerful consent of the tutti. Who does not recall Wieland's words[26] as the strings soar in flight?

> Once more saddle up my hyppogryph[27]
> For a ride into that ancient romantic land.

And already there rings down to us (from the airy wind instruments) a hallowing assent as if from higher regions,

OP. 92
Poco sostenuto, mm. 23–26

OP. 92
Poco sostenuto, mm. 25–27

and the voice of the high strings joins in fondly. The strings repeat the assent to the still doubting ear (in addition, the stirring song of the second violin),

OP. 92
Poco sostenuto, mm. 29–31

and when the primary content of the invocation is heightened and intensified through repetition, the high sounding flutes, oboes, and violins cast their spell. And, as if through a thunderclap of magic, we find ourselves transposed into a more beautiful, warmer region. From all the winds (only the trumpets together with the drums are still silent), there rings down upon us an almost rustic, fresh, spirited melody as if from bright mountains crowned with vineyards. The chorus of string instruments, opposing decisively the chorus of the winds, seems to want to interrupt and take the lead, and when the first chorus has completed its subject, then all the string instruments soar in mighty octaves, and the entire orchestra bursts forth tumultuously, wildly exuberant with reckless daring and pulsating vigor. Who would presume to count how often the choruses of the strings and winds outdo each other with interruptions and imitations, how often the melody soars more boldly in an airy dance and continuously takes new turns! How often do even the silent spots in the melody (p. 26 [mm. 144–50]—also p. 65 [mm. 394–400] in the [first edition 1816] score from Steiner's publishing house), shocked by flashes of lightning, prepare for even bolder soaring! It is a thankless effort to dissect a work of art into individual, beautiful features. It would also be ineffectual for anyone who wasn't able to get to the meaning of the work according to the most general suggestions. However, whoever follows our suggestions and, in particular, follows the work precisely, will not feel that he is in the glowing south, will not see a rustic people inspired by war, rushing unrestrained along the fast, bold path of a warrior's life. This is the glorious age of the Moors, an age whose image in this movement and in the entire symphony was not sought out by us, but to the contrary forced itself upon us.

The second movement, titled Allegretto, is marvelously suited to this. Even the principal idea

OP. 92
Allegretto, mm. 3–10

bears a strange, romance-like character. Its sublime, mournful tempo is joined by a yearning lamentation,

OP. 92
Allegretto, mm. 27–34

at first in the middle tone range of violas and cellos, then an octave higher by the second violin, and finally by the first violin another octave higher.

Remarkably, the winds stand in contrast to this melody of the strings. After they have begun with the call "listen!" they fall silent. Not until the end of the plaintive melody in the second violin do they join in, uncertain and insignificantly as it were, and do not join the melody in the first violin with certainty and complete power until they counter the melody with a funeral song. Thus it could come about if lamenting prisoners are led before the victor and their lament moves the hearts of the warriors. And thus there now follows in our romance a consoling, mildly invigorating reply, too sweet for the voice of even the gentle victor. Is it the intercession of a being tender and dear to him?

This author knows that a large part of the readers will, indeed will have to, consider this suggestion to be unfounded, enthusiastic dreaming since the education of most people has taken such a decisive orientation toward reason that an intimate surrendering of one's entire soul, one's entire being, and trust in the results of such an attitude have become very rare. Also, it is easier to present proof to reason in its secluded, brightly illuminated domain than to an undivided mental facility that desires to attain satisfaction in all the endless directions in which it has expanded. The direction that favors reason above all can become dangerous to the artist. It certainly makes many a talented but weaker disciple of art mistrust the inspirations of genius whenever he doesn't see them supported at least by authority, rules, or tradition. It also stands opposed to an objective and a more comprehensive understanding of works of art when it is a matter of recognizing a significance in them that has not yet been recognized or perhaps that didn't appear in early works of music. The latter is a case that appears so frequently in Beethoven in particular and already has been touched upon directly in this periodical (in the evaluation of the 111th sonata).[28]

The author of this essay believes that he has already achieved much for a more intellectual understanding of music (dissemination is the major purpose of the first volume of our periodical), if only it is generally recognized that something higher is manifest in works of music. This manifestation goes beyond the mere reasoned understanding of the form of a work of art and beyond the mere sensual and general stimulus of feeling. However much the readers are found inclined to accept the image in which the idea of a work of art is to be made visible as suitable and satisfying, it will be sufficient for now if it is only recognized that a piece of music was capable of stimulating an idea or definite representation. Since the present essay is designed to point the way to this recognition and thus induce those capable to investigate works of art vigorously, there is therefore little need for any further observations on the Symphony in A Major or on the *Eroica*. Nevertheless, we will reserve the right to return to both as soon as we are justified by some extrinsic occasion.

Finally, if there is a need to reassure those concerned with the question why this point of view, which we hold to be true, was not expressed or not so definitively in the works of older and highly distinguished philosophers of art, we offer for their consideration the following fact. The preliminary works of philosophers of art are useful to us, and we find the way paved that they first had to prepare laboriously. Above all, however, we make reference to the fact that art first had to reach the stage of perfection where it provided material for a higher point of view and that it quite naturally happens that Sulzer[29] did not comprehend art in general or the symphony (to return to our theme) in the way it took shape after his death. To provide an illustration for that, we have endeavored to present here the gradual development of the symphony in cursory outlines.

NOTES

1. Adolf Bernhard Marx (1795–1866) was an early biographer of Beethoven and the founder of the *Berliner allgemeine musikalische Zeitung*. In his periodical and his many other treatises, he developed a systematic theory of aesthetics. In regard to Beethoven, he stressed the necessity of considering each work as a totality representing a uniform complex of images that are evoked by tone painting. Marx considered Beethoven as a genius whose progressive development began a new epoch in the history of music. An interesting perspective on Marx and his critical writings is found in Sanna Pederson, "A. B. Marx, Berlin Concert Life and German National Identity," *19th-Century Music* 18 (1994): 87–107. See also Wallace, *Beethoven's Critics*, 45–64.

2. In Roman mythology, Minerva—Greek Pallas Athena—leaped forth from the brain of Jupiter in full armor. She was the patron of defensive war and the useful arts (i.e., of spinning, weaving, needlework, etc.). The metaphor in this statement expresses a concept of German Idealism that art has its own cultural existence that is not dependent on any given individual.

3. "Our Jean Paul was referring to this or another view of the overture when he says somewhere: overtures are a musical embellishment which transfers the noise of the public to the musicians who then call out: assemble, honorable guests, we are about to begin! The Berlin public at least is usually as deaf to overtures and acts as if the music were to begin *only after* they are finished."

4. "Even now the Italians and French, who concern themselves very little with symphonies (as we call them) mix up both names."

5. 1736.

6. A familiar example of the fugal overture style, which Marx clearly views as superior to the more loosely structured Italian-style overtures found in many works of the same period, is found in the overture to Handel's *Messiah*, which Marx cites above as a work of unique seriousness and purity.

7. "That also explains the development of other compositional forms, e.g., the aria. Handel, for example (mentioned here because we have constantly made reference to him and will soon be discussing him even more), wrote exactly only as many themes as the text necessarily demanded and was not afraid to repeat the principal theme often. After him came the Hasse-Graun period in which usually the first part of an aria was followed by a foreign interlude and then the first part was repeated note for note—proof that people of that time didn't comprehend and weren't satisfied as quickly as now when such repetitions (e.g., in Graun's *Passion*) are perceived as boring."

8. Johann Adolf Hasse (1699–1783) was one of the foremost composers of Italian serious opera. He is known for his association with Metastasio, many of whose libretti

he set to music, and who seems to have preferred Hasse's settings to all others. See entry no. 24, n. 11.

9. Marx offers here a rudimentary description of what is now called "sonata form" or "sonata-allegro form." Marx himself played a critical role in defining the new form. What is particularly interesting here is that Marx describes sonata form as conditioned by melody. Most previous discussions of this Classical period form had emphasized the tonal and harmonic structure instead.

10. "Sebastian Bach's and Handel's great variations must be regarded as models here."

11. That is, sonata form.

12. "Beethoven's 54th and 111th sonatas shall be considered as examples for the latter case." Here Marx seems to be referring to the Piano Sonata in F, op. 54, and the Piano Sonata in C Minor/Major, op. 111. Actually he means "Appassionata" Sonata (titled "LIVe Sonata" in the first edition), op. 57, and Sonata in C Minor/Major, op. 111. For information on the misnumbering of ops. 54 and 57, see Hans-Werner Küthen, "Pragmatic Instead of Enigmatic: 'The Fifty-First Sonata' of Beethoven," *Beethoven Newsletter* 7 (1992): 68–73.

13. K. 550.

14. K. 543.

15. The reference is to Haydn's Symphony No. 95. The third movement, however, was labeled a minuet by Haydn.

16. Johann Ladislaus Dussek studied under C. P. E Bach and became close friends with his student, Prince Louis Ferdinand of Prussia. See entry no. 9, n. 5.

17. Prince Louis Ferdinand of Prussia (1772–1806) was a nephew of Frederick the Great and a student of Dussek. On Beethoven's opinion of Prince Ferdinand, Ries reports: "His [Friedrich Heinrich Himmel's] piano playing was elegant and pleasant but not to be compared even with that of Prince Louis Ferdinand. [To] the Prince he had once paid a great compliment . . . when he observed that he did not play at all like a king or prince, but like a skillful pianist" (*Beethoven Remembered: The Biographical Notes of Franz Wegeler and Ferdinand Ries*, trans. Frederick Noonan [Arlington VA: Great Ocean, 1987], 97; trans. of *Biographische Notizen über Ludwig van Beethoven* [Coblenz, 1838]). Beethoven also showed some appreciation of Prince Louis's compositions and dedicated the Piano Concerto No. 3, op. 37, to him.

18. "Zeitung, no. 19, p. 168." This article by Marx appears as a series in three consecutive issues, and the reference here is to the last column of the article in issue 19, which begins in my translation with "if one asks about the intellectual meanings of these symphonies" and ends with "these are the main features of Beethoven's accomplishments in the area of the symphony."

19. Symphony No. 1, op. 21, and Symphony No. 2, op. 36.

20. "The symphonies do not follow in chronological order and are not accounted for completely but accordingly, as they most suitably serve to illustrate our view. On the evolution of Beethoven's genius with examples from his complete works in chronological sequence, another time." The reference here is to Symphony No. 5, op. 67.

21. Ernst Theodor Amadeus Hoffmann (1776–1822) still ranks as one of the most prominent critics of Beethoven in the nineteenth century. His reviews of works by Beethoven, particularly that of the Fifth Symphony (see vol. 2 of this work) did much to enhance recognition of Beethoven's unique accomplishments and to place his music within the context of literary Romanticism. Although he always had a special affinity for music (he changed his middle name to Amadeus because of his admiration for Mozart), Hoffmann was active in virtually every field of artistic endeavor. His fluency with both music and language thus equipped him to be one of the most perceptive and articulate music critics of all time. *Fantasiestücke in Callots Manier* (1814–15) is a collection of prose tales and essays dealing with various themes on music or composers. Hoffmann rewrote the review of the Fifth Symphony, which appeared in AMZ in 1810 (cols. 630–42 and 652–59) for

Fantasiestücke, omitting much of the technical analysis and the music examples. For more on Hoffmann's contributions to music criticism, see Peter Schnaus, *E. T. A. Hoffmann als Beethoven-Resenzent der Allgemeinen musikalischen Zeitung* (Munich: Emil Katzbichler, 1977); and Wallace, *Beethoven's Critics,* 20–26 and 126–43.

22. *Wellingtons Sieg oder die Schlacht bei Vittoria,* op. 91.

23. For an extensive discussion of Marx's interpretation of the *Eroica,* see Scott Burnham, "Marx and Beethoven's *Eroica:* Drama, Analysis, and the *Idee,*" in his "Aesthetics, Theory, and History in the Works of Adolph Bernhard Marx" (Ph.D. diss., Brandeis University, 1988), 189–229, and his *Beethoven Hero* (Princeton: Princeton University Press, 1995).

24. This passage seems to have engendered similar reactions by other contemporaries of Beethoven as well. Ignaz Moscheles (1794–1870), who participated in the premiere performance of the Seventh Symphony (conducted by Beethoven), wrote the piano score of *Fidelio* under Beethoven's supervision (1814), and performed the *Missa solemnis* in 1832, wrote in his autobiography (*Life of Moscheles,* ii, 186) that as he stood at the deathbed of his former student, Felix Mendelssohn, this exact passage passed through his mind during the final pulsations of his breath. Moscheles also translated Schindler's biography of Beethoven in 1841.

25. Symphony No. 7, op. 92. A more extensive discussion by Marx of the Seventh Symphony appears in his *Beethoven,* 2 vols. (Berlin: O. Janke, 1859), II: 191–207.

26. See entry no. 24, n. 17.

27. A mythical creature like a griffin or vulture, but with the body and hindquarters of a horse, it is sometimes referred to as a "winged horse."

28. The author is undoubtedly referring to Piano Sonata in C Minor, op. 111.

29. Johann Georg Sulzer (1720–79) was a popular philosopher and aesthetician of the Enlightenment who theorized on the moral values of aesthetic effects. On Sulzer's influence on Beethoven, see Owen Jander, "Exploring Sulzer's *Allgemeine Theorie* as a Source Used by Beethoven," *Beethoven Newsletter* 2 (1987): 1–7.

~

30.
"The Lower Rhine Music Festival, 1824,"[1]
Kölnische Zeitung 87 (30 May 1824).

Just as the first day of the festival belongs exclusively to the creations of the maestro who has become a dear acquaintance to us (F. Schneider), so too will the second provide a worthy cornerstone and at the same time recall to mind names that long have belonged to the Rhineland as a proud heritage and therefore should be particularly dear to us at this Rhenish festival. They are the excellent sons of the Rhineland, whom we gladly honor for their accomplishments, thereby honoring ourselves. Namely, Beethoven, this ancient hero and the real creator of instrumental music, as one knowledgeable author on music calls him, and his student Ries.[2] Both of these sons of our neighboring city Bonn will consecrate this day with their genius, and everyone familiar with these composers will be grateful to the thoughtful organizers of our national festival that they made such a significant choice for this festival with such patriotic understanding.

1. The Lower Rhine Music Festival was perhaps the most prestigious and certainly the longest-running institution of its kind in nineteenth-century Germany. Begun at Elbersfeld by Johannes Schornstein in 1817, it quickly became an annual event, held at the time of Pentecost in Elbersfeld (until 1827), Aachen, Düsseldorf, or Cologne until 1922. The most famous of its later directors was Mendelssohn, who led the festival seven times between 1833 and 1846. Several descriptions of performances at the Lower Rhine Music Festival appear in vol. 2 of this work.

See entry no. 27, n. 5 for F. Schneider, mentioned in the first sentence of this entry.

2. Ferdinand Ries (1784–1838) was the oldest son of Franz Anton Ries, who gave Beethoven violin lessons in Bonn and served as concert master in the Electoral orchestra in Bonn. From 1802 to 1804 Ries studied the piano with Beethoven in Vienna and at times acted as his secretary and copyist. From 1813 to 1824 he lived in London, where some of his works were performed and where he acted on Beethoven's behalf. He collaborated on a biography of Beethoven with Franz Gerhard Wegeler, published in 1838 as *Biographische Notizen über Ludwig van Beethoven*.

⌇

31.

"Ludwig van Beethoven," *Abendzeitung nebst Intelligenzblatt für Literatur und Kunst* 88 (21 July 1824).[1]

Mentioned: *Fidelio*, op. 72, and Overture to *Prometheus*, op. 43

Beethoven belongs among those men who glorify not only Vienna and Germany but Europe and our entire era. Together with Mozart and Haydn he forms the unexcelled triumvirate of contemporary music. The ingenious depth, perpetual originality, and the idealism that in his compositions flows forth from a great spirit assures him the recognition of every admirer of divine Polyhymnia, in spite of Italian cacophony and modern charlatanism (and other pitfalls). But here we are not dealing with his work, only with his personality.

Beethoven's life, as he himself puts it, is a life of tension. The happenings of the world outside hardly affect him. He belongs entirely to art. Late in the night he is at his desk, and the earliest morning hours awaken him to return. Perpetually at work, he is affected by letters of demand (not letters of indebtedness) in a very unpleasant way, for he is only willing to produce products of his mind that are free and not forced. He considers art as divine and not as a means to achieve fame and fortune. He despises everything that is pretext and insists on truth and character in art as well as in life. When *Fidelio* was offered for the first time, the proper overture could not be performed. Another (Prometheus) had to be presented.[2] "People applauded," he said, "but I stood ashamed; it wasn't suitable for the entire piece." He is incapable of dissembling.

TO LUDWIG VAN BEETHOVEN

The realm of music is opened,
The masters select their part:
It winds, like young spring blossoms,
The wreath of songs, which pain and good
Gently bedew with poets' tears.

Whoever penetrates to the distant clouds,
And with solemn sounds
Brings peace to hearts
On the pilgrimage of this life,
Dedicates himself to sublime song.

Another genius has chosen
the pictures of nature,
He has given them a new birth in song,
The soft kiss of truth rewards him
Who has faithfully devoted himself to the master.

Indeed, from the flowery meadows of the heart
Everyone takes a leaf of life for himself,
And uses it with bold self-confidence
In his time and place
To edify the artist's bower.

But out of the bright circle of masters
One man rises forth,
His eye gleams in its unique way,
And searches in the choir of stars
And sinks back quietly and seriously.

He climbs into the realms of the heart,
Recognizes there the essence of beings,
And in a stream of songs makes known,
How things churn and foment there,
Even the dark dreams of premonition.

He has discovered the key
To the sacredness of all life,
He knows the wounds of the tender soul,
Knows its clarity, its fame,
And sings it to us in rare tidings.

Like he who with his fist
Paints life in all its branches,
Paints the gloomy and cheerful striving,
And how it becomes dark and bright
And how they intertwine.

Thus the master has boldly wound
His wings around the wide world,
Has boldly penetrated the firmament,
From the abyss of hell to heaven's heights,
And sung to us sublimely inspired.

And now the soul is lifted high
On wings of mighty harmony
In the fast spiral flight above,
And now melancholy thaws
The loud raging of wild hearts.

How have you, master, achieved that?
Did it come to you in a dream from the firmament?
Alas! if they had not departed from you,
So many flowers of your world—
Such things you would not have achieved.

Only where bitterness of experiences springs
From the deep well of the heart,
Only there where through your own pains
Longing swells in a foreign breast,
Only there do such candles of heaven burn.[3]

NOTES

1. In his *Erinnerungen an Beethoven* ([Stuttgart, 1913], 2:68), Friedrich Kerst attributes a slightly different version of this article to Johann Sporschil (1800–63), as published in the Stuttgart newspaper *Morgenblatt für gebildete Stände* (no. 265, November 1823).

2. The author is in error here. While it is true that the original overture (*Leonore* No. 1) had been found unsatisfactory at a private performance, *Leonore* No. 2 was actually performed and not the Overture to *Prometheus*. In Kerst's version, the title *Prometheus* is not mentioned.

3. This poem closes the article. Preceding it are several anecdotal accounts on Beethoven's appearance, his eating and drinking habits, his sources of income, in addition to other notions about his personal character and feelings, all of which are recounted in Thayer-Forbes.

~

32.

"Morceaux choisis de Louis van Beethoven, arr. à grand orchestre—par Ignace, Chevalier de Seyfried,"[1] *Allgemeine musikalische Zeitung* 27 (5 January 1825): 15–16.

Since music leaders now always want something different but certainly not bad nor pedestrian, and since good, choice works cannot be produced as easily and in such numbers as potatoes, there is therefore no end to arrangements of such works. Whoever doesn't arrange this way, arranges that way, that is to say, from other instruments for the fortepiano, or from the fortepiano for other instruments, etc. Whatever can be said against that, it is, nevertheless, better than accepting something bad and pedestrian and getting used to it. Mr. von S. has proven in his arrangements of large keyboard works by Mozart for the orchestra that he understands how to do this perfectly. In fact, several of his passages sound as if they were originally written for orchestra and even increase expressiveness according to the nature of the instruments. The pieces transformed here are as well selected and as capably and diligently worked out as those by Mozart. Since they are excellent in the originals, they also appear just as beautiful in the arrangements as Mozart's were. For that reason they can most easily be recommended to orchestras, primarily as interludes in concerts or plays. The first issue contains three pieces, the second two. The parts have been made much easier by means of frequent, small notes instead of rests, both for directing without a score as well as for those who do not like or are not sure about handling the rests. Everything: ad hominem. Well, that's the way people want it!

NOTE

1. "Select pieces by Ludwig van Beethoven, arranged for grand orchestra by Sir Ignaz Seyfried."

Ignaz Xaver Ritter von Seyfried (1776–1841) was a student of Mozart and arranged works by Mozart and Haydn, as well as Beethoven. He was the Kapellmeister at the Theater-an-der-Wien from 1797 to 1825 and came into frequent contact with Beethoven. He left an amusing account of turning pages for the premiere of Beethoven's Third Piano Concerto (see Thayer-Forbes, 329–30) and conducted the premiere of the 1806 version of *Fidelio.* He was also the author of an inaccurate account of Beethoven's contrapuntal studies (*Beethovens Studien im Generalbass, Contrapunkte und der Compositionslehre,* 1832), as well as a review of the Ninth Symphony, the *Missa solemnis,* and the String Quartet in C♯ Minor, op. 131, which appeared in *Cäcilia* 9 (1828): 217–43.

～

33.

S. v. W. "Miscellaneous (Submitted): Beethoven's Symphonies," *Berliner allgemeine musikalische Zeitung* 2 (19 January 1825): 24.

Mentioned: Symphony No. 3, op. 55; Symphony No. 5, op. 67; and Symphony No. 7, op. 92

1. IN C MINOR

(Allegro)[1]

Frightened heart, annoyed, oppressed with grief,
You almost disdain the gentle solace of lament.
Does not yet hope dawn on your night?
And healing come to the torment of your wounds?

(Adagio)

See a bright figure ignited before you—
Religion!—It will not let you lose courage,
It will enlighten you about many questions,
Trust in God!—that alone can profit you!

(Menuetto)

Even if fate emptied its quiver of arrows against you,
And the fury of pain increased a thousandfold,
You will now struggle resolutely, indeed, with defiance and disdain.

(Finale)

Join in the victory hymn of blessed spirits
With jubilation, master of providence,
And reap, patient one, the well-deserved crown!

2. *EROICA* SYMPHONY (HERO'S LIFE)

(Allegro)[2]

Rock against rock the heroes stand fighting!
Shield to shield and knee pressing knee,
And helmet to helmet, and bush crowding bush,
Strength struggles with counterstrength midst the menace of death.

(Marcia funèbre)

Dreadful fall of the earthly sublime!
Here a procession approaches, pain delays it oppressively,

And melancholy, barely checking the tears,
Restrains the hero's word, with which the spirit has fled!

(Scherzo)

Flourish now, you heirs of that great name,
In child's play to the songs of the shawm[3]
And joyful fanfares of the hunting horn!

(Finale)

Then rush forth, like eagles in flight,
And hasten to tournaments and serious games,
In gratitude to the most beauteous ladies—often winning!

3. IN A MAJOR

(Poco sostenuto—vivace)[4]

Heaven's abundant blessing in the southern regions
enlivens the glee at the festival of the grapes,
The gold of the fruit glitters in the huts and the bower,
The wineskin is passed around to dispense the mellow wine.

(Allegretto)

A fresh young couple knows how to avert
Accusation and admonishment which mock in whispers,
They must first steal these moments,
So that their delights are consummated later.

(Presto)

Youth, beautiful, agile, unconstrained,
Loves to become entangled in fun and games,
The aged watch with pleasure and in cheerful spirits.

(Allegro con brio)

Longing nods to native dances,
Come forth then, tambourine and castanets
That charm and beauty may compete for the prize.

NOTES

1. The poet seems confused about the movement headings and cites them inaccurately; they are: Allegro con brio, Andante con moto, Allegro, and Allegro.

2. The four movements are Allegro con brio; Marcia funebre: Adagio; Scherzo and Trio: Allegro vivace; and Finale: Allegro molto.

3. The shawm was a conical-bore, double-reed woodwind instrument used in Europe through the seventeenth century. The German *Schalmei* was a transitional form of the instrument that was replaced by the oboe.

4. Because the form of this poem, the Italian sonnet, traditionally has two quatrains, in iambic pentameter, followed by a sestet (in the same meter) whereas the symphony has four movements plus a slow introduction to the first movement, the poet assigned the slow introduction and first movement tempos to the first quatrain and divided the sestet into two separate strophes to accommodate the last two movements. The four movements are Poco sostenuto, Vivace, Allegretto, Presto, and Allegro con brio. Before Mozart's death, the sonnet was almost completely neglected in eighteenth-century Germany. It was revived and gained popularity during the Classical and Romantic periods in German literature. The poet uses the same form for all three symphonies.

~

34.
G. C. F. Lobedanz, "Composers," *Cäcilia* 3 (1825): 231–32.

"COMPOSERS"
DISTICHS BY G. C. F. LOBEDANZ[1]

Mozart

You darling of the Muses, humorous, gentle, sublime,
Has your genius granted you, magician, almighty power?

J. Seb. Bach

Whoever opens new avenues with sure steps,
Will certainly not please many, but connoisseurs will still treasure him highly.

C. P. E. Bach

Not fearing to attain to the style of your father,
You have created your own self, worthy, powerful and pure.

Gluck

When a giant mightily breaks the chains of fashion,
Narrow-mindedness cries out loud, destined to wear chains.

Handel

Hallelujah, the choruses of the heavenly hosts sang,
When you sang of the Messiah with German strength.

Haydn

With Hesperian[2] abundance you unite rustic simplicity,
Grandeur with cheerful humor, and strength with the merriest fun.

Cherubini

Creatively in new romantic ways your spirit forms
Characters as no one knows how to paint them.

Zumsteeg[3]

Many a pleasure was given to us through you, always the greatest,
When you sang melancholic songs to us in Hölty's[4] spirit.

v. Beethoven

Like a raging forest river[5] storming down from mountain rocks,
Your majestic spirit appears; even less great you still would be beautiful.

Spontini[6]

Stir up the flames, glorious spirit, and receive the holy fire,
For truly as long as you sing, it will not be extinguished.

A. Romberg[7]

(Vivo voco, mortuos plango, fulgura frango),[8]
Even though we at once lament you, your glorious work lives indeed.

R . . . i[9]

He piles one style upon the other, this affected artist,
If the father sings like this, what have we to fear from the son?

NOTES

1. Distichs are traditionally couplets consisting of one verse line in hexameter and the second in pentameter. Originally they were used in elegiac or epigrammatic poetry. Here the German meter is a loosely constructed hexameter. Distichs were popularized in Germany by Klopstock, Goethe, and Schiller, all three of whom Beethoven admired at different points in his life.

2. The term *Hesperian* derives from an ancient Greek word for "evening" or "west" and refers here to the Occident, which in English and Latin refers to the part of the world where the sun sets.

3. Johann Rudolf Zumsteeg (1750–1802) was concertmaster in Stuttgart. The comparison of Zumsteeg, popular for his *Lieder,* to Hölty is apt as he also was known for his lyrical poetry written in a tender and melancholic style. See also entry no. 6, n. 2.

4. See entry no. 24, n. 2.

5. A similar water metaphor to describe Beethoven's music appeared several years before in an article that rhapsodizes on music in general with images drawn from the planetary system. See entry no. 18.

6. See entry no. 24, n. 22.

7. See entry no. 8, n. 2, and entry no. 9, n. 3.

8. Slightly distorted Latin, which should read: Vivos voco / Mortuos plango / Fulgura frango (I call the living / I weep for the dead / I smash the thunderbolts).

9. This is probably a reference to the Ricci family, the most well known of whom were Luigi (1805–59) and Frederico (1809–77). Both gained recognition for their buffo style and fantastic comedies but were too young to be considered here. Francesco Pasquale Ricci (1732–1817), who performed his greatly varied compositions from Italy to Holland, is a more likely candidate.

35.
"Critique: History of Music, for Friends and Admirers of This Art (from the French of Mrs. Bawr, freely translated by August Lewald)," *Allgemeine musikalische Zeitung* 27 (7 December 1825): 812–13.

Mentioned: Symphony No. 3, op. 55; Symphony No. 6, op. 68; *Fidelio,* op. 72; and Overture to *Egmont,* op. 84

Ludwig van Beethoven, born in 1772[1] in Bonn, a master whom we mention next to Mozart, who penetrated the most profound secrets of the world of music, has mightily stirred all the strings of the soul in all of his poetic works without words. He has rightly been called the Jean Paul of composers. His works are so rich, so new, and so imaginative that it is almost unbelievable that the art of instrumental composition can be advanced any further. However, it is often the case with him that in his intention to create something even more original he becomes incomprehensible to the listener and degenerates into bizarrerie. His *Eroica* Symphony, his Pastoral Symphony (only these?), his opera *Fidelio,* several of his songs, and the music for Goethe's *Egmont* belong to the most exquisite things we have in music. His works alone are at the top, from which just a small step leads downward again. To want to surpass Beethoven without wanting to surpass his genius, since it could hardly be done otherwise, must produce a caricature.

NOTE

1. Actually 1770. See entry no. 1, n. 2. The section on Beethoven is embedded in a general history of music covered in cols. 809–17.

36.

Gottfried Wilhelm Fink,[1] "On the Question: Is It True That Our Music Has Declined So Far That It No Longer Can Stand Comparison with the Old and Oldest Music?" *Allgemeine musikalische Zeitung* 28 (25 January 1826): 56–59.

Here we will have to pass over many great things that prepared the way for the modern.[2] Haydn lifted up a great people into the new, friendly course of his life. Mozart arose with splendor. His light is clear like the light of reason, which, like a good father, allows the children of his heart to play around him, to cry, to shout with joy, and to be praised with well-cultivated joy and unconcealed uniqueness. Beethoven ascended like youth decorated with all the colors of spring. He seats himself upon mountains. Wildly his steeds rush forth. Brooding, he holds the reins firmly so that they rear at the precipice. He, however, peers into the abyss as if he had buried something down there. Then he bounds across the gaping crevices and proceeds home, playing as if in mockery or blustering as if in a storm. And that something in the depths strangely gazes after him—that is also life. And I think that our age can boldly take up the challenge in many respects when it is a matter of the struggle of art.

Has indeed any age been richer and more diverse than ours in the area of *Lieder,* in particular and most of all among the Germans? Amid this abundance who could expect otherwise than that there is much that is unsuccessful? Every age has in common with others that most of the works don't hit the mark. There are obviously so many good and first-rate things in this area that I will have to pass over many who otherwise also have the right to see their names here.[3]

However, we have more than *Lieder* that will assure us the fame of a truly artful age. What can't be said (and, unfortunately, not unjustly) against today's frequently extravagant instrumentation if we examine the majority of the larger musical works that are appearing now? How often haven't we had to hear the little tiny, meticulous figures (please forgive the expression!), which are imposed on effective instruments, censured as tasteless bombast? Nevertheless, one can by no means fail to recognize that precisely because of the perfection of instruments in the area of the sonata, trio, quartet, and quintet for instruments, etc. we are so far advanced that no earlier age can be compared with ours. Also in this area J. Haydn is the originator of true instrumental quartets, and very many of his works will remain masterpieces forever. Here his inexhaustible flow of good-natured humor distinguishes him significantly above all others. *No one with musical spirit* is capable of hearing Beethoven's trios for strings without delight, presuming (as one must everywhere for every kind of music) that they are played well. Here too, extremely high honor is due the genius of Mozart. What other works would I not have to cite if it could be my intention to ramble!

Furthermore, honor is due our age for having created real artistic pleasures in the area of concertos. One of the first and greatest in this area is again Mozart with his concertos for fortepiano. It is a great disadvantage for art that performers, who now prefer to see all their fingers engaged in wondrous movement, no longer like to perform them frequently, or perhaps are no longer able to. Beethoven's works in this genre, a few by Moscheles,[4] for example, the Concerto in G Minor, many works by C. M. v. Weber, Spohr[5] etc. are each in their own way unsurpassable.

The magnificence of the symphony, what is that otherwise than a product of our age? However much could still be said about that, the essentials for a brief overview have already been stated. On the other hand, I feel and know quite well how much an admirer of ancient church music, of the esteemed works of Durante, Scarlatti, Lotti, Caldara,[6] Handel etc. still has to look back on. Much of that is also not without foundation. However, what seems to result from the great revolutions of an age is not always the real result. Often what was feared, and not unreasonably, is the opposite of what happens.

Often something unheard of comes about only so that the strength lost among the masses may re-enter life more solidly. If some artistic genre has reached its apex, that often signals the great turning point where the almost terrified younger artist believes he sees himself obligated to develop more ingeniously another, even entirely opposite genre. Admittedly, I cannot wish that larger musical institutes, yielding to their general and only too natural preferences, declare themselves only for the marvelously and, indeed, occasionally mockingly fantastic elements in Beethoven's works, which they would like to perform almost exclusively to the neglect of all other masters of the symphony. Nonetheless, given the appropriate alternation of symphonies by Haydn, Mozart, and others, I can just as little agree with the apprehensions born in the hearts of many, even if they don't dare express them out of shyness of general opinion. Beethoven is great, but he is no titan. Also, the heavens are too solid and too high for there to be anything legitimate to fear for him and for us. The mists approach, the horizon becomes dark, weather is forming, and everything is bright. Refreshed, nature breathes out healing aromas tenfold. I do not comprehend why one cannot enjoy something where there is truly something noteworthy to enjoy. Cypresses are beautiful, and myrtles and oak trees too. Wherever there are fruit trees, it is delightful, as in the forest. In brief, our symphonies do our age as much honor as masses do the age of Palestrina.

NOTES

1. Christian Gottfried Wilhelm Fink (1783–1846) studied theology and wrote extensively on music. In 1827 he became the editor of the AMZ. In an editorial note attached to

Friedrich Rochlitz's defense of the String Quartet in C♯ Minor, op. 131 (AMZ, 30 [1828]: 488–89), Fink compared the outcry against Beethoven's late works with the initial reaction to some of his earliest compositions. The mythologized images in this essay reveal Fink's indebtedness to contemporary literary aesthetics.

2. The first five columns of this article present a historical overview of the conditions for the flowering and decline of good music beginning with ancient Egypt.

3. Fink now proceeds to discuss the *Lieder* of Schulz, Reichardt, Kreutzer, von Weber, Zelter, and Spohr without reference to Beethoven. For that reason, this section as well as the beginning and end sections of the article have been omitted.

4. See entry no. 29, n. 24.

5. Louis Spohr (1784–1859) was an important German violinist and composer of both instrumental music and operas. Although his music was basically conservative in style, certain aspects of his operatic writing anticipate Wagner, whose early music he championed. He is also known to violinists as the inventor of the chin rest. Spohr initially held Beethoven's music in high esteem until he performed Beethoven's works in front of other well-known artists and found himself criticized for his taste in Beethoven's music: "Now called upon to perform, I believed that nothing more dignified could be offered to such connoisseurs and artists than one of my favorite quartets by Beethoven. But soon I was forced to notice that as earlier in Leipzig I again had made a blunder: for the musicians of Berlin knew these quartets just as little as those in Leipzig, and therefore they neither knew how to play them nor to appreciate them. After I had ended, they indeed praised my playing but spoke disdainfully about what I had played. Romberg [Bernhard] asked me straight out: 'But my dear Spohr, how can you play such baroque stuff?'" (dated October 1804, in Louis Spohr, *Lebenserinnerungen* [Tutzing: H. Schneider, 1968], 88).

6. The author lists Italian composers of the early eighteenth century known primarily for their sacred and operatic music.

~

37.
C. K . . . s. "Miscellaneous: Request of Beethoven," *Berliner allgemeine musikalische Zeitung* 3 (5 July 1826): 220.

Might it please maestro Beethoven to write cadenzas for his fortepiano concertos![1]

One stumbling block that explains why Beethoven's fortepiano concertos are performed so rarely is the fact that it is not everyone's business to create a cadenza that is compatible with Beethoven's muse. Besides, it has always seemed to this writer that whenever he has heard Beethoven's concertos performed with *ipse fecit*[2] cadenzas, or (just between you and me, Mr. Editor!) played them himself, it is as if one were wearing a velvet evening dress with calico flaps.

NOTES

1. In keeping with the performance practices of the Classical period, Beethoven's original cadenzas for the first four piano concertos were not published as part of the first editions, but appeared in print for the first time in 1864.

2. "Do it yourself!"

38.

"A Feature in Beethoven's Portrait" (*Minerva als Beiblatt zum Allgemeinen musikalischen Anzeiger*), *Allgemeiner musikalischer Anzeiger* (Frankfurt),[1] 1 (6 September 1826): 73.

Just as Beethoven's works carry the stamp of the highest and, no doubt, often bizarre originality, we also see the master moving about within, or rather outside, the bustle of the world with the greatest peculiarity. His works receive all the more value precisely because of the fact that they are pure, unadulterated products of his innermost spiritual life, weakened and modified as little as possible by external impressions. Therefore, it must be of great interest for every admirer of Beethoven, indeed in this way it must be absolutely necessary for a better understanding of his musical compositions, to examine his external life, at least in its individual characteristics.[2]

NOTES

1. There were actually two periodicals published simultaneously under the title *Allgemeiner musikalischer Anzeiger*, one in Frankfurt and the other in Vienna. The periodical published in Frankfurt appeared in only two years, 1826–27; the Vienna publication ran from 1829 to 1840.

2. The author then narrates popular anecdotes on Beethoven's personal life, most of which are recorded in Thayer-Forbes.

~

39.

F. "Open Essays: On the Relationship of Form to Content in Recent Music,"[1] *Berliner allgemeine musikalische Zeitung* 3 (4, 11, and 15 October 1826): 317–18, 325–26, and 333–34.

If the casting off of old, traditional ideas is a sign of an imminent or even completed production of new ideas in art, as well as in science and life, then it would be difficult to deny, as far as music is concerned, that we stand at the beginning of a revolution. Everyone unanimously admits that new forms have developed in music. However, only an unthinking person can separate this admission from the other that new forms must be created through new ideas. The primary and most indispensable understanding for opening the door to art is the fact that in art form and idea are inseparable. Form is not simply a vessel for an idea or a container for storing an idea. To the contrary, it is the *entire idea itself* that has manifested itself and become definite or *formed*. What prospects can be gained for the music of our time, according to this way of thinking, will not be considered here. It will suffice that we are forced to admit that musical ideas that are stimulated now, or in part already created, are not simply renewed or changed because their forms also simply seemed to be renewed or changed. To the contrary, with those forms that never existed or were undiscovered until now, an ideal realm has been entered, which remained undiscovered until now and for which the concern for its care and cultivation is commended to those of the vocation.

The inability to make one's way through the new forms, or better, even to use them to break through to the new ideas, is the difficulty that quite generally stands in the way of understanding the music characteristic of our epoch. It seems imperative to initiate an investigation of the source from which these new and misunderstood forms have emerged. For the time being, we will be content with suggesting a guideline for them without intending to assert that it is the only one that will reach its goal. It cannot be determined in advance from which point in time later scholars will begin dating the transformation. From the point of view *we* are assuming, Beethoven indisputably represents the person to whom we must attribute the discovery of new fields, or at least the blossom-covered paths leading to them. If we understand this great composer correctly, we can characterize his artistic deed as one by means of which he, for the first time, opened the romantic world, in which Mozart's dramatic music moves, for instrumental music too.[2]

Just as *human* behavior and action, awakened by love and passion, is the richly agitated foundation upon which Mozart's poetic creatures appear, so also is the inexhaustible abundance of *natural life* in instrumental music (according to its original meaning) the basis (no less creative) to which Beethoven has attached his artistic views.

One will have to admit that the governing force in dramatic music is moral, and in instrumental sensuous; or, what amounts to the same thing, the idea of the first belongs to history while that of the latter belongs to nature. Accordingly, however, the form of these ideas, or to speak in our jargon, the expression thereof will at once be divided into similar distinctions: the one form will be represented in a historical element, the other in a natural element. To locate both in music presents no difficulty. Everything whose perception occurs in time belongs to history, in which phenomena exist in *succession*. Everything whose perception occurs in space belongs to nature, in which phenomena exist in *juxtaposition*. If now, in general, the succession of sounds constitutes the concept of melody, but their juxtaposition the concept of harmony, thus it follows that the form of the historical element is melodic and that of the natural element is harmonic. No one will hesitate to recognize the predominance of melody in Mozart's music and harmony in Beethoven's as the feature that in particular differentiates the forms of both. To cite more details about this would go beyond our intention. It may appear more important to note how soon the separation of melody and harmony ceases to be valid, even after the distinction indicated above has been made. For anyone who looks more closely, it disappears just as much as does the separation of nature and history, each of which has an aspect of the other.

Given the thoughtlessness that is now displayed toward works of art, particularly musical works, one will certainly turn one's back, in the absence of further motivation, on the commencement of an investigation that endeavors to derive the justification for phenomena in the area of the beautiful (which is only designed to entertain and to divert) from such distant regions. But whoever is not motivated by artistic interest should at least be moved by the scientific need for cooperation that demands that every single significant phenomenon of a time be related to all others. The direction toward nature, which in our opinion more recent music has taken and which also can be discovered in the poetry, painting, and philosophy of our day, is certainly not a matter for great reflection.

This preoccupation of recent music with the abyss of harmony is what makes the adherents of older music dissatisfied with it, since they see in it merely a formal and therefore only extrinsic change without substance. They perceive not so much the power of harmony as rather the apparent lack of melody. Removed from the hitherto prevailing point of view, the old rut they were used to wandering in comfortably and that they now look for in vain, they feel annoyed. They are somewhat like an old logician looking about in vain for the usual syllogisms in the deductions of recent philosophy. They have, so to speak, lost track of the relationship of the hypothesis to the conclusion, of the first theme to the second theme and miss the regular entrances of the dominant and return to the tonic key. And they regard all the recent changes as a *defection* from old, sacred customs that will avenge itself and end in *decay*.

After our attempts to derive the characteristics of the forms that have become dominant and that we have designated in general with the name harmonic forms, we must proceed one step further to the assertion that, through Beethoven, instrumental music has gained just as real a basis in nature as dramatic music has in history. If earlier it was only the expression of a purely inner emotional state, an act of completely subjective feeling, it has now been raised to the representation of a completely objective perception. Judicious men have long since viewed Haydn's much-discussed tone-painting (which has often been censured as ambiguous) less as an aberration than as a naive and awkward foreshadowing of what was to become known and actualized in our times as the true meaning of instrumental music.[3] Wherever similar reminiscences of nature appeared previously, they were always realized only in instrumental music. However much or little truth can be found after this in the assertion that music of the earlier period was more inclined toward poetry and in the later period more toward painting can be derived from what has been stated here. But we must dismiss the investigation, which is suggested here, of what influence the new direction of instrumental music would exert on the traditional form of dramatic music as being beyond our objectives. If, however, we look even here for a suggestion of what can be expected amid what is already at hand, Karl Maria von Weber can supply useful material for observation. In his next to last opera (and supposedly even more in his last opera, which is unknown to us),[4] he made valid the natural element in which his drama develops, the individuality of time and place, and, above all, in music too. On this matter, note what Mr. Marx has cited in his "Art of Song" (section 793)[5] in agreement with this and in reference to Mozart.

The basis of instrumental music, which we have called the historical, not only explains the prevalence of melodic forms in particular; in *general,* it also provides the key for understanding the entire *structure* of works of art that are based on the historical. The presentation of symphonies, concertos, and sonatas in three or four successive parts, separated from one another extrinsically, cannot be something accidental or arbitrary. Each of these parts is maintained in a key different from the others and stimulates a different feeling. Nevertheless, they are disposed to forming an entirety together and are therefore not independent of each other but rather are connected internally and sustained by a common idea. That fact and this demand should therefore be reconciled, and without distorting music we cannot do that any other way than by asserting, true to our basic view, that the division of such works into several parts is nothing more than the necessary consequence of the underlying historical type. The instrumental compositions of this genre contain, namely, the history of one and the same musical thought, of one and the same internally stimulated feeling that appears modified this way and that and must go through all the changing levels of formation before it can be presented in a completed form as the reproduction of the effectual disposition of the soul of the author. The first appearance of the theme in its simplicity, the quickly following modulatory turns of phrases, the combining with other themes, the contrapuntal complexities, the entrance of the adagio, the scherzo, and the finale, which once again picks up all of the elements: to what is that more closely related than to the history of a greatly agitated mind? Such a mind first appears in youthful vigor and openness, is soon drawn into the diverse confusion of life, and finds itself in strange surroundings, makes new connections, and must go though all the intricacies of the world, through sad and happy things, and experience the charm of the pleasant and the might of the powerful before it is tested and ennobled enough to achieve the maturity that breaks its passion and forms its character. In this manner, the historical idea has called forth a form that in turn is itself historical. On the whole it thus appears justified and substantiated. If it is still maintained individually and is respected as a firmly established norm, the reason for that can probably only be a misunderstanding. How much do habit, patriotic love for the traditional, and the increasingly widespread acceptance of mediocrity of talent participate in the pursuit of the path that was once taken by great geniuses? It would be strange to assume that each musical idea is in need of expansion into a certain number of parts or could even tolerate it! It is obvious that, as a result of similar misunderstandings, in symphonies, sonatas, etc. of even the greatest masters one or the other part is inferior to the others in worth and significance and indeed often appears to be superfluous. This provides proof that the author has paid homage to custom more than he has yielded to inner necessity.

Instrumental music of recent times, whose foundation has been called the world of sensuous perceptions,[6] on the whole has had to maintain the same structure that we saw developed in works with a historical basis. For nature, just like history, is a manifestation of the spirit, and the way the former is represented is but a reflection of the representation of the latter. If in the instrumental works of the earlier period the various parts into which the composition was divided were just so many expressions of the same idea modified by the various levels of feeling, then in the works of the present time they are just so many impressions of the same image modified by the various levels of perception.

This relationship of history to nature just discussed above enables nature to be understood by poetry, as well as art, as a grand eternal symbol of human nature. To see in nature pain and joy, struggle and harmony, desire and satisfaction is not something violently imposed on nature but something offered freely. But the expression of these forces is not given in lifeless form, as the sensuous eye perceives them; the power of poetry must elevate them. Nature appears enlivened and spiritualized to the organ of art, and with one stroke the entire, great magical world of fantasy is revealed. For that reason she has become the sovereign of the new realm that, as we said, Beethoven has opened up.

In those works whose idea is historical, the melodic forms were the ones retained to call forth the various conditions of the heart according to the relationships to time. Here, the more limited listener could also comprehend individual elements by himself and thus gain something from it. In those works whose basis is made up by the perceptions of nature, it is the harmonious forms that are retained to place the figures before the imagination, more according to the relationships of space. Here the individual disappears completely in the entire, more encompassing, perception. Here, where it is imperative to penetrate the intention of the author and to draw up a similar, indeed the same, total picture as he did, here, the listener—who would like to take hold of a single melody and follow it calmly as nourishment for his memory—will gain very little benefit. But a person with such a demand is at the lowest level of musical judgment, not just for this but for every kind of composition.

With this recently discovered direction of the musical idea there is a new relationship of the details to the whole in light of which the new forms can be understood. If we have already noted above that the development into several extrinsically separated parts could not be suitable for the expression of every subjective feeling, then that must be even much more valid for the presentation of an objective perception, which cannot be pulled apart arbitrarily or limited, but has a completely circumscribed content. Beethoven also has often thrown off the shackles of custom if no inner reason induced an association with the traditional, and he did not add to two parts a third when he had already said what he wanted to say.[7] The fact that many works of music, even famous ones, have been put together out of several parts, which the author composed at various times and which originally didn't belong together, cannot negate the claim of criticism that works of art ought to be formed as a perfect whole and developed from one idea. That every author with a mind and intelligence will let himself be guided by the idea he wants to present throughout the entire piece when selecting whatever parts are at hand also confirms the truth of these remarks.

NOTES

1. In this essay the author attempts to offer philosophical reasons for the failure of many critics to understand new German music and its major representative, Beethoven. His arguments derive from Enlightenment aesthetics (especially from Lessing's differentiation between the concept of the successive series of narration and the juxtaposition of objects in the plastic arts) and German idealism (e.g., Kant, Schiller, Schelling, and most importantly, Hegel, whose epistemology profoundly affected BAMZ's editor A. B. Marx's understanding of music and its historical development).

2. In other words, the author views Beethoven's instrumental music as the first Romantic instrumental music and Mozart's operas as the first Romantic operas. This forms an interesting contrast to E. T. A. Hoffmann, who saw Haydn, Mozart, and Beethoven as Romantics, but concerned himself almost exclusively with their instrumental music.

3. Marx's Hegelian view of music is clearly manifested in this paragraph, which presents the development of the expressive potential in instrumental music in terms of a Hegelian triad, in which the initial employment of subjective expression and "painterly" techniques by composers like Haydn led to a far more powerful and "objective" music expression rooted in nature.

4. The author is probably referring to *Euryanthe* (1823) and *Oberon* (1826), both noted for their natural and supernatural elements.

5. Marx's *Kunst des Gesangs* was published in 1826, the same year this article appeared.

6. See in the introductory essay on Alexander Baumgarten and the foundations of aesthetics.

7. The author probably refers here to Beethoven's two-movement piano sonatas, which seemed to Beethoven's contemporaries to be lacking a third movement. The publisher of the first edition of the last sonata, op. 111, wrote to Beethoven on receiving the sonata to inquire "if a third movement is not to be added" (see the letter from A. M. Schlesinger to Beethoven from 13 July 1822, in *Letters to Beethoven,* 2:225; and Brandenburg, letter no. 1481).

～

40.

"Beethoven and Jean Paul!—Mozart and Goethe!—A Parallel" (*Minerva als Beiblatt zum Allgemeinen musikalischen Anzeiger*), *Allgemeiner musikalischer Anzeiger* (Frankfurt) 1 (25 October 1826): 134–35.

Beethoven is without a doubt the most ingenious composer of our time. He rules over his genius like it is a slave, now soaring high with it in the spiritual realms of pious faith, now plunging into the deepest abyss of the most fiery feelings. Then he plays a trick on his genius by putting a fool's cap on it and making it do the craziest caprioles. The perfect mirror image of Beethoven's spirit is found in Jean Paul. Should one not believe that one inspiration inflames both of them, that *one* beat of the wings carries them upward and *one* drop of the wings carries them downward? Do they not both magically enchant *fire* and *ice, laughter* and *tears* to become united as they please, or to emerge one from the other, floating without drive and force from the spiritual to the sensual with certainty and speed, like a beam of light reaching the earth? Are we not overpowered by both equally, deluded, made tense, teased, and finally lifted up to the greatest admiration?

Mozart, on the other hand, finds his true spiritual likeness in Goethe.[1] He possesses a regulated, orderly simplicity, a wealth of melodies, which he lets inundate our hearts, and a fidelity of character, which ranges with the greatest certainty and boldness from roguery to horrifying terror. His Mediterranean vitality more or less inflames everything but is kept in check by Nordic strength and solidity. Both rise equally before our eyes, and, however high their soaring carries them, their flight constantly seeks a fixed goal and never misses it. If we follow both of them with our emotions, they draw us ever higher and higher. We dally and are soothed with them, we weep at their laments, we reel at the celestial heights to which they draw our gaze, but in the midst of astonishment they descend to us, and a simple, final chord, a simple truth of life tells us: "You are dreaming."

NOTE

1. The author's assertion that Beethoven was a musical Jean Paul, but Mozart a musical Goethe is echoed in Beethoven's rejection of Goethe's courtly manners. In a letter of 9 August 1812, written soon after spending time with the poet in Teplitz, Beethoven wrote that "Goethe delights far too much in the court atmosphere, far more than is becoming to a poet. How can one really say very much about the ridiculous behavior of virtuosi in this respect, when poets, who should be regarded as the leading teachers of the nation, can forget everything else when confronted with that glitter—" (Anderson, letter no. 380, and Brandenburg, letter no. 591).

For a discussion of the tradition of linking Beethoven to Jean Paul (and other literary figures), see Elisabeth Bauer, "Beethoven und der musikalische Jean Paul: Anmerkungen zu einer Analoge," *Beethoven / analecta varia,* 83–105.

~

41.

Philomelos, "Correspondence—Article: Dear Mr. Woldemar"[1] (*Minerva als Beilage zum Allgemeinen musikalischen Anzeiger*), *Allgemeiner musikalischer Anzeiger* (Frankfurt) 1 (24 January 1827): 240.

It has long since been my intention to write to you to demonstrate my approval of the beautiful essay on the *new* Beethoven works, which you inserted in the morning paper some time ago. Until now various circumstances have prevented me from carrying out my intention. Since, however, to my distress, I have heard a *new* musical rhapsody by this *great* man today, I can no longer remain silent. I must pour out my heart to you, you who are, after all, one of the few who protects our miserable art of music against the unfortunately prevailing unnaturalness and stupidity. The present-day chaos of Mr. B. has again convinced me that this good man must have fallen into a state of mental disturbance, or at least must be suffering from an attack of high fever when he composes. There is such confusion in his ideas that it is just as impossible to derive a healthy total concept from them as from the confused speech of someone sick with delirium. There is neither design nor unity in the total work, but rather he continually leaps, as they say, from one extreme to the other, and his fire is the raving of a madman. To be sure, the poor man can be excused because, from what one hears, he is deaf and can therefore only compose with his eyes. Much that seems wonderful on paper sounds offensive to the ear. This is unfortunately the case with all composers who only have music in their head and not in their heart and soul, and whose products are examples of cold calculation. If the composer is completely *deaf*—alas! For a deaf musician is like a blind painter, for like the latter he is also lost to his art. Like you, dear Mr. W., I am also entirely of the opinion that our good B. is qualified according to B. In the meantime, there are enough human beings (even ladies) who are lifted up to seventh heaven by his rhapsodies and claim to understand them completely in order to lend themselves the appearance of great, profound connoisseurs. What can be done? Nothing but remain silent: one cannot wash a Moor white. After all, it is the fashion of the new school to replace the natural and simply noble with extreme artificiality and floridity and to suppress poor melody beneath a very heavy harmony, and to look for the total value of music in mathematical calculations.[2] Who can swim against the current? Let us patiently bear the nonsense that therefore rules in our dear fatherland and console ourselves with the hope that with time people will turn back from that and realize that music is on a path that will lead to barbarism. For the time being, we should console ourselves with the relics of the great composers of earlier times and the works of composers still alive but who have not yet embraced such vulgar taste. When this evil is at its worst, perhaps a revolution will come about and make everything good again. Amen!

NOTES

1. The reference is to Ernst Woldemar, a Berlin music critic known for his vehement opposition to the works of Beethoven's late period. For more information, see Helmut Kirchmeyer, "Der Fall Woldemar; Materialen zur Geschichte der Beethoven Polemik seit 1827," in *Beiträge zur Geschichte der Musikkritik,* ed. Heinz Becker (Regensburg: Gustav Bosse, 1965), 19–25. See also Robin Wallace (*Beethoven's Critics,* 66–67) for a discussion of Woldemar's critique of late Beethoven as music of the "insane," which sparked a lively debate on the late music during the 1830s (which goes beyond the time limits of this collection, 1790–1830). See entry no. 53 for an example of this debate. *Deutsches biographisches Archiv* claims that Woldemar is a pseudonym for Johannes Adolph Overbeck, a writer and composer, but offers no further information in support of the claim.

2. The German term "das einfach Edle" (the simply noble) received its literary validity as a formulaic expression for classical beauty in the work of the art historian Johann Winckelmann (1717–68). The complete statement has often been quoted as the keystone to neoclassical aesthetics: "The general and most distinctive characteristics of Greek masterpieces are, finally, a noble simplicity and quiet grandeur, both in posture and expression" (*Reflections on the Imitations of Greek Works in Painting and Sculpture* [La Salle IL: Open Court, 1987], 33). For the origins of the term, see the introductory essay.

$\backsim$

42.
R. B. . . . K, "The Musical Observer in Berlin, First Letter" (*Minerva als Beiblatt zum Allgemeinen musikalischen Anzeiger*), *Allgemeiner musikalischer Anzeiger* (Frankfurt) 1 (7 February 1827): 254–55.

Finally, you will get another overview of what is being accomplished for music in Berlin in a critical sense. In the first place there is A. B. Marx as editor of the *Berliner allgemeine musikalische Zeitung* or, as the express mail service writes with ghastly wit: the *Berliner*(!) *allgemeine*(!) *musikalische*(!) *Zeitung*(!). In three volumes Mr. Marx has now proven that he seeks only to promote the subject matter, free of any partiality. And precisely this striving, even if it had been without success, deserves recognition, even more so since he really has done so much good in such a short time. For the first time, Beethoven and Spontini became more comprehensible and accessible through his essays, which are articulated with intelligence and expert knowledge. Gradually, the most preeminent concert producers have considered it beneficial to open their concerts with symphonies, also the work of the same editor. That most of the coworkers at his journal are young men and themselves composers is still a stumbling block for many. This is, however, not the place for wide-ranging discussions about that.

43.

Johann Friedrich Rochlitz,[1] "Necrologue," *Allgemeine musikalische Zeitung* 29 (28 March 1827): 227–28.

Beethoven is no longer among us. The news of his death just arrived from one of his most loyal friends in Vienna. On 26 March, at sunset, B's great, extremely strong spirit fought its way free of its mortal frame, which in many respects surrounded him as a burden, but which he victoriously overcame with the energy of his entire being and, at the end, with quiet resignation. He reached his fifty-fifth year [*sic*]. People will hear regrets about his death as far as the notes of music reach, and they will be echoed for a long, long time. To him belong the greatest, richest, and most unusual qualities that modern instrumental music possesses and, above all, also the freer, bolder, and mightier energy that it has assumed in our times in general. In it, he is the foremost inventor of his contemporaries. In his works, so numerous and significant, he disdained to resemble even himself; rather, he wanted to appear as a new man in each work, even at the risk of making an occasional blunder, or of sometimes being scarcely understood by even a few people. Wherever his most bold, powerful, and energetic works are not yet revered, enjoyed, and loved, the reason is a lack of a noteworthy number of people who are capable of comprehending them and forming a public. This number will grow and together with it his fame will increase. Wherever his works are understood and enjoyed, people will become more and more familiar with them, and his fame will grow to its full extent. For some time already, his relationship with his competitors is such that on the turf he has conquered as his own favorite spot, no one even tries to dispute his sovereignty. The strong avoid him there, and the weak submit to him by struggling to imitate him. The few who earlier misjudged and railed at him are long since forgotten, and those who are still alive can't understand now how they ever could have railed at him. Like hardly any other, he devoted the full sum of his powers, innate or acquired, exclusively to the art for which he was created. Whatever else life offers, he never sought it, and if he did find it, it only served to make his existence tolerably secure; otherwise it meant almost nothing at all to him. He didn't understand people and for approximately the last fifteen years not even their words, and as he did not understand them, neither did they understand him, except in his musical notes. He was separate from them, and since the time his unfortunate fate had befallen him almost totally, he created his own world, wonderfully made up of musical notes that were only thought and not heard. He gave his world life and made it complete. That is truly the meaning of being what one can be through nature, providence, and one's own power of the will! That is the meaning of manfully running the course of this earthly pilgrimage staked out by a higher power. Whoever is successful in his own domain, as Beethoven was in his, and, likewise, whoever is successful in leaving behind at all stations of that course such worthy monuments of his presence, for that person, once he is finished, there will be no lamenting. Instead, there will be a loud confession of respect and lively gratitude. To be sure, we will all feel his truly irreparable loss, but what he has created will remain ours; it will continue to exert influence, directly or indirectly, for an unlimited time. And he will gloriously be remembered in every history of music, even in the latest and most general one, by having provided the essential content for its present period, and by having made it himself, this period and its history, to his own personal domain.

NOTE

1. Johann Friedrich Rochlitz (1769–1842) was editor of the AMZ from 1798 until 1818 and remained a contributor thereafter. In 1822 he visited Vienna and later claimed to have met Beethoven on three occasions. His descriptions of their meetings, however, contain many fabrications, and it is doubted whether he even met Beethoven (see Solomon, "Beethoven's Creative Process: A Two-Part Invention," in *Beethoven Essays* [Cambridge MA: Harvard University Press, 1988], 126–54). Rochlitz's elegant obituary for Beethoven, however, is one of the most important contemporary documents from the period surrounding Beethoven's funeral and is often reprinted along with Franz Grillparzer's funeral oration.

∾

44.
Friedrich de la Motte Fouqué,[1] "To Beethoven," *Berliner allgemeine musikalische Zeitung* 4 (2 May 1827): 137.

To sing songs together with you once, MAESTRO,
This longing dwelled deepest in my heart,
Ever since the mysterious wonders of your songs captured
Me in raptures, horrors, and agonies.
Earlier seraphic pinions sprouted from you,
Carrying you from the worldly air, darkened often by mist,
Home to the glittering light of spiritual candles,
Where eternal hymns resound at the crystal sea.
Full of melancholy I stared far away toward YOUR grave.
From thence arose a sound with caresses pleasing to the west,
Rich—and you often sang like that—in ecstatic horrors.
I dare it, I sing this meaning through the air:
"Yes, we two shall once awaken antiphonies,
High above the mossy grave beneath heavenly roses."

NOTE

1. Friedrich de la Motte Fouqué (1777–1843) was a German poet of French heritage. Fouqué gained much acclaim in Romantic circles for his courtly novels based on motifs from Germanic antiquity, and although most of his works were quickly forgotten, he still maintains an important place in German Romanticism for his fairy tale *Undine,* which the great Beethoven critic E. T. A. Hoffmann used as the basis of an opera of the same name, published in 1816.

~

45.

Dr. Wilhelm Christian Müller, "Something on Ludwig van Beethoven," *Allgemeine musikalische Zeitung* 29 (23 May 1827): 345–54.

Mentioned: Three Trios for Piano, Violin, and Cello, op. 1; String Quartets, op. 18; Septet, op. 20; *Die Geschöpfe des Prometheus,* op. 43; *Adelaide,* op. 46; Six Songs by Gellert, op. 48; Symphony No. 5, op. 67; Symphony No. 6, op. 68; *Fidelio,* op. 72; *Herz, mein Herz,* op. 75, no. 2; *Egmont,* op. 84; *Christus am Ölberg,* op. 85; Mass in C Major, op. 86; *Wellingtons Sieg oder die Schlacht bei Vittoria,* op. 91; Thirty-three Variations on a Waltz by Anton Diabelli, op. 120; *Missa solemnis,* op. 123; Symphony No. 9, op. 125; Grosse Fuge, op. 133; Three Sonatas for Piano, WoO 47; and Twenty-four Variations on "Venni amore" by Righini, WoO 65

In the past weeks, newspaper readers have read many interesting things about this famous composer: his illness, gifts from the English for his care, his death, and the funeral ceremony. Every friend of art, indeed, every cosmopolitan person must be concerned with learning about further particulars regarding this extraordinary genius. For that reason, the following few notes would probably not be out of order. They are from a reliable source because we had carried on a correspondence with him and his most loyal friends for many years and made his personal acquaintance in 1820.

B. was born on 17 December 1770 in Bonn. We know this from the baptismal certificate in the church register. The general statement that he was born two years later is therefore wrong. He himself was in error about that. He was not concerned with years; in the world of music in which he lived, periods of time overlapped one another without divisions according to days and years. His father was a tenor in the chapel of the Prince Elector of Cologne, Maximilian, one of the brothers of Emperor Joseph II. This prince was a great friend of music, like all the children of the Empress Maria Theresa, and maintained one of the most complete chapels of his time. The fathers of the famous Rombergs were also members. Two members are still alive: the father of the well-known fortepianist and Beethoven's major student, Ries; and the music dealer Simrock in Bonn. From these two we also know essential details of Beethoven's youth.[1]

His father gave him his first instruction on the pianoforte and violin in his earliest childhood. He was encouraged to do almost nothing else, and for that reason B. wrote a poor hand and had poor spelling. As a boy he was strong, but with a rather pudgy body. Even as a youth he was devoid of finer worldly habits, and he was still regarded as such in his fiftieth year. His nature was, therefore, contrary to Mozart's.

Because of his lonely life as a boy and the strict orders of his father that he occupy himself continuously with music exercises in his room, he was too preoccupied to feel the loss of social intercourse. He remained shy and taciturn because he exchanged few ideas with people, observed and pondered more than he spoke, and abandoned himself to the feelings and brooding fantasy awakened by music and later by poets. Mozart, on the other hand, was already introduced to the world as a seven-year-old boy, which explains his versatile, affable, communicative, friendly nature, his early skill in composition, and his universal, highly structured, and pleasing, cosmopolitan music. On the contrary, as a boy Beethoven did not think about writing down his creations for others or himself. He improvised at an early age on the pianoforte, and even more on the violin, so that in his loneliness he forgot all of the necessities of life and often had to be fetched to the table by his threatening mother.

On one such occasion she saw him standing in the middle of the room playing on the violin, and to her horror she noticed that a spider had lowered itself down from the ceiling and was hovering above the violin. With angry disgust she hurled the little musical beast to the floor and crushed it with her foot. Her choleric son, acting overhastily in anger, threw the violin at his mother's feet, trampled it to pieces, and never again played on this instrument, for his only listener, the only playmate in his lonely world whom he could enchant to come down to him with musical notes, like Amphion, had been murdered.[2]

After he had given up this melodic instrument, he practiced his beloved art on the *harmonious* one. It is very probable that by his twelfth year, he had learned all the forms of the composers of that time, Haydn, Mozart, Sterkel,[3] etc. for they appear as such in the three sonatas that his father published in his son's eleventh year and that he dedicated to the Prince Elector of Cologne.[4] How much is uniquely his own in these pieces is difficult to determine. They aren't different from the style of that time, but they clearly demonstrate the young beginner; the figures are borrowed from the above-mentioned masters, and the rhythm of his phrases lacks smoothness. The character of his pianoforte trios, which are known to us as his first published work, is quite different. In these works, not only is the form very different, but also in each one there is a tone painting that one can grasp in one's imagination and picture vividly.[5] In his fourteenth year, he became a cembalist in the orchestra; that is to say, he accompanied on the general bass for symphonies. In his sixteenth year, he became the Prince Elector's court organist.[6]

Once he incurred the displeasure of his gracious lord. In order to humiliate an Italian singer who liked to show off his confidence and despised all

German music, Beethoven had let himself get talked into throwing him off-key and off-beat in an aria. To the delight of the members of the orchestra, it worked, but since it happened during a musical mass in the church, he received a sharp rebuke. Nevertheless, he didn't betray those who put him up to it.[7]

Up to that time his manner of playing was merely powerful, raw, and without refinement, though already rich in new, fantastic forms. He was universally admired, but because he was simple, modest, and without pretensions, he was not envied. In his eighteenth year [*sic*], a few of his colleagues took him to Mainz in order that he be heard as a virtuoso.[8] The Abbé Sterkel was known to him as a great keyboard player, and Beethoven wanted to hear him. Fortunately they were invited by Sterkel as director of the orchestra. The Abbé played one of his sonatas with great delicacy. B. stood in the corner with intense attentiveness; he had never heard a refined keyboard player. Now he too was supposed to play, and since he continuously refused, his companions dragged him to the pianoforte by force. He began shyly, but finally he forgot where he was and lost himself in endless fantasies so that the Abbé could not praise him enough. Then he was asked to play his published Variations, but since he didn't know them all by heart, he played seven new variations, which were more beautiful than the published ones.[9] The amazing thing for his friends was his refined playing with the same delicacy as the Abbé's. That he intended to mock his patron, as someone believed, is something of which we do not believe his good nature to be capable.

The Prince Elector sent him to Vienna in 1792 at the prince's own expense to perfect himself in counterpoint under Haydn. He became the favorite of the maestro and was met with respect and affection everywhere, so that in 1794 he decided to stay in Vienna. He also may have decided at this time not to marry in order to dedicate himself completely to music with absolute freedom. He may often have regretted this intention, for we know that once he fell in love with a pretty, diligent student.

One of his most distinguished students was Baroness Ertmann, the most perfect keyboard player we have heard.[10] She gave those of us who never heard him play an idea of how he may have played. He led us to his English instrument, but we couldn't persuade him to play it.[11] He knew what noble thoughts we had about his playing. He certainly didn't want to diminish our beautiful thoughts with his playing that now was harsh, a quality that he would of course demonstrate due to his deafness. Therefore we left him with the same noble idea in our imagination, because in his conversation and friendliness he imparted to us a more pleasant idea of his mind, his heart and an unbiased, free philosophy of life full of truth and justice. In his cramped, somewhat disorderly quarters, he appeared to us like a Diogenes rising above commonness and without the desire of some Alexander, except to grant him light.

His major patron was the Archduke Rudolph, Cardinal and Archbishop of Olmütz. This man, who was his pupil and whose compositions are not unknown, and two other distinguished gentlemen had managed to keep him in Vienna with an annuity of 2,000 gulden after he had twice received an offer from Cassel.[12] The circumstances are known, however, why he did not enjoy the two other patrons' share of the annuity for long, but only that of the first, which amounted to 700 gulden. Two years ago concerts of his latest compositions were arranged, a few times for his benefit, but the costs were so large that only 200 of the 2,000 gulden were left over for him.[13]

Earlier, he had saved some capital that he lent to his brother, a businessman or official in Linz, and which was used to vindicate his honor.[14] Nevertheless, he failed and the capital was lost. Since this brother also died soon, B. took over the support of his widow and son. He had this nephew with him in 1820. However, with his solitary life devoted to art, he wasn't able to watch over the boy properly and probably didn't understand how to raise him at all. To be sure, he did everything possible for him in order to create support for himself someday, but apparently his plan was frustrated.

How little he knew about the world and how little he concerned himself about conventional forms and earthly things is demonstrated by his physical appearance during the time when he was doing most of his composing. For example, he did not know the fashion of wearing frills. Once he asked a lady friend who had dress shirts with this particular decoration made for him so that he would appear more respectable for his female pupils, "What are these for?" "Of course, to keep me warm!" he answered himself, and stuffed his adorned shirt under his vest.

As an unsuspecting man unfamiliar with the intrigues of the world, he may well have been a disorderly and frequently deceived housekeeper. Out of several bottles of excellent wine he drank only one and believed his servant when he said that the others had exploded. It is certain that with his modest way of life, he sometimes lacked the most basic necessities.[15] But he never complained about that, and he never accepted charity from friends of his rank. Indeed, he didn't even take help or favors from his most loyal friends, and in his final years he no longer accepted dinner invitations because he did not want to feel limited in his freedom and because he did not want to become a burden to others because of his deafness. Accordingly, the Viennese may well not have known when he was in want,[16] and one can imagine how difficult it was for the poor sick man to write to Moscheles for support.[17]

This sense of cosmopolitan freedom and this consideration of others may have been the reason why in restaurants, where he occasionally enjoyed a frugal noon day meal, he would carry on with any given conversation and, free of prejudice, express himself critically or satirically about everything: about the government, about the police, about the morals of the aristocracy. The police knew it but he was left in peace, either because they thought him a dreamer or out of respect for his distinguished artistic genius. For that reason it was also his opinion or assertion that no one could be freer than in Vienna. His ideal system of government, however, was English. He examined every political phenomenon on the basis of the English model. He had also heard often how highly he was regarded in England. Ten years ago the management of the London Concert gave him a beautiful Clementi [*sic*] pianoforte.[18] Also, just before his death he received a gift of money for his care. This was probably his last delight from life. He was allotted little else of what one calls external fortune on earth. Music alone was his comforter for unsuccessful wishes and a world full of heavenly pleasures. For that reason, no greater misfortune could befall a human being than his deafness, which was brought on by a cold. Nothing had helped him, and, as he asserted, his ear trumpet had only worsened his ailment with excessive vibrations to the hearing nerves. During the performance of his *Schlacht bei Vittoria,* someone asked him whether he heard the music. "Yes," he answered, "I can certainly hear the bass drum." Nevertheless, he could almost always understand us whenever we stood in front of him and articulated in a clear tone since he had already more or less become accustomed to lip reading. He had others write in a pocket-sized book.[19]

In regard to his morality, he indeed stood high above the vast majority of his contemporaries and artists in that luxurious city. To give an example of his peculiar, strict, moral way of thinking, he once fired his housekeeper, who otherwise was good, because she had told a lie to protect him. To a lady friend, who had obtained this good person for him and now questioned him because of his harshness, he answered: "Whoever tells a lie, does not have a pure heart, and such a person cannot cook pure soup either."

This strange sounding expression of his moral principles corresponds to the strange sounding chords and modulations in his music, which are regarded by many listeners as incomprehensible, affected, or bizarre. Many such passages in his last works must be attributed to his deafness, for on paper much seems harmonious to the imagination but does not quite turn out to be beautiful in real musical tones, above all when difficulties and imperfect players and singers obscure the performance. In his earlier compositions, strange combinations create new aspects of beauty, at least for connoisseurs who have become accustomed to his poetic works.

In almost all of his works, one can discover how rich B's music really is in distinctive, inexhaustible, and unrepeated forms of beauty. We need only recall a few passages in his passion *Christus am Ölberg,* in his opera *Fidelio,* in his masses, in Gellert's songs, *Adelaide; Herz, mein Herz,* etc.,[20] and his Pastoral Symphony, his music for *Egmont,* his first fortepiano trios, his first quartets, and his Septet, etc.

Everywhere he penetrated into the most profound secrets of the world of music and listened to the most tender sounds as well as the most powerful movements of nature itself. During his walks he composed and often took his themes from birds, for example, the G–G–G–E♭, F–F–F–D in the Fifth Symphony.[21] At his favorite summer residence we thought we heard a bird singing this theme from his symphony. There, the ravine behind his place suited his nature: the steep rocks with overhanging pine trees, the murmuring brook, the pretty evergreen meadow between the shady little patch forest of birch trees, and up on top of the mountain peak the infinite view of the fertile plains of Hungary and the rugged, snow-covered mountains of Steiermark.

Beside the single, accurately conceived passage in the Pastoral Symphony, where he has the nightingale, the cuckoo, and the quail sing in jest, one cannot find a prosaic imitation of nature anywhere. It wasn't merely the external aspect of nature that he knew how to interpret, but rather as a philosophical poet he touched all the strings of the soul. He was called the Jean Paul of composers. We would rather compare him with Shakespeare in regard to original sublimity, profundity, strength, and tenderness with humor, wit, and his constant, new, fantastic variations. Occasionally he also loses himself in excesses, but is more organized and has more diverse characters, and exhausts every idea: the most sublime majesty, the deepest melancholy, the warmest delicacy, the most capricious jesting, the most childlike simplicity, and the craziest merriment.

The art of composing for instruments can hardly be promoted any further. How could one develop a theme of three notes with greater variety? Who could enlarge a movement more without exhaustion? More difficulties, more dissonances and ornamentations, more noise, greater duration of a piece— all of that would be unpleasant, boring, oppressive, crazy, and exceed the abilities of the performers. He himself exceeds aesthetic limits in a few pieces, for example, in his 37 variations, in the last violin quartet, in the symphony with Schiller's song about joy.[22] To desire to surpass his genius will lead to adventurous nonsense and to monstrosities. Therefore, in our poem *Pentaide* we assert that, with Beethoven, music reached its apex and can rise no higher, although it can expand infinitely in breadth. We also assert, however, that this master himself has provided the motives for the decline of music. Among his 130 larger, numbered works, in addition to which there are more than 100 choral works, songs, variations, sonatinas, ballets, and dances not so designated, we find, as is known, works of every kind: 2 masses of the most sublime solemnity, a Passion *Jesus am Kreuze,* the opera *Fidelio,* which has been performed in large cities with great splendor, 12 known and unknown symphonies, each of which contains a characteristic tone painting of a romantic story, 16 violin quartets and quintets, approximately 50 works for the pianoforte with and without accompaniment.[23] Of his theater ballets, only *Prometheus* is known.

This may suffice for us to sympathize with the lament of friends of music at his death. Every educated German regrets the loss of Maria von Weber and now even more so L. van Beethoven, for through them we now stand above our musical neighboring countries. But this glory can die out after a few years, and music can sink into general mediocrity.

Beethoven's closer friends mourn his loss most, particularly those who knew him personally and loved him in spite of his peculiarities and only regretted that they weren't able to give him more proof of benevolent love. Now the Viennese friends of music and patrons[24] will erect a monument to him to confirm Kästner's epigram on the English poet Buttler:[25]

> The poor poet asked for bread,
> They gave him a stone.

Poor Beethoven! You too had to be satisfied in life with the riches of your creations and the joy of their dissemination. However, only our grandchildren will understand and enjoy your works properly and revere the master as the prince of the world of music.

> As far as the countries of the globe reach,
> Haydn ruled the kingdom of tones;
> Only Mozart could be compared with him:
> Beethoven is still equal to both.
> His unrestrained rule surpasses both
> With the creative power of fantasy;
> With ghostly ethereal shapes
> His spirit rules, as if by magic.
> He is served by darkness and brightness,
> The abyss, the celestial heights,
> The thundering ocean, the trickling spring,
> The brook, the moonlit sea.
> The forest, the song of nightingales,
> Listened to attentively by tender lovers;
> And a thousandfold voices resound
> To the storm that roars in the leaves.
> Sublime splendor and the charm of beauty
> Revealed in quartet and symphony;
> Feelings, thoughts resound
> In melody and harmony.
> Enchanted delight and sweet longing
> Are awakened by his song, his gay jesting;
> He melts delicate feeling to tears,
> And then awakens the heart to joy.
> Like the spherical tones of Aeolian harps,
> Magic songs, songs of the world continuously

Stream forth from his fantasy;

Man perceives and never forgets them.

The breath of his flutes, the flow of his strings,

Animated by his magic hand,

Shall disseminate heaven in the world—

For that reason God sent him to us.

He sang his loftiest song

In Kyrie, Sanctus, Gloria;

He won the highest goal of art

And stands there as the prince of the music world.

He couldn't live here any longer;

He already was living centuries advanced.

His higher striving was in vain here;

Therefore he hastened from the world.

Bremen, 15 April

NOTES

1. The reminiscences of Ries (who met Beethoven in 1800) and Dr. Franz Wegeler (a childhood friend) were first published in 1838. They are generally regarded as accurate, although several dates and other information are recorded incorrectly. The first complete English translation is titled *Beethoven Remembered: The Biographical Notes of Franz Wegeler and Ferdinand Ries* (henceforth Wegeler-Ries). Nikolaus Simrock (1752–1833) was twenty-eight when Beethoven was born and is a reliable witness to Beethoven's years in Bonn. Simrock's reminiscences are unpublished, although his account of Beethoven's encounter with the pianist Sterkel in 1791 is published in H. C. Robbins Landon, *Beethoven: A Documentary Study* (New York: Macmillan, 1970), 51. Some of his reminiscences appear in section C of the Fischhof manuscript (see Clemens Brenneis, "Das Fischhof-Manuscript, Zur Frühgeschichte der Beethoven-Biographik," in *Zu Beethoven* [1], ed. Harry Goldschmidt [Berlin: Neue Musik, 1979], 90–116, and his "Das Fischhof-Manuskript in der Deutschen Staatsbibliothek/Text und Kommentar," in *Zu Beethoven* 2 [Berlin: Neue Musik, 1984], 27–87). For further information on Sterkel, see n. 3, this entry.

2. According to Thayer-Forbes (p. 58), Beethoven was unable to recall this incident. Apparently the spider story first appeared in AMZ 2 (June 1800): 653–54, but without direct reference to Beethoven. The source of the anecdote is Quatramère Disjonval's *Araneologie* (sic, the author means *Arachneologie*, the science of spiders), which according to the author, D. Hager from Altenburg, refers to Beethoven: "The young artist at that time is the now famous Beethoven." In support of his claim, Hager cites as his source "his [i.e., Beethoven's] teacher at that time citizen Le Mierre in Paris." Jean Frédéric Lemière de Corvey (1770–1832) was a composer and teacher of music; he served as a general under Napoléon in Germany from 1796–97 (Treaty of Campo Fòrmio between Austria and France, 17 October 1797) and again in the Prussian campaigns of 1806. Friedrich Rochlitz continues the tale with his own account of the influence of music on spiders. Amphion was a Greek mythological character, who with his lyre enchanted the stones lying around Thebes to form a wall to protect the city.

3. Johann Franz Xaver Sterkel (1750–1817) was a court chaplain in Mainz as well as a composer with more than 100 works. Of Beethoven's relationship to Sterkel, Wegeler writes: "Sterkel's playing was very light, highly pleasing, and, as the elder Ries put it,

somewhat ladylike. Beethoven stood beside him concentrating intensely. Then he was asked to play but only complied when Sterkel intimated that he doubted whether even the composer of the Variations could play them all the way through. Beethoven played not only these Variations, as far as he could remember them (Sterkel could not find the music), but also a number of others no less difficult and, to the amazement of his listeners, he played everything in precisely the same pleasant manner with which Sterkel had impressed him. That is how easy it was for him to adapt his style of playing to someone else's" (Wegeler-Ries, 23).

4. WoO 47.

5. "We have tried to describe an example of this in the tenth song of the *Pentaide,* which will appear in print shortly."

6. Beethoven served as cembalist for the court orchestra in 1783 when he was twelve years old. A court document dated 27 June 1784 establishes that Beethoven was thirteen when he was first paid 150 florins for serving as the second court organist. He had apparently served at least two years prior to that date (beginning in 1782) for no pay. See Thayer-Forbes, 68, 79.

7. A more complete version of Müller's anecdote here is given in Franz Wegeler's account of the story first published in 1838. Wegeler identified the singer as Ferdinand Heller and notes that it was Beethoven's own idea to try to throw off the singer. See Wegeler-Ries, 20–21, and Thayer-Forbes, 81.

8. The visit with Sterkel and Beethoven's performance of the Righini Variations is recorded in a letter from Simrock to Anton Schindler. Müller's version is inaccurate in almost every detail, including the fact that the trip actually occurred in 1791 when Beethoven was twenty. For Simrock's account, see H. C. Robbins Landon, *Beethoven: A Documentary Study* (New York: Macmillan, 1970), 51.

9. As Simrock reports, the variations were the twenty-four Variations on the Arietta "Venni Amore" by Righini, WoO 65, composed in 1790 and published in 1791 by Götz in Mannheim. Simrock reported that Beethoven "added a couple of new variations for good measure" in the style of Sterkel. See Robbins Landon, *Beethoven,* 51.

10. Baroness Dorothea von Ertmann, née Dorothea Graumann (1781–1849), knew Beethoven well by 1804, studied the piano with him, and later championed his music. In 1817 Beethoven dedicated the Piano Sonata in A Major, op. 101, to the Baroness, whom he affectionately called his "Dorothea-Cäcilia" as a way of honoring her for her stature in the world of music performance. See Thayer-Forbes, 412–13, and Beethoven's letter of 23 February 1817, in Anderson, letter no. 764, and Brandenburg, letter no. 1093.

11. Müller refers here to Beethoven's Broadwood six-octave piano, given to him in 1818 (today in the National Museum, Budapest).

12. The two other signers to the agreement, which promised 4,000 florins to Beethoven, were Prince von Lobkowitz and Prince Ferdinand Kinsky. The Archduke Rudolph pledged to contribute 1,500 florins annually, to be supplemented by 700 florins from Lobkowitz and 1,800 from Kinsky. By February 1811 the sum was reduced in value to only 1,600 florins, and in September Lobkowitz stopped payments for four years. Beethoven was far from alone in having to pursue financial compensations after the disastrous "Finanz-patent" act of 1811; court records in the Ministry of Justice in Vienna contain thousands of petitions from ordinary citizens seeking more favorable rulings regarding their assets. See Max Reinitz, "Die Prozesse gegen die fürstlichen Mazene," *Beethoven im Kampf mit dem Schicksal* (Vienna: Rikola, 1924), 40–49. On Beethoven's major patron, see Susan Kagan, *Archduke Rudolph, Beethoven's Patron, Pupil, and Friend: His Life and Music* (Stuyvesant: Pendragon, 1988). In 1812 Kinsky died, but after some legal wrangling his heirs backdated payments to November 1812. By 1815 Beethoven received 3,400 florins per annum. The second offer referred to here was from the king of Westphalia. For details of the annuity agreement, see Thayer-Forbes, 453–58, 522–24, and 551–54.

13. Müller probably refers here to the benefit concerts of 7 and 23 May 1824, at which the Ninth Symphony and portions of the *Missa solemnis* were first performed in Vienna. The gross receipts for the first concert were 2,200 florins and the profits were less than 420 florins. See Kinsky-Halm, 911–12.

14. Casper Anton Carl van Beethoven (1774–1815) had had a stormy personal and financial relationship with his brother. His last will and testament, which awarded guardianship of his son, Karl, to his wife, Johanna, and his brother, became the instrument for a prolonged legal battle between Johanna and Beethoven over custody of Karl. Contrary to Müller's statement, Beethoven won the legal right to a share of his brother's estate and did not assume the support of Johanna. For a recent full-length study of Beethoven's relations with his nephew, see Stefan Wolf, *Beethovens Neffenkonflikt: Eine Psychologisch-biographische Studie* (Munich: Henle, 1995).

15. "As is well known, this has been publicly contradicted in Vienna.—Ed."
Müller's statement, already corrected by the editor, is indeed inaccurate. For an extensive and well-documented report on Beethoven's real financial circumstances and the economic situation for musicians in Vienna, see Julia Moore, "Beethoven and Music Economics" (Ph.D. diss., University of Illinois at Champaign-Urbana, 1987).

16. "As one might suspect from the boastful letter from Vienna in the *AMZ*.—M." (*AMZ* 27, 288–90).

17. On 22 February 1827, Beethoven wrote to Moscheles to request that he influence the Philharmonic Society of London to give a benefit concert for his behalf (responding to an offer he said they made a few years before). Beethoven wrote, "For a long time composing has been out of the question for me, and thus unfortunately I could find myself in the position of being in want—" (for the complete text, see Anderson, letter no. 1554).

18. Müller refers here to the Broadwood piano sent to Beethoven in late 1817, which arrived in July 1818 in a damaged condition. The piano was a gift from Thomas Broadwood, who had visited Vienna earlier. A plaque on the instrument contained Beethoven's name, Broadwood's as donor, and the names of several important English well-wishers, including Kalkbrenner, Ries, Ferrari, Knyvett, and Cramer. Clementi's name was not included. For a chronological survey of Beethoven's pianos, see William S. Newman, *Beethoven on Beethoven,* 50–67.

19. After he became nearly completely deaf in 1818, Beethoven began to carry paper notebooks in which he would ask people to write questions and comments. Conversation books from 1818 to 1827 survive.

20. The songs mentioned here are ops. 48, 46, and op. 75, no. 2 (or WoO 127). Opus 46, *Adelaide,* is based on a poem by Friedrich von Matthison (1761–1831), teacher, lecturer, and popular poet, respected by Friedrich Schiller and other contemporaries for his euphony, gentle melancholy, and sentimental landscape descriptions. Opus 75, no. 2, is based on Goethe's *Neue Liebe, neues Leben,* written during his *Sturm und Drang* period.

21. Carl Czerny, Beethoven's piano student, also reported that the motive of the first movement of the Fifth Symphony came from the call of the yellowhammer. See his *On the Proper Performance of All Beethoven's Works for the Piano,* ed. Paul Badura-Skoda (Vienna: Universal, 1970), 13. The anecdote that follows probably refers to the hills outside Baden (Steiermark is another name for Styria).

22. None of Beethoven's variation sets were titled "37 Variations." The author probably refers here to "33 Veränderungen über einen Walzer," op. 120, now called the "Diabelli" Variations, published in 1823 by Cappi and Diabelli in Vienna. The "last violin quartet" probably refers to another extended work, the *Große Fuge,* op. 133, published posthumously in May 1827 as "Grande Fugue/tantot libre, tantot recherchée/pour/2 Violons, Alte, & Violoncelle." The *Große Fuge* originated as the first finale of String Quartet, op. 130, which was removed by Beethoven because the earliest performers and audience found it extremely troublesome. Similarly, after the premiere of the Ninth, Beethoven contemplated replacing the choral finale with a purely instrumental finale (Thayer-Forbes, 895).

23. The author's statement about *Jesus am Kreuze* refers to *Christus am Ölberg,* op. 85, Beethoven's only oratorio, written in 1802–03 and published in 1811 by Breitkopf & Härtel. Müller's assertion that all of the symphonies contain a "characteristic tone painting of a romantic story" is of some importance for the reception of these works, given that only the *Eroica* and Pastoral Symphonies bear descriptive programmatic titles.

24. The reference is probably to Gesellschaft der Musikfreunde in Vienna. The plan to erect a Beethoven monument in Vienna did not materialize until 1880; the first Beethoven monument was erected in Bonn in 1845. The 1880 official Viennese monument was designed by Caspar Zumbusch. For a history and survey of Beethoven monuments, see J. A. Schmoll gen. Eisenwerth, "Zur Geschichte des Beethoven-Denkmals," in *Epochengrenzen und Kontinuität/Studien zur Kunstgeschichte,* ed. Winfried Nerdinger and Dietrich Schubert (Munich: Prestel, 1985), 217–62.

25. Samuel Butler (1612–80) gained recognition as a satirist with his *Hudibras,* which is often called the English *Don Quixote,* as well as as an aphorist. Abraham Gotthelf Kästner was a professor of mathematics and physics at the University of Göttingen and a leading figure of the German Enlightenment. He also published several volumes of didactic verse.

The verse cited has its origins in Matt. 7:9: "Or what man is there of you, whom if his son ask bread, will he give him a stone?"

~

46.
"An Opinion on a Piece of Music by Beethoven from No. 4, 1827 of the
Berliner musikalische Zeitung, Which Deserves Greater Dissemination,"
*Allgemeine Musikzeitung zur Beförderung der theoretischen und
praktischen Tonkunst, für Musiker und Freunde der Musik
überhaupt* 1 (8 August 1827): 101–02.

In regard to the most recent works of this great composer, one has to become accustomed to being cautious with one's opinion after listening to them for the first three to six times. This is not because the work is by the famous Beethoven, and as such he already has gained a favorable opinion for himself, or because other famous men will publicly make favorable and laudatory judgments about his work. The reason is rather that thereafter one usually becomes not a little embarrassed when the work begins to become accessible to a mind that initially was so ready to pass judgment against it. Such a mind even believed to have the evidence in hand by daring to declare individual passages as harmonious nonsense or as outbursts of a strange mood that, just for novelty, intentionally snatches at something illicit in order to astound and disturb.

For all that, one is strangely disposed to exactly such works by Beethoven. Just as soon as one knows that a new Beethoven work has drawn near the simple threshold of one's home, one pushes aside all of one's favorite inclinations, indeed even all professional business, just to hear whether the wind, which is to propel the willing ship of the soul and its sails, our feelings, is going to blow northeast or southwest. And behold! after playing it through once, one stands up exasperated and has heard nothing even though one has seen everything, and has felt nothing even though there was no elasticity of feeling lacking. I prefer to go for a walk, up on the high lake shore. There I will know what I am seeing and feeling when I am feeling and that I am hearing something when I am hearing. Indeed what good are the echoing sounds to me up on the high mountains: (here there follows a short passage from a quartet), how did it go after that? It wouldn't have come to mind if the highest branches of the beech tree weren't always swaying so gregariously and friendly in the evening breeze and in freedom. And I have nothing further from my two-hour effort in order to enjoy something suitable. Is it worth the effort; is that the thanks that Beethoven gives his performers for their effort? Why does the man write just this way and not otherwise? How many ugly passages have I had to work out, against my entire sense of hearing, against all beauty? The man makes a useless effort; he is finished and knows nothing more. He is deaf and can't hear anything any more. I wonder whether he can play the violin. I hardly believe that. How oppressive all of that is, so sublime; how awkward it sounds. He ought to learn to play the violin, etc.

One returns home. Nevertheless, the passage is indeed beautiful, that has to be true, and from that one knows that he wrote it, something like that someone else could—how was the ending, quite strangely vivacious.—So gigantically grand. And a strange finale—the theme: it seems to be ably worked out. How obbligato the parts develop, as if they had no concern for themselves, but they do have that. And the striking contrast: the thing does seem to be worth the effort. One has to hear it more often. Well, once more. Also, one has to go through it *à quatre mains,* each week one movement quite gratefully.[1]

NOTE

1. Beethoven's string quartets and other works were frequently published in four-hand ("à quatre mains") arrangements for piano.

47.
Tobias Haslinger,[1] "A Notice Regarding the Larger Portion of Beethoven's Bequest," *Allgemeine Musikzeitung zur Beförderung der theoretischen und praktischen Tonkunst, für Musiker und Freunde der Musik überhaupt* 1 (20 February 1828): 119–20.

Mentioned: large number of miscellaneous works, including Septet, op. 20, *Der glorreiche Augenblick,* op. 136, and *Leonore* Overture No. 1, op. 138

In the auction of Beethoven's bequest, which took place here on 5, 6, and 7 November, I acquired by purchase many manuscripts of known, engraved works (e.g., symphonies, concertos, quartets, sonatas, songs) of this famous master and also the original manuscript of his well-known Septet.[2] In addition, I obtained *many* partially lesser, partially greater, but very significant and *still unknown original compositions* of this famous master. Among them there are preeminently five packets of studies written down in *Beethoven*'s own hand on the theory of composition and counterpoint, which the deceased studied with his master *Albrechtsberger*.[3] Further, a pianoforte trio that he composed when he was still an organist in Cologne, a sonatina for four hands, several marches for military music, a few larger choral pieces, songs, and other things.[4] In addition to these, there are also a still unknown *Grand Characteristic Overture for Orchestra by Ludwig van Beethoven*, which consists of a large introduction to an Allegro, with a splendid Adagio as the middle movement, and with a complete working out of the first Allegro as the concluding movement.[5] Art experts are quite delighted by the beauty and great worth of this ingenious and easily comprehensible work and cannot explain to themselves how this great composer could withhold such a masterpiece from the world of art for so long.

I am now disposed to pass on this noteworthy product to the art-loving world and to have it engraved for publication before all the others and, to be sure, under the title indicated in *Beethoven's own hand* and in the following editions as indicated:

GRAND CHARACTERISTIC OVERTURE BY
LUDWIG VAN BEETHOVEN, OP.138

1. In complete score, in a deluxe edition
2. for the entire orchestra, with individual orchestra parts;
3. for full-voiced Turkish music;
4. for nine-part harmony, with trumpet ad lib;
5. in quintet for two violins, two violas, and cello;
6. in quartet for pianoforte, violin, viola, and cello;
7. for two pianofortes;
8. for the pianoforte for four hands with violin and cello accompaniment;
9. for the pianoforte for four hands (without accompaniment);
10. for the pianoforte alone.

Work has already begun on the engraving of these editions.

The purpose of this notice is to entreat you to make this notice known in your area and to let me know as soon as possible how many copies of each of the indicated editions I should send to you.

At the same time I further report to you that I am in possession of *several manuscripts by Beethoven* that the founder and my business predecessor,

S. A. Steiner, bought as his personal property from the deceased in 1814.[6] Among these is the grand cantata *Der glorreiche Augenblick,* which was performed only twice in Vienna in the large Royal Redouten-Saal during the presence of the highest ranking allies, and is distinguished in particular as Beethoven's greatest posthumous masterpiece.[7]

I have also purchased the London complete edition of Handel's works (in forty folio volumes), excellently preserved in leather (with Handel's portrait, ingeniously executed and very exact), also from the bequest named above. To be sure, it is the same complete edition that the deceased received as a gift from England shortly before his death.[8]

Vienna, December, 1827.

NOTES

1. Tobias Haslinger (1787–1842) worked his way up in the Sigmund Anton Steiner Company eventually to become sole owner. Steiner and Company published a number of Beethoven's works, and Haslinger, who for a time had a friendly relationship with Beethoven, planned a deluxe collection of Beethoven's scores in sixty-two volumes in preparation for a published edition of his works. Although his plan was never realized, a handwritten copy of Beethoven's works, prepared by two calligraphists engaged by Haslinger, is currently in the Gesellschaft der Musikfreunde in Vienna.

2. On the circumstances surrounding the auction of Beethoven's music estate, see Georg Kinsky, "Zur Versteigerung von Beethovens musikalischem Nachlaß," *Neues Beethoven-Jahrbuch* 6 (1935): 68–96; and Douglas Johnson, "The Artaria Collection of Beethoven Manuscripts: A New Source," in *Beethoven Studies* [1] (New York: Norton, 1973), 174–236. At the auction the publisher, Domenico Artaria, bought about 80 of the first 188 items in the catalogs (the manuscripts in Beethoven's hand); Haslinger bought about 40. According to the report here, primarily he (and Spina, representing the Diabelli firm) bid on unpublished autographs.

3. The packets of compositional studies in Beethoven's hand were no. 149 in the *Nachlaß* catalog, where they were described as "Contrapuntal essays, apparently by other masters, with his own notations, 5 packages." The collection sold for 74 florins. Haslinger gave the task of editing the studies to Ignaz von Seyfried (a student of Albrechtsberger), who then compiled them as *Ludwig van Beethovens Studien im Generalbasse, Contrapunkte und in der Compositions-Lehre* (published by Haslinger in 1832). The publication is very flawed because Seyfried did not realize that only some of the studies were from Beethoven's own studies or that the rest were transcriptions of excerpts Beethoven had written out in 1809 from composition textbooks by Johann J. Fux, Albrechtsberger, and others for the Archduke Rudolph's composition lessons. The Beethoven sketch scholar Gustav Nottebohm straightened out the exact nature of the studies and provided accurate transcriptions of them in "Beethovens theoretische Studien" (1863) and *Beethovens Studien* (1873). For information on Seyfried and on Beethoven's knowledge of counterpoint, see Warren Kirkendale, *Fugue and Fugato in Rococo and Classical Chamber Music,* 2nd rev. edn. (Durham NC: Duke University Press, 1979), 203–06.

4. The "trio" mentioned here was almost certainly WoO 37, a trio for piano, flute, and bassoon, first published by Breitkopf & Härtel in 1888. The autograph was no. 179 in the *Nachlaß* catalog and was purchased by Haslinger for 20 florins (see n. 1, this entry). The title on the autograph reads "Trio concertant a clavicembalo flauto, fagotto composto da Ludovico van Beethoven organista di S.S. Electeur de cologne [*sic*]," which may explain

Haslinger's mistaken claim that the work was composed while Beethoven was an organist in Cologne.

As Beethoven wrote no sonatina for piano four-hands, the "sonatina for four hands" may possibly refer to Beethoven's four-hand set of variations on the song *Ich denke dein,* WoO 74. The autograph was listed as no. 184 in the *Nachlaß* catalog and is described there as "Clavierstücke mit Begleitung, z.T. unbekannt." Artaria, not Haslinger, however, purchased it for 6 florins, 34 kreuzer.

Haslinger purchased no. 159 ("Zwei Zapfenstreiche in Partitur") together with no. 158 ("Lied und Kirchenstück") for 6 florins, 36 [30] kreuzer; he also obtained no. 162 ("Marsch für die Harmonie") for 2 florins, 20 kreuzer. The two Marches are WoO 19 and 20; the "Marsch für die Harmonie" may be the Ecossaise, WoO 23.

Haslinger purchased *Nachlaß* catalog no. 169 (Music to *King Stephen,* op. 117) for 3 florins and catalog no. 143 (*Germania,* song from Treitschke, *Die gute Nachricht,* WoO 94) for 4 florins, 30 kreuzer.

5. Regarding the Leonore Overture, op. 138, see Kinsky-Halm, which cites and discusses this article.

6. The contract between Steiner and Beethoven is dated 29 April 1815 and is given in Anderson, app. F6. The contract stipulates that Beethoven was turning over thirteen works to Steiner, including *Fidelio,* op. 72; the Cantata, op. 136; the String Quartet, op. 95; *Tremate, empi, tremate,* op. 116; Symphonies Nos. 6 and 7, ops. 68 and 92; the "Archduke" Trio, op. 97; the Violin Sonata, op. 96; the Overtures, ops. 113, 115, and 117; and possibly Twelve Songs, WoO 157.

7. Haslinger published the first edition of *Der glorreiche Augenblick* in 1837, noting on the title page that the work had been performed before all the assembled monarchs and nobility in the Congress of Vienna in 1814.

8. Beethoven's receipt for the arrival of the forty-volume set of Handel's works is dated 14 December 1826 (see Anderson, app. G19). They were a present from Johann Andreas Stumpff in London. Beethoven's thank-you letter is dated 8 February 1827 (see Anderson, letter no. 1550), wherein he notes that the gift was even mentioned in the Viennese papers (according to Thayer, the notice appeared in the Vienna *Modenzeitung*). Beethoven valued Handel above all other composers. Haslinger purchased the set at the *Nachlaß* auction (where they were listed as no. 239) for 102 florins.

48.
"Recent Church Music," *Münchener allgemeine Musik-Zeitung* 23
(8 March 1828): 361–64.

Mentioned: *Missa solemnis,* op. 123

RECENT CHURCH MUSIC

Even though the idea of a holy, ruling church, a victoriously achieved freedom of faith, and the scriptures have not remained dominant in the area of art in more recent times, and even though the totality of human life has become the more distinguished object of art, in preference to a singular direction toward religion, nonetheless this direction has still not lost its intrinsic attraction and uplifting power for composers.[1] Nevertheless, in their works we see more and more the influence of their individuality, and more and more the strict separation of sacred and secular music is disappearing. However, here we still have to characterize *three* artists for the most part, not as the only ones worthy of being mentioned, but as those whose creations definitely demonstrate three directions from which further matters could be explained.

JOSEPH HAYDN

In him we see a youthfully happy human being, at peace with himself and the world, and in the gentle stirring of unsullied joy we see how his heart and eye open up to all surroundings. Now (as it is) he senses, he recognizes the spark of life in every object of nature. All creatures, all births in the plant kingdom, the elements that form the earth and frame the heavens—all of this is animated to him, and he feels like a happily playing child among happy playmates. Every violent passion slumbers, even the horrifying is only the sweet shudder of a playful fantasy, and the mildly soothing rays of the evening sun at once penetrate the storm cloud. In his *Creation,* Haydn sang of *the first recognition of the spark of life in every creature of nature,* and in his *Seasons* he sang of *the joy of existence.*[2] And all of his sacred compositions are full of the most cheerful, childlike gratitude and delight in life so that more serious generations will hardly know how to unite it with the dignity of the church and the text of the mass and other prayers.

His entire being is *joy.*

MOZART

In his individuality there emerged, after the joy that *Haydn* had called forth, a delicate, indeed, a preeminently tender feeling. With gentle compassion and ardent, sacred love, his soul devoted itself to humanity, which he preferred to portray and visualize in the brilliance of an intuition, which rises above the individual, rather than in the full light of truth. Alongside the exultation of writing songs for a consecrated place, his works for the church (and nowhere more perceptibly than in his *Requiem*)[3] express this *spirit of love* that characterizes him.

BEETHOVEN

If we dare to express words here that suggest something about this greatest instrumental composer before we have become acquainted with his greatest composition of sacred music, the great mass for solo, chorus, and orchestra,[4] it is done in the opinion that in the works that are already known, and even in his predominant tendency toward instrumental composition alone, his distinctiveness has been sufficiently indicated so that in delaying the dissemination of that great work we will not be allowing any lacuna to occur. So that our statement does not appear to be blindly risky, we must mention beforehand that we will endeavor to recognize the distinctive controlling forces of every mind in its choice of themes and cannot regard it as any more accidental or insignificant that *Beethoven* preferred to occupy himself with instrumental music than that *Raphael* became a historical painter and someone else a landscape painter. In song, however, human nature seems to be represented, and in instrumental music superhuman nature.[5]

Wherever possible, *Beethoven* became preoccupied with the world of instrumental music (also in the greatest part of the sacred compositions known to us) so that, instead of a definite human element, the particular content of his tone poems seems to be made up of a *presentiment* that emerges from a total intuition of nature and whose command extends to mysticism in a way that never occurred in any composer.

Now, what we have suggested up to now about the trend of sacred works of music (an exhaustive treatise must be reserved for a special work) cannot and must not be regarded as a scientific presentation of the various creeds and views of faith, which lies completely outside our province. To the contrary, it is a point of view that the works alluded to have secured for us.

If the characteristics outlined above, which by necessity are incomplete and general, must be regarded as still too insufficient for the immediate purposes of singers, that will only confirm our opinion about the infinitely greater insufficiency of the general determinations that were regarded earlier as satisfactory. Only widespread familiarity with the works and an intimate investigation of their essence can make fruitful such an account, whose nourishment our mind has absorbed from the various works. Without that, it must remain unfruitful, indeed, even misunderstood.

NOTES

1. Religious music during Beethoven's lifetime in Vienna was seriously affected by Josephian reforms. See John Rice, "Vienna under Joseph II and Leopold II," in *The Classical Era*, ed. Neal Zaslaw (Englewood Cliffs NJ: Prentice-Hall, 1989); and Bruce Mac-Intyre, "Church Music in the Context of Musical Life in Eighteenth-Century Vienna," in *The Viennese Concerted Mass of the Early Classic Period* (Ann Arbor MI: UMI Research, 1986), 13–26.

2. Here the reference is to Haydn's oratorios *The Creation* (1798) and *The Seasons* (1801).

3. "Compare the *Berl. allgem. mus. Zeitung*, vol. 2, no. 46, 47, 48."

4. "Whose publication is forthcoming from Schott in Mainz. (It has now appeared and can be obtained in several arrangements.)" The first edition of the *Missa solemnis* was published by Schott in March/April 1827.

5. "In the wind instruments that imitate human voices perhaps the animal kingdom is represented—compare the *Berl. allg. mus. Zeitung*, vol. 3, no. 20, p. 78."

~

49.

Gottfried Wilhelm Fink, "An Opinion on Beethoven from the *Revue musicale*, Associated with Our Views," *Allgemeine musikalische Zeitung* 30 (12 and 19 March 1828): 165–70, 181–85.

Mentioned: *Fidelio*, op. 72; *Christus am Ölberg*, op. 85; Mass in C, op. 86; *Elegischer Gesang*, op. 118; and *Missa solemnis*, op. 123

Viewed from many different aspects, it cannot be anything less than extremely important for us to examine the opinions of the most cultivated nations about our music in general. In particular, we should listen to opinions about those men we justifiably rank among the best *choregi* and geniuses of our fatherland.[1] It would also afford not just simply light entertainment but a many-sided, mutual perfection if men from all kinds of nations, trained in their fields, were to compile their varying opinions and present them for examination in a humane way. We want to try to do that now, with, we hope, the approval of our countrymen as well as those abroad, for we live in the full confidence that no truly educated man from each of the different nations can still labor under the misconception that he alone is wise. We can only learn mutually from one another, and those will be the best who have always remained childlike enough to regard precisely this learning as a human honor, in spite of all manly activity and individual creativity. They will have good reason for their conviction that no one on this earth can ever be finished learning, least of all in the field of music where, as we know, there are so many things that still have to be discovered. We all understand very well that more diversity must exist precisely in our opinions about music than in many other things, because music is based primarily on feeling. It is so because here we are talking about a tone language that by its nature cannot be characterized with words in a way that makes it universally understandable, as, for example, a logical conclusion is. Therefore, we truly rejoice that Mr. Fétis,[2] a man who has shown himself to be worthy of being the head of a music journal, has made such fortunate progress in France and abroad, which can only serve to promote art.

And thus we will now put together as briefly as possible those points that contain Mr. Fétis's opinion of Beethoven and examine them in juxtaposition with our point of view.

In his sketch of the life of our immortalized composer, he thinks that it was too late for Beethoven, who had already begun to compose in his eleventh year, to achieve a great purity of style and to become a learned composer, in spite of his studies with Albrechtsberger, because his manner was already established. However, he continues, the beauty of his genius makes one forget his aberrations and digressions. He held himself back capriciously and bizarrely and had only a small number of friends who forgave his gruffness. He had only zealous opponents, just as he had only zealous friends. The first accused him of ruining art and the others were grateful to him for his errors and exalted him above all his predecessors. Gradually they became calmer and recognized his originality. But they also noticed affectation and artificiality. In the midst of faulty harmony they discovered the elegance of his accompaniment, the novelty of his forms, and the wealth of his modulation. Next to intolerable harshness one hears melodies of great tenderness, and in the midst of disconnected and strange phrases they saw a wisely conceived plan and the brilliance of simply natural ideas. Although he was less comprehensive than Mozart and less gifted in his capacity to sing happily always, he still occasionally equaled Mozart and excelled him in the sonata, whose form he perfected. If he doesn't possess Haydn's purity and, like the latter, is not able to produce great effects with few means, he still has more rapture and abandon (*véhémence et abandon*) and his manner is more varied. His Adagios and Andantes are all excellent; his keyboard sonatas often approach perfection; his quartets, quintets, and symphonies are full of first-class beautiful qualities and are unique. In instrumental music he has a place next to Haydn and Mozart that is as close as possible. In the works of his youth,[3] one finds the most natural singing, the least originality, and the most pleasant modulations. By means of a bedazzlement, which is just too natural, he despises these works and values only the later ones, some of which are nothing more than lengthy absurdities ("extravagances"). He has also tested himself in theatrical music, but here he is beneath himself. *Fidelio,* which was performed in November of 1805 without success,[4] is almost entirely lacking in melody and dramatic interest. The serious style was more suitable to him, and for that reason he was also more fortunate in his oratorio *Christus am Ölberg* and in his masses. On the whole, one can confirm that Beethoven is one of the greatest musicians of whom Germany can be proud.

In the same journal, a man who signs his name Porro testifies appropriately to the same opinion as expressed here but with less gravity. We will summarize the major points of his opinions in the following.

Beethoven is richly talented by nature, always original, enthusiastic, proud, serious, eloquent. Joy and satisfaction were not in his soul. He knew little of love, which appears to be the first element of all the arts. Just as fruitfully and independently, he prescribed new paths for himself and found enchanting effects that belong only to him. He replaced what he didn't have with thousands of dazzling works. His numerous supporters have almost deified him. Which real artist will ever dare to censure such wise foolishness? Does not such reasonable lunacy amount to the admiration that one owes to genius? He possessed to the highest degree the power to sweep everyone along with him who could only understand him. He knows all the depths and secrets of art, and perhaps he has gone far beyond that which constitutes actual art. Since I am only speaking from my heart, my weak voice must seem suspicious to all who practice art according to principles. His holy music will long be studied as exemplary.

On many essential points our subjective point of view is not only different from these foreign opinions, which in many respects are noteworthy, but we are also confident that the conviction of most Germans is different. Therefore, we believe we will be able to count on some sympathy if, according to our best conviction and with succinct brevity, we offer our opinion of Beethoven alongside the foreign opinions so that our public can compare it with the viewpoints of both of them.

As far as Beethoven's character is concerned, we cannot deny that a few essential points have been correctly described. Since we are hoping for a good portrayal of the life and work of this master, we also recognize the difficulty for a foreign critic, say, for example, an Englishman who will concur in Beethoven's nature many things, which might be suggested to a certain degree by Beethoven's own utopian preference for England. However, we must confess that by no means has he yet been as completely understood as we must expect and as he should have been according to the known reports about him and according to his works. People seem to deny completely that he is good-natured and benevolent and that he has a sense of pleasantry (even though in his later years the latter had to be rarer because of his misfortune, as he so painfully lamented in his last will and testament, which was reported in this journal). This was not true about him, and for that reason we must refer to the description by Fr. Rochlitz in the first number of this volume.[5] His character is thoroughly wonderful, jovial, outstandingly original, and he is just as independent as he is philanthropic and friendly. To be sure, he has a liking for solitude, but he is, nevertheless, communicative and sociable, and given his sense of self-worth, he is modest. Only on the outside was he untroubled and without worry because his mind lived and moved in the higher sphere of musical art. He not only knew how to revere the excellence of other masters but also to take delight in their works, and until his death he studied Handel, a related spirit in many things. Therefore, when Mr. Fétis says of him that he achieved neither the purity of style nor learned composition, we need only point out that among his papers were found exercises that he had worked out under the direction of the famous Albrechtsberger. As promised and as is proper, they will be disclosed publicly to the friends of music. Even more compellingly we can refer to his works. One can hardly deny a deep knowledge of everything belonging to erudition in composition to someone who, like him, understands how to cause a single, predominant idea to permeate an entire, long symphony in the most diverse turns of phrases, complications, strettos, inversions, and in the richest blendings. (We exclude in this case the fugue that he did not favor because of its thoroughgoing regularity.)[6] He accomplishes this so thoroughly with new thoughts that often, unexpectedly but effectively, he shapes the most varied abundance into a completed total image, in accord with the model of nature. Even though in the masses of chords in his fullest scorings he occasionally piles notes upon notes, like a giant piling mountains upon mountains, this is certainly not done according to the traditional rules. Indeed, it is occasionally grotesque, but always splendid (excluding particular points such as the last movement in his last symphony) and completely worked out to the clearest level possible, as if one were led away from the wild craggy rocks of the river bank down into the most charming valley. Even when he occasionally is where he wants to be in four steps, like Neptune, no matter how far the goal, his gigantic pace is indeed amazing and surprising. But the strange promenade in the storm is immediately most sweetly soothed by the greatest charm of his melodies and the ramification of the parts, and the now pleasant stroll in the fields of quiet and peace thereby becomes all the more charming. Therefore, what for others is incorrect and affected is not that for him. Those wild masses have become so distinctively rooted in his nature, as it were, that it would be unnatural for him if what is called aberration were not found in him.

One can name very few who are as great in the mastery and the most effective use of all instruments as our Beethoven. In the application of special features of all tools of music I do not know a single person who is more masterly, and in instrumental music he is the richest. If one were to restrict oneself to the collection of details without regarding the mostly exquisite totality, one would only do an injustice to him, art, and oneself. To be sure, many a frog hops in the grass, many a mosquito buzzes around the ear, and all kinds of wildlife run through the green forest while the sweet flock of feathered singers let their song of praise resound from their blossomy branches in the most beautiful month of May and inspire us to joy and gratitude. If he occasionally leads us through small swamps, it happens only in order to show us soon thereafter even more charming groves. It is only to release and free us from the profound impression of some part of the world of beauty so that we do not become lost and exhausted in a one-sided emotion and sink into apathy and lassitude. He does this so that we again become more receptive to a new and more attractive pleasure that, while different from the preceding, is still related to it and exalts it even more. Then suddenly he sweeps us with wonderful force across thorns and thickets into a new field of higher beauty.

His nature is predominantly romantic, something that people have always thought an otherwise well-educated Frenchman was least able to acquire. Nevertheless, in life itself (even if until now less in art) they have provided shining examples from time to time that they are indeed capable of it. Beethoven has frequently been compared to all kinds of writers, but never to a Frenchman. Who doesn't remember having read about him being compared to Jean Paul (Fr. Richter)? The comparison wasn't bad, for Beethoven truly does possess that humoristic quality that essentially distinguishes the writer. They are also alike in that both of them impose the same fate on their imitators, and not to their advantage. As many similarities as the comparisons of both men offer, the dissimilarity of both is so great that it would have to be regarded as strange if the fondness for comparisons had not been directed at other distinguished men. One of our most recent music authors (Karl Christian Krause[7] in his interpretations from the history of music etc.— see the review in no. 2 of this volume of our newspaper) compares him to Michelangelo among painters and to Lord Byron among poets. Both comparisons contain much that is apt and both are splendid. The painter who made the Final Judgment visible for us, who himself cut off Amor's arm in order to give it the stamp of a pretended antiquity for some time, and the wonderful architect of famous bridges and the frontal side of the St. Peter's Cathedral in Rome, has many qualities similar to our Beethoven. Lord Byron does correspond to him in his infernal ideas and particularly in his almost horrifying revolutionary nature. It cannot be mistaken that Beethoven's solid independence quite distinctly reveals the spirit of a mighty battle against tradition. That explains his occasionally beginning with the fifth leaving the fundamental tonality undermined in the absence of the mediating third, which doesn't placate the uncertain waiting of the astonished listener until later.[8] So many phrases that run counter to the traditional order, and which Mr. Fétis counts among the inconsistencies and other such things, verify this without a doubt. However, this is only a part of his nature, even if, of course, it is the most pronounced; but it is by far not the magnificent, elevated totality of his nature. Therefore we must find this comparison insufficient too. There is no solidly frozen manner in Beethoven. How could he have accomplished such extreme charm in juxtaposition to violence, even in the *Lied?* How could he have accomplished such perfection and delight in the sonata? How could he be so engaging, stirring us now in deep melancholy and now in plaintive desire, as in the Adagio and Andante? Here above all, the love of his benevolent spirit is most intimately expressed. How could someone who could produce something like that have been without love, assuming that one doesn't understand love in the sense associated with Louis XIV and Louis XV. In short, his works and his life offer the most expressive evidence of that goodwill and that deep good-naturedness that pay honor to a better human being. For that reason we would not like to compare him with Byron, but would prefer most of all to compare him with Shakespeare, of whom Jöcher states in his *Gelehrten-Lexikon* that "he had a jocular spirit but he could also be very serious," or our Goethe.[9] To be sure, French critics do not hold this tragedian,[10] so highly praised among us and his countrymen, in special regard. It is only all too well known which judgments about him have taken place in France and for the most part still take place. We will have to wait to see whether the English theater, which for some time has enjoyed a larger public, will contribute much to change its opinion about the great dramatist to his favor. However, whoever knows *Lear* or *A Midsummer Night's Dream* will indeed have to judge quite differently, even if he, and not just a few of us (including even our Goethe too), belonged to those who are unable to consider every single swear word as worthy of admiration and universally valid. So, too, it is with our Beethoven. Indeed, his nature stands in such a striking contrast to the spirit that still generally prevails in French art, that we should not by any means be surprised by the rebukes against him.[11] To the contrary, we should learn how properly to respect the justness that willingly recognizes the moving quality of his romanticism. Nevertheless, a German can best be compared with a German and is therefore, in our opinion, more suitably compared with Goethe than with anyone else. We must, however, leave the comparison itself to each and every person so that we don't go on too long and only repeat things that are generally known among us; and that we can do.

Now, as far as Mr. Fétis's judgment of Beethoven's *Fidelio* in particular is concerned, we consider ourselves obligated to express an entirely opposite opinion. Precisely this opera proves to us with what great sublimity our master was capable of handling the most divergent things and comprehending and reproducing highly distinctive features to the point of ardor, which the unsurpassable scenes in the prison prove most of all. On the other hand, we do not hold his oratorio *Christus am Ölberg* in at all as high regard as is done there. Rather, we find something far more secular in it than is befitting this genre if the presentation is to be masterly. Also, Beethoven has proven his greatness and depth much more splendidly in several other religious works than in this one, for example, in his elegiac song "Sanft, wie du lebtest, hast du vollendet,"[12] and in several hymns and masses.

Beethoven can be compared with Haydn and Mozart just as little as for example, Klopstock and Schiller with Goethe, and in a comparison of any great men with others in their field injustice of any kind should not be inflicted on one or the other. If comparisons are made in order to make the characteristics of one or the other all the more apparent, then it is well done. If, however, comparisons are made in order to gauge the degree of their stature, the preference of the person making the comparison for this or that genre will fix the value of the one or the other too one-sidedly. That is too human to be able to expect anything different from anyone. Greatness remains great in any form.

If, however, one should select foremost for study from the recent masters, we will definitely grant Mozart and Haydn the preference over Beethoven, for these masters are not inferior to our Beethoven in any skill that can be acquired by diligence. If one or the other such skill should be found, Mozart and Haydn, each by himself, would yet again show advantages, which in comparison would be capable of compensating for anything. Since, however, the originality of both follows a much more orderly path, which is easier to overlook, then, if our assumption is found to be as irrefutable as we believe, our opinion is directly confirmed. Nevertheless, both are equally masterful in their methods of presentation, which in many artificially traditional forms are probably even more at their disposal. Here, there can be no question of imitations, which are in no way desirable. One will also not be able to say: "Conform to one or the other." Rather, everyone needs only to become familiar with the characteristics of the masters so that his own nature becomes strengthened by already existing masterly qualities and so that afterward he is in a position to present his inner being more freely and diversely, with complete clarity and independence in accord with his acquired ideals. The greater the given model, the more troublesome the imitation is. According to such presuppositions it is hoped that after everyone has become familiar with Haydn and Mozart, he will regard the study of Beethoven's works as highly influential and necessary. This is not in order that he may follow in the footsteps of one of these men, but rather that he may become familiar with the various ways that lead to the temple of fame for his own edification. However, we would stray from our present plan to a subject matter too far afield if we did not stop now and leave the rest for everyone to contemplate.

There remains nothing further for us than to summarize briefly our humble opinion about Beethoven. In him a powerful force and an almost unbounded majesty of uniqueness in masses of ideas and in their individual groupings in the most diverse parts, to which all must respond as individuals of nations obey a consistently heroic ruler, are wonderfully united with the most intimate tenderness and love of a benevolent heart. Directly through these two extremes, which true greatness more or less always knows how to control, a deep longing complains in a painful lamentation, like a bride over the early grave of her beloved. Again, manly courage struggles and, holding firmly to terrestrial beauty, cradles love peacefully for a brief moment to achieve a better home. Or, in the roaring storm of life he struggles to play soothingly and flirtingly to achieve his rest until a more beautiful morning has risen blissfully for him.

NOTES

1. The German term *Chorführer* derives from the Greek idea of the *choregos,* that is, the elite patrons of art who were responsible for the education and support of the members of the chorus in ancient Greek theater.

2. François-Joseph Fétis (1784–1871) was a Belgian scholar and theoretician of music. Concerning his contributions to music criticism, see Peter Anthony Bloom, "François-Joseph Fétis and the *Revue musicale*" (Ph.D. diss., University of Pennsylvania, 1972). See also Wallace, *Beethoven's Critics,* 108–19.

3. "That is, not his very earliest but beginning with the trios, which he wrote primarily for the pianoforte, which appeared in Vienna, and which Beethoven himself declared as his first work [i.e., op. 1]."

4. "That is, in Vienna; in other places *Fidelio* is not just liked, but delights by far the majority, even if not everyone."

5. Almost the entire first issue referred to here (AMZ 2 [January 1828]: 4–16) is devoted to communications from Friedrich Rochlitz, the journal's former editor. Appearing under the title "Zusatz aus einem spätern Briefe," these communications contain an often-quoted account of a meeting Rochlitz claimed to have had with Beethoven in Vienna. The authenticity of this report has been questioned; see Maynard Solomon, "On Beethoven's Creative Process: A Two-Part Invention," *Music & Letters* 61 (1980): 272–83. Except for the introductory verse, the entire article is a reprint of letters from *Briefe aus Wien vom Jahre 1822* by Friedrich Rochlitz. See Thayer-Forbes, 246, for an example of one excerpt from the material reprinted in the article.

6. The commonly held perception that fugues and fugal writing were not employed in the Rococo and Classical periods is false. Warren Kirkendale has demonstrated how extensive were Beethoven's, Mozart's, and Haydn's knowledge and use of counterpoint in his *Fugue and Fugato in Rococo and Classical Chamber Music.*

7. See entry no. 24 for comparisons of poets and composers.
Karl Christian Krause (1781–1832) studied philosophy with Fichte and Schelling. He worked as a freelance scholar, writing on the philosophy of music and art. His principal work was *Das Urbild der Menschheit*. Krause is credited as being the founder of panentheism, a reconciliation of theism and pantheism. His two publications on music are his *Darstellungen aus der Musik: Nebst vorbereitenden Lehren aus der Theorie der Musik* (Göttingen: Dietrich, 1827), reviewed in AMZ 30 [1828]: 17–26, and *Anfangsgründe der allgemeinen Theorie der Musik nach Grundsätzen der Wesenslehre,* ed. Victor Strauss (Göttingen: Dietrich, 1838).

8. Fink is perhaps referring here to the famous opening of the Ninth Symphony, where the third of the opening A chord is missing. Fink mistakes Beethoven's aesthetic intent for a "battle with tradition."

9. Christian Gottlieb Jöcher (1694–1758) studied theology and philosophy, and as a professor of history at Leipzig he also taught the philosophical systems of Leibniz and Wolff. Among his most well-known works is his *Allgemeines Gelehrten-Lexikon,* 4 vols. (Leipzig: J. F. Gleditschen, 1750–51).

10. That is, Shakespeare.

11. The classic text on French reception history is Leo Schrade, *Beethoven in France* (New Haven: Yale University Press, 1942). Three recent contributions of note are Jeffrey Cooper, *The Rise of Instrumental Music and Concert Series in Paris, 1828–1871* (Ann Arbor MI: UMI Research, 1983); Katharine Ellis, *Music Criticism in Nineteenth-Century France: La revue et gazette musicale de Paris, 1834–80* (Cambridge: Cambridge University Press, 1995); and Robin Wallace's chapter "French Beethoven Criticism" in his *Beethoven's Critics,* mentioned in the introductory essay (see n. 12).

12. The *Elegischer Gesang,* op. 118.

∾

50.
"On Beethoven and Mozart, from the *Revue musicale,*" *Münchener allgemeine Musik-Zeitung* 36 (7 June 1828): 573–75.

Mentioned: Symphony No. 5, op. 67

On the occasion of a report on the concerts of the Royal School of Music in Paris, our capable editor expresses the following about these heroes of German art.[1]

"Again we have heard echoes of the immortal sounds of the great master Beethoven, whose music the Royal School of Music caused us to listen to as a worthy offering to his memory on the anniversary of his death. Then, his worthy interpreters made the decision to place flowers on the grave of Mozart, who was his first model and whose works stir and move every heart. His name and works will never perish and will withstand all time and influence in everlasting beauty."

Then our author expresses the differences between these two masters in the following way:

There are two things that are particularly prominent in musical composition. The first is the author's intention and idea, this inspiration that one cannot define but which is exactly the same in all arts. This is the design, the interpenetration and unity of feelings and ideas, the association and opposition and, therefore, the poetic quality in a work of art in general. The second is the way in which composition is artistically represented in notes, or actually the technical forming, the external shaping of the inner life by natural means, that is, through the sounds of music. Although this second part is very much subordinate to the first, its influence is nevertheless great, and in regard to the effects upon the masses very much is dependent on it. For the latter, such minor points are often everything, even the music itself, whereas educated people regard them only as a means to an end. They view them as a transitory addition in so far as it does more than is even necessary in order to reveal with the victorious power of art the inner life of the artist in complete clarity.

In my opinion, of all the musicians who ever lived, *Mozart* was the greatest poet, the most fortunate, richest musical genius. In him everything was united that brings about any humanly perfect works. He is a model for all times in every respect. Sweet, delightful melody, the most tender expression and the most powerful unity of ideas and clarity in design, the most perfect taste and the purest style, an endless abundance of external forms, and the most skillful, effective utilization of instruments: these are the gigantic inner means with which this great mind worked. For that reason he needed few external means in order to be great in small things. Not so with *Beethoven*. He needed rich, external means and walked the path he pursued to the very end either conscious of the necessity (therefore intentionally) or unconscious of the necessity (therefore unintentionally), because this way did indeed correspond especially to his essence. We believe that we must assume the latter, for in despising all external constraints he abandoned himself to the boldest adventures of his passionate fantasy without concern and called forth phenomena from which any other prudent mind would have recoiled. Fortunately, however, these products of his fantasy are of such a sublime, indeed, gigantic nature that they overwhelm the listener with their magic power and are dispersed before he has time to reflect on them and to bring their appropriateness and significance before the eye of reason. *Mozart,* with all his mental superiority, would never have found such a grandiose, colossal motion as the one that opens the last movement of the Symphony in C Minor. This phenomenon lies outside the realm of notes; those are not flutes, horns, violins, or basses that one hears; this is the world, the universe trembling. *Beethoven* does not know if he should stop. Unlike *Mozart* and *Haydn*, he does not know how to give his works that beautiful proportion in individual sections. All too often he strays into areas from which he can only return with cold and chilling effects. Just take a look at and compare Mozart's overture to the *Magic Flute*. What grand and continuously new ideas. How one thought displaces another with more and more beauty and power! And nevertheless, what unity, what appropriateness! Odd indeed! Many of our artists feared, after sampling his work, that *Mozart* would lose greatly to the memory of Beethoven's last great works and have no effect. How wrong they were! *Mozart*, who, one would like to say, was the creator of our orchestra, did not possess *Beethoven's* means to any degree. How far behind, for example, were the wind instruments in his day and how much less did the orchestras accomplish then. He couldn't use such means as these for his intentions because he didn't know them himself. If then *Beethoven* knew all of this and knew how to utilize it all, *Mozart* understood how to do without them.—

Beethoven* and *Mozart* are infinitely great human beings in quite different ways. The one is a brilliant genius, he rises like Homer and falls like him. The other doesn't make his fantasy astonish you, but he does move your heart and reason to admiring enchantment. The former has novelty to his credit, the other a freshness that after fifty years has not yet lost anything of its charm. *Mozart* is a charming seducer;—*Beethoven* triumphs with the victorious power of his proud boldness. *Beethoven* remains a great musician whenever he does without grand means as, for example, in his quartets, etc. But *Mozart* is without his equal here: he is a god.

NOTE

1. The author is referring to François-Joseph Fétis (see entry no. 49, n. 2), the editor of the French periodical *Revue musicale*.

51.
"News: Stuttgart: On Our Concert Music," *Allgemeine musikalische Zeitung* 30 (20 August 1828): 560–61.

The first concert opened with a symphony by Beethoven. Since Rochlitz's interesting notices came to us in your *AmZ* and since I heard even further things about his life from people personally acquainted with him when the notices were read aloud in a music circle, I now believe I understand his peculiarities somewhat more. Nevertheless, I am well aware that any kind of originality always remains somewhat incomprehensible.

If an art (or science) has been bound by certain natural laws for a long time and its masters have striven to liberate it here and there, a man will finally come who will break all the bonds and on his own authority will stretch the limits so far that theory is shocked and all existing reference books become useless or at least appear to be insufficient.

Musical fate has selected a genius richly endowed by nature who, neither bound, borne, nor oppressed by middle-class or familial relationships, made music his kingdom, his world. With self-confidence he transferred this peculiarity in his way of thinking and acting to art in a peculiar and singular manner. He was attracted, honored, and supported by an enthusiastic musical amateur and his circle.[1] His slightest musical developments were listened to intensely, his artistic moods were received sympathetically, and he saw the sounds of his poetry immediately performed publicly in the liveliest form by a circle of excellent artists. With the passing of years, he was excluded from friendly, soothing human contact because of his loss of hearing. He sought to compensate for everything that fate did to aid and injure him, for all the privations of this man who rejected the sweet, prosaic happiness of family life, in his inner feeling that listened only to itself, in a musical dream world that could no longer adjust its phantoms to reality.

NOTE

1. Beethoven was supported by the nobility in various ways from his teens in Bonn until his death. See entry no. 45, n. 12. The author's description of an "enthusiastic musical amateur and his circle" probably refers to the Archduke Rudolph, Beethoven's most significant patron and only composition student.

～

52.
"II," "Arrangements for Pianoforte by Carl Czerny,"[1] *Allgemeiner musikalischer Anzeiger* (Vienna) 1 (January 1829): 17.

Every lover of music knows that *Beethoven* wrote magnificent symphonies; indeed, we would like to say that in regard to energy, fantasy, and impressive greatness, he wrote the most magnificent. Most fortepianists know as well that Mr. *Carl Czerny* is quite suited to translate an orchestra piece in full harmony, effectively, and in the most appropriate way for pianoforte for four hands. Therefore we can cast the most favorable horoscope for this complete collection of all of *Beethoven's* symphonies, arranged by C. Czerny. This first volume justifies the favorable prejudice that we held for this work. The publisher has done his part with clear engraving, good paper, and tasteful cover, and thus we hope there will not be a lack of sales for the entire work.

Indeed, *Pacini's* operas for four hands are also finding enthusiasts and, what is more, buyers.

NOTE

1. The article heading also contains the following publication description: "Collection complète des sinfonies de L. van Beethoven, arrangées pour le pianoforte à quatre mains."

Carl Czerny (1791–1857) was an Austrian pianist, composer, and pedagogue; student of Beethoven and teacher of Franz Liszt. Although Czerny composed more than a thousand works, which were published by Probst in Leipzig, he is remembered today primarily for his technical exercises for the piano. According to Kinsky-Halm, Czerny's arrangements of the first eight symphonies for four-hands piano were published in 1827 by Probst (all eight with the plate number 360) and by Schott in Mainz (plate number 3164). Probst's plate number 360, however, suggests an 1827 date for the Ninth as well; see Otto Erich Deutsch, *Musikverlags Nummern* (Berlin: Merseburger, 1961), 18. An announcement of a "ganz correcte Ausgabe," "sauber gestochen" (entirely correct edition, cleanly engraved), of all nine symphonies in Czerny's arrangement appeared in no. 15 of the *Intelligenz-Blatt zur allgemeinen musikalischen Zeitung* in October 1829. For the text of the announcement, see Richard Linnemann, *Fr. Kistner 1823/1923* (Leipzig: Fr. Kistner, 1923), 18–19. This notice is particularly interesting and claims that Czerny had arranged the symphonies with "our new fortepianos" (i.e., the fortepianos of the late 1820s with an expanded range and larger tone) in mind.

Czerny studied piano with Beethoven from 1801 to 1803 and taught Beethoven's nephew from 1816 to 1818. He knew all of Beethoven's piano works by memory and gave detailed instructions on their performance in vol. 4 of his *Complete Theoretical and Practical Piano Forte School*, op. 500. His memoirs from 1842 contain many important details about Beethoven.

~

53.
"A Few Additional Words to the Many on Beethoven's Last Works," *Allgemeine musikalische Zeitung* 31 (29 April 1829): 269–73.

Mentioned: *Missa solemnis*, op. 123; Symphony No. 9, op. 125; *Große Fuge*, op. 133; and a string quartet

PRELIMINARY REMEMBRANCE

Let us grant just a few introductory words to the editorial staff because of the watchful Eris[1] who continuously strolls above the heads of human beings and loves to let enticing apples of discord with constantly changed inscriptions glide down into the halls of joy. To be sure, it is not essential to cause discord, because it is already there. However, where two parties decisively oppose one another, one will praise what the other censures. Every party can do that according to his conviction, but humanely, as is proper for educated people. If, on the other hand, one party were to demand that the other simply be treated like Papageno and have a lock placed on his mouth, that would indeed be behaving somewhat less respectably than did the black ladies.[2] We want both sides to be heard and heeded, and we want them to speak to each other in a *manly* way, that is, they should meet reasons with reasons and abstain from superficial declamation. The time of primal rapture, which reasonable men allow, is past. It does honor to man to listen calmly to the opposite of his own assertions and likewise to be able to reply with something worthy so that truth is fostered. The opposite is a disgrace for him. Let us not fear that Goethe's rhymed aphorism can be applied to many in this respect.

> Come, let us print everything:
> And let us prevail forever and ever.
> Only no one should grumble,
> Who doesn't think like us.[3]

May this essay, which is at the least decent and spurns passions, also speak this way, and may it have the effect of which it is capable.

Editorial Staff

Since the death of the great master, people have fought about his last works frequently and on occasion with bitterness. One side exhausts itself in praise and believes that the public is not yet ready for these works that are far beyond their times. They believe that only later on, after frequent listening, will people discover and enjoy their qualities of beauty. The others dismiss them as baroque, too lengthy, unclear products of an overheated fantasy. I admit that I am on the side of the latter, but animated by true respect for the departed, I would like to see the matter discussed more with calm reasons derived from the essence of music and not by means of harsh attacks and invectives.

Beethoven's defenders admit that his last compositions have not yet been understood, but as proof that this will happen in the future they cite *Mozart,* for whom things didn't go any better. I have seen many strike their sails at this comparison, but perhaps seldom has a less tenable comparison been chosen. Mozart's career was short, and if during that time he was misjudged by *a few,* never by the *masses,* at *the end* he enchanted the entire world. Beethoven, on the other hand, lived much longer. In the beginning and in the course of his journey among us, he created exquisite works that also charmed us universally. Only toward the end of his journey did he enter a path on which only a few followed him, and these few probably not out of *pure* love for the direction he was going. Where is the similarity between Mozart and Beethoven here? And even if the comparison were entirely true, that would only be admissible as proof if we could assert that art is capable of *eternal advancement*. The history and structure of mankind sufficiently contradicts that, however.

The purpose of every work of art can be no other than to infuse our inner being with the highest possible degree of bliss in those moments when it engages us. This purpose is achieved when reason and feeling, equally occupied, are brought into harmonic play. In instrumental music, which we are concerned with first in regard to Beethoven's music, *reason* is satisfied through order, symmetry, and relationship to a major idea—theme and execution—in one word: through skilled thematic work. *Feeling* is satisfied through the *beauty* of the melody and through *harmonious sound*. When modern music was beginning to develop into an art, for a long time it was the child of mathematical, calculating reason, and therefore satisfied only reason and couldn't awaken any broad-based interest. Little by little the magic power of melody and harmonious sound began to be sensed and subsequent masters tried to unite that with mathematical art. The person who knew how to unite both characteristics in the most beautiful symmetry, the art of thematic work with melody and harmonious sound, was Mozart. And which composer's works would ever have had a larger public, satisfying and charming both laymen and connoisseurs? Beethoven, richly equipped like Mozart with everything that makes a great master, stepped up and into Mozart's footsteps. He did not imitate him in his ideas (that would have been mimicry), but rather in the pursuit of his two primary maxims, which the latter had recognized as flowing from the essence of music and had developed. Their correctness also proved to be right in Beethoven as long as he followed them, for his public was not smaller than that of the preceding master.

Unfortunately, Beethoven lost that gem that for a musician is invaluable: hearing. Becoming melancholic and gloomy, he withdrew more and more from the external world and no longer *heard* music; he only saw it, and the longer this lasted the more *the actual charm* of music faded in his memory and the more the consequences of this became evident in those of his works that now began to appear. Anyone who has walked the difficult path from the first attempt to a painful birth will know that there is *eye-* and *ear-music*. He will know that often what looks quite exquisite in the *score* has no effect at all in performance, and vice versa. Gradually, Beethoven became an *eye-composer;* indeed, he had to become one because of the circumstances. More and more he enjoyed inventing odd motives and working out and interconnecting them in an artificial and strange way. He piled idea upon idea, and on paper they appeared very clear and delighted his eye, but in working them out they often become a *chaotic image*. Many passages in his last works appear as such to me, as often as I hear them. In conjunction with his loss of hearing, Beethoven was also led on that false path by the major striving of his life for originality. He wanted to be *new at any price,* especially in the last years. Earlier, when the rich shaft of his inner being provided him with the most noble and exquisite metals, it became easy for him to shape products that are both original and beautiful at the same time. Over the years this wealth naturally decreased, all the more so when *external stimulation* departed. He found fewer noble qualities and sought to replace this loss with the *most baroque structures.*[4] His fugal overture,[5] his *Missa,*[6] quartet, and last symphony came about this way. I ask all impartial people how many actual spoils (taken in the more noble sense of the word) for the *ear* do they find outside of simple *strangeness*. To be sure, *strangeness* attracts, the more so according to its intensity, but it does not bring about a true artistic impression. Indeed, one can get used to *strangeness* after more frequent contact with an object, even if it is the ugliest, but that can never be used as proof of its value. Don Quixote also gained a taste for the monstrous tales of the knights of his times by means of repeated reading, so much so that he became a fool and regarded windmills as giants and a barber's bowl as the helmet of a mandarin.

NOTES

1. Eris, the ancient Greek goddess of Discord, was enraged at her exclusion from a wedding festival and threw a golden apple among the guests with the inscription "For the fairest." The end result of the contest over the apple was the abduction of Helen by Paris, the judge in the contest, and Homer's Trojan war.

2. In act I of Mozart's *Magic Flute,* three ladies, representing the Queen of the Night, kill a serpent (or dragon) that had been pursuing Prince Tamino. Papageno, who witnesses this event, later claims to have killed the serpent himself. In return for telling this lie, the ladies place a lock on his mouth.

3. The quotation is from an eight-line strophe in Goethe's *Zahme Xenien II* (*Goethes Poetische Werke* [Berlin: Aufbau, 1965], 1:653). The word "Xenia" derives from Greek and refers to gifts given to guests. At first, Goethe and Schiller published *Xenien,* a collection of epigrams, in response to hostile criticism directed against Schiller's periodical *Die Horen.* Gradually they grew in scope to give expression to Goethe's critical views of contemporary literary culture. *Zahme Xenien* appeared in 1820 in "Über Kunst und Altertum" (II, 3).

4. Because the word *baroque* was not widely used in the early nineteenth century as a description of what is commonly known as the Baroque period in music history (ca. 1600 to ca. 1750), the author probably intends the adjective to signify the use of bizarre or incongruous details, dramatic, overstrained effects. Grimm's *Deutsches Wörterbuch* (1854) claims that it agrees with "bizarre" and cites the image of a multicolored garment from the eighteenth century as an example. The works cited in the following list are characterized by excessive length by the standards of the day, complicated and lengthy fugal writing and fugues, unexpected rhetorical juxtapositions, and complex music forms.

5. The "fugal overture" is probably the *Große Fuge,* op. 133, the opening of which is described on the autograph and first edition as an "overtura."

6. *Missa solemnis,* op. 123.

54.
"News: Paris," *Allgemeine musikalische Zeitung* 31 (30 December 1829): 863.

A certain Hector Berlioz gave a concert on the first of November in which items of his composition were put on.[1] They exceeded everything heard up to now that is crazy, bizarre, extravagant. Here, all the rules were trampled on, and only the unbridled fantasy of the composer dominated throughout. Nevertheless, with all that, one could not deny that he has an innate feeling for music. It is just too bad that it is without any education. If he had this, perhaps he would become a Beethoven.

NOTE

1. This was Berlioz's first concert in Paris. Given at the Conservatoire, it included the "Concert of Sylphs" from his *Eight Scenes from Faust, Les Francs Juges* and *Waverly* Overtures, and the *Resurrexit*. The concert was also auspicious in that it included the first Paris performance of Beethoven's "Emperor" Concerto, with Ferdinand Hiller as soloist and Habeneck as conductor. The comparison to Beethoven was timely for two other reasons: the Conservatoire had begun performing Beethoven's symphonies to great critical acclaim in 1828, and Berlioz was widely known as a composer who "only cares about that wild fellow Beethoven." See the *Memoirs of Hector Berlioz,* ed. David Cairns (New York: Knopf, 1969), 117, 125.

~

55.
"Review: Fantaisie brillante sur trois Thèmes de Haydn, Mozart, et Beethoven pour le Piano, comp. par Ch. Czerny,"[1] *Allgemeine musikalische Zeitung* 32 (27 January 1830): 52–53.

A fantasy on these themes? Well, if one improvises like this on themes, it is the easiest piece of work in the world for a man of so much talent and such great proficiency as Mr. Cz. to do it and write it down. He modulates and ornaments here for three pages, as the case may be here, suitable or unsuitable to everything and everyone. There now follows Haydn's beautiful theme (from one of his quartets). If it is played out, he sets down two lines as if for a variation, but immediately he moves on again to modulation and ornamentation, three and a half pages, *ut supra.*[2] Now comes the Mozart theme (the song "When love . . .").[3] Now it is performed with rich ornamentation, and then for a short time a phrase from it is continued. Then he modulates and ornaments for a few pages again, ut supra. Now Beethoven's theme (in march tempo: from the "Bagatelles"). Now he modulates and ornaments for four pages so that one is reminded only occasionally of the theme in a quite fortuitous manner. Only in the last lines, which end the piece, does there appear a jocular idea that recalls a little bit of the Mozart and Beethoven themes. It goes without saying that Mr. Cz. does all of this quite nicely, that it proceeds in a very skillful, rounded, and nice manner, and that it sounds quite pretty. However, we are indeed sorry that a man like Mr. Cz. wants nothing more than just this. He will find many keyboard players, and even more female keyboard players, who likewise want nothing more. Of course, there will not be a lack of publishers who will gratefully accept these compositions and offer rich rewards for them. We should wholeheartedly be delighted for him. Nevertheless, it still is too bad when an artist distinguished by nature and practice aims solely for that.

NOTES

1. "A brilliant fantasy on three themes by Haydn, Mozart, and Beethoven for the piano, composed by Ch. Czerny."
The final section (twenty lines) of this article has been omitted as unrelated to the content.
2. "As above."
3. This is probably a reference to Mozart's song *An Chloe,* whose text, by J. G. Jacobi, begins "Wenn die Lieb aus deinen blauen, hellen, off'nen Augen sieht."

~

56.
Wenzel Johann Tomaschek,[1] "Autobiography," *Libussa* 4 (*Jahrbuch für 1845*): 374–75.

Mentioned: Piano Concerto No. 1, op. 15, and Piano Concerto No. 2, op. 19

In the year 1798, when I continued my law studies, Beethoven, the giant among keyboard players, came to Prague. In the *Konviktssaal,* he gave a very well-attended concert, at which he performed his C-Major Concerto, op. 15, then the Adagio[2] and the graceful Rondo in A Major, op. 2, then concluded with an improvisation on the theme from Mozart's *Titus,* "Ah tu fosti il primo oggetto," given to him by the Countess Sch.[3] My soul was shaken in a strange manner by Beethoven's splendid playing, and particularly by the bold execution of his improvisation. Indeed, I felt myself so profoundly humbled in my innermost being that I didn't touch my fortepiano for several days. Only my indestructible love for art and then rational deliberation induced me to continue my pilgrimages to the fortepiano, like before, and, to be sure, with intensified diligence.

I heard Beethoven at his second concert, where neither performance nor composition made this powerful impression on me. This time he played the Concerto in B♭ Major, which he had just composed in Prague.[4] Then I heard him for a third time at Count C's, where besides the graceful rondo of the A-Major Sonata he improvised on the theme "Ah vous dirai-je Maman." [5] This time I followed Beethoven's artistic performance with a calmer mind. To be sure, I admired his strong and sparkling playing, but I did not fail to note his more frequent bold leaps from one motive to another, whereby organic association, a gradual development of ideas, is disrupted. Such drawbacks often weaken his most splendid works of music, which he created with overly exuberant inspiration. Not infrequently, the impartial listener is violently dislodged from his supremely blissful mood. Peculiar and original elements seemed to be the chief points in his composition, as is sufficiently confirmed in the answer he gave to a lady when she asked him whether he frequently attended Mozart's operas, namely: he doesn't know them and also doesn't like to listen to the music of others since he doesn't want to jeopardize his originality. [6]

NOTES

1. Wenzel Johann Tomaschek (1774–1850) studied law and music in Prague. He gained recognition for his chamber and piano music as well as for his success as an instructor of composition. Tomaschek became acquainted with Beethoven during his studies in 1798 and has provided detailed descriptions of both Beethoven's piano performances and his judgments of other composers. See Thayer-Forbes, 207–08 and 597–98.

2. Tomaschek here used the word "Adagio" as a synonym for "slow movement"; the second movement of op. 2, no. 2, is marked Largo appassionata.

3. The reference is to Mozart's opera *La clemenza di Tito*.

4. The genesis and history of the early performances of the Second Concerto are very complex. Using paper types for dating purposes, Hans-Werner Küthen has recently shown that Beethoven worked on op. 19 in four stages: an initial version written in Bonn by 1790 at the latest; a second version written in 1793 for Vienna with the Rondo, WoO 6, as its finale; a third version from 1794; and a final fourth version prepared in Prague as Tomaschek notes here. See Küthen, preface to *Beethoven/Konzert für Klavier und Orchester*, no. 2 (Munich: G. Henle, 1991), v.

5. Mozart wrote a famous set of variations on the theme (K. 265 [300e]) known to English speakers as "Twinkle, twinkle, little star."

6. Both parts of Tomaschek's statement are contradicted by Beethoven's letter to the Abbé Stadler, dated 6 February 1826, in which Beethoven wrote, "I have always counted myself among the greatest admirers of Mozart and shall remain so until my last breath—" (Anderson, letter no. 1468, and Brandenburg, letter no. 2113). By 1798 Beethoven was intimately familiar with many of Mozart's works and had used some of them as models for his own compositions. He specifically knew *Die Zauberflöte, La clemenza di Tito, Le nozze di Figaro,* and *Don Giovanni;* Seyfried reported that Beethoven considered *Die Zauberflöte* Mozart's greatest work. An extensive but partial list of the music of other composers that Beethoven knew and studied (including Palestrina, Byrd, J. S. and C. P. E Bach, Handel, Graun, Haydn, and Mozart) is given in Kirkendale, *Fugue and Fugato in Rococo and Classical Chamber Music.*

The remainder of the article describes Wölffl's performance on the piano.

∼

OP. 1
THREE TRIOS FOR PIANO, VIOLIN, AND CELLO IN
E♭ MAJOR, G MAJOR, AND C MINOR

See also op. 104, arrangement of the C-Minor Trio

57.

Wiener Journal für Theater, Musik und Mode 1 (Vienna, 1806): 53–54.

Mentioned: Trio for Piano, Clarinet, and Cello, op. 11; Sonata for Piano and Horn, op. 17; and Variations for Piano and Cello on a Theme from Handel's *Judas Maccabeus,* WoO 45

Beethoven made a powerful, mighty, and stirring appearance as a keyboard composer with those beautiful trios that he dedicated to Prince Lichnowsky. Novelty and depth, ease in using harmonic devices, and a certain peculiarity of style and treatment led us to expect this still youthful man to become an original and gifted composer; and his great instrumental compositions, a few of his symphonies and concertos have confirmed this hope.[1] However, many of his later works for pianoforte are not as worthy as his earlier ones. Because of an obvious desire to be completely novel, B. is not infrequently incomprehensible, disconnected, and obscure, and much of his work is extremely difficult without compensating with distinguished beauty. Nevertheless, wherever B. made his goal beauty and not strangeness, he also created excellent works, and these can be earnestly recommended to all strong fortepianists. Along with the trios mentioned, I also include the "Variations on a Theme by Handel" for p.f. and violoncello, a trio with a clarinet and violoncello, further a very beautiful sonata with an obbligato horn, and finally Beethoven's concertos in which a beautiful and effective instrumental accompaniment is dominant. There are also many individual moments of beauty scattered among the remaining works of the composer.

NOTE

1. By 1806 only the first two symphonies and first three piano concertos had been published. The *Eroica* was published in October 1806, but had been performed earlier.

∼

58.

Adolf Bernhard Marx, "Reviews," *Berliner allgemeine musikalische Zeitung* 4 (13 June 1827): 186–87.

That these excellent products of the past period reached a second edition after such frequent repeated distribution by the first publisher attests to the well-deserved continuing general interest in them, which will also certainly reward their discerning and industrious publishers.[1]

The placing of Beethoven's first work next to a similar one by Mozart (Grand Trio, op. 19 [*sic*]), reminds us how disproportionately greater the interest in him was, as long as he stayed in the familiar regions of Mozart's music. It is understandable that not everyone was able later to follow his new paths.

It is more difficult to comprehend how so many presumed, and still presume, to revile his misunderstood works instead of at least suspecting, if not honestly confessing, their own incapacity to understand them. Should not the highly praised and already unparalleled works of his first period have awakened that much piety and awe? Nevertheless, in order to sense God, one must not be godless oneself.

NOTE

1. In 1825 the Viennese publisher Cappi & Co. issued a "Nouvelle édition" of the Trios, op. 1. As Marx notes, the first edition, by Artaria, was reprinted with minor variants at least six times prior to 1825. Editions were also issued by Simrock (1797), André (1803), A. Kühnel (1810), and Breitkopf & Härtel (1816).

～

59.

"Short Notices," *Allgemeine musikalische Zeitung* 31 (4 February 1829): 86–87.

When it comes to such a new and good edition of a generally known, esteemed and beloved work, there is essentially nothing else to say other than, it is there.[1] However, a few unessential and superfluous things may probably be added. We are delighted that a new edition of this work has become necessary after so many earlier ones. And it really was necessary, for besides the fact that one must assume that an experienced publisher will know very well what he is doing, this is proven to the reviewer by the presence of two copies of earlier editions, whose plates are so worn out that they have hardly reproduced even the most necessary essentials, and it is necessary to half guess at many things in the impressions.[2] What an immense number of people must have taken truly beautiful and joyful pleasure in this work, and how often, in the thirty and some years since it appeared! And truly, who wasn't in need of such a pleasure from time to time, precisely in these years? But the work itself in this new edition also brought us great joy when we performed it before friends again after it had not come up for performance for a long time. First, as may be taken for granted, because of its content and value in general. Second, and in particular, because in this opus as in few others, the cheerful youth of the master is still clearly reflected, lightly and frivolously, notwithstanding that already his later profound seriousness and tender intimacy at times come over the composer (and then, how beautifully!). Also, regardless of the fact that one recognizes Mozart's fortepiano quartets as models, Beethoven's peculiarities and independence unmistakably shine forth and emit electrifying and inflaming sparks. May many share the latter joy with us! If they do feel it, may they remember the outstanding master with renewed love, be it only for his sake, because this work was given over to the first publisher almost for the copying fees, just so that it would be available to the public. In return, it was bungled not just a little by the reviewers at that time.[3]

NOTES

1. Breitkopf & Härtel in Leipzig had released a second edition of their 1816 print of op. 1 in May 1828.

2. The author refers here to the deterioration of the soft metal plates on which music was engraved during Beethoven's lifetime. Each impression made from a plate weakened it; after substantial use, the printing of the music became lighter and lighter and the plates often cracked. The cracks collected ink and were printed along with the notes, further obscuring the musical text.

3. The publication history of Beethoven's first works to be given an opus number (thereby signifying that they belonged to his series of greater works) is complicated by the fact that Beethoven himself arranged for the first publication by enlisting subscribers to underwrite his costs in an advertisement in the WZ on 9, 13, and 16 May 1795. In fact, Beethoven made a tidy profit from the sale, for he paid the printer only one florin per copy and charged one ducat. See Thayer-Forbes, 175; and Kinsky-Halm, 4–6.

~

OP. 2
THREE PIANOFORTE SONATAS IN F MINOR, A MAJOR, AND C MAJOR

See entry no. 56

OP. 4
STRING QUINTET IN E♭ MAJOR

See also entry no. 86

60.

M. "Reviews," *Berliner allgemeine musikalische Zeitung* 4 (6 June 1827): 182.

Arrangement for piano four-hands

Beethoven's Quintet in E♭ Major, whose minuet with two trios and finale promises every patron of the arts delightful pleasure, is a welcome publication in this arrangement and can thus attain a broader circulation than in the original publication, which requires five players.[1] The format is very appropriate and the edition respectable.

NOTE

1. Breitkopf & Härtel published J. P. Schmidt's arrangement for four-hand piano in April 1827. An arrangement for piano trio, possibly made by Franz Xaver Kleinheinz but without Beethoven's involvement, had already been published in 1806 (listed as op. 63 in Kinsky-Halm).

～

OP. 6
PIANO SONATA FOR FOUR HANDS IN D MAJOR

61.

r . . . r . . . , "Brief Reviews," *Allgemeine Musikzeitung zur Beförderung der theoretischen und praktischen Tonkunst, für Musiker und Freunde der Musik überhaupt* 1 (31 October 1827): 280.

Since the great maestro of music van *Bethoven* is no longer among the living, people are beginning to dedicate more attention to his works than before. Indeed, they are looking up his first productions in order to recognize the course of his musical development and to see how he gradually became the great master. Many want to assert that his earlier works by far surpass the more recent ones and are particularly distinguished by clarity. We do not wish to investigate this assertion here, since this topic will probably receive a closer examination elsewhere. However, this is especially a reason why several of his earlier works have been published in new editions since his death. To the latter belong also the sonata for four hands mentioned here. To be sure it is modest in size, but in intrinsic value it nevertheless still outweighs many of the fattest tomes. For this reason it is also quite proper that it be distributed to the music public again in a new edition.[1] Indeed, it would be unfortunate if it should be lost. For those who agree that one should have students learn by heart the compositions of recognized masters, the above-mentioned sonata is recommended in particular.

NOTE

1. The second edition of op. 6 (described on the title page as a "IIde" edition) is dated "around 1825" in Kinsky-Halm. Joseph Czerny reissued the work under a new title after 1828. By 1822 the sonata, whose first edition appeared in October 1797, had already been reprinted by at least thirteen publishers, which probably explains the appearance of the second edition published by Cappi et Comp. in Vienna.

~

OP. 7
PIANO SONATA IN E♭ MAJOR

62.
. . . s, "Music," *Zeitung für die elegante Welt* 6 (14 June 1806): 572–73.

This sonata is considered by the reviewer to be among the most splendid by this original composer.[1] It forms a great, noble totality. A heroic fire constitutes the dominant feature of its character and is also demanded of the performer of the first Allegro con brio in E♭.[2] A strong passion also holds sway in the subsequent Largo con expressione in C major, although it is interrupted by moments of a calmer feeling and finally seems to dissolve in quiet resignation.[3] The following Allegro in E♭ major in $\frac{3}{4}$ time expresses concentrated power and spirited resolution; the *minore* seems to reveal wild storms within and progresses entirely in eighth-note triplets in both voices. Finally, this sonata closes with a soft pleasant rondo without entirely denying its passionate effect, which in a minor key (C minor) becomes almost turbulent until the exhausted heart is gradually rocked into a state of repose.

This composition is full of great effect when it is played by a skilled hand with just as much overpowering passion as tender complaisance. It requires approximately the same skill and similar expressive playing as *Mozart's* familiar Fantasy and Sonata in C Minor with which, to a certain degree, it forms a companion piece.

NOTES

1. The first edition of op. 7 appeared in October 1797 from Artaria in Vienna. Two subsequent editions, one of which may have occasioned this review, appeared in 1805: the Bureau de Musique, Hoffmeister & Kühnel, in Leipzig; and J. Andre in Offenbach (not listed in Kinsky-Halm).

2. Actually, Allegro molto e con brio.
3. Largo, con gran expressione.

~

OP. 10
THREE PIANO SONATAS IN C MINOR, F MAJOR, AND D MAJOR

63.
"Reviews," *Allgemeine musikalische Zeitung* 2 (9 October 1799): 25–27.

It cannot be denied that Mr. v. B is a man of genius, has originality, and goes entirely his own way.[1] In addition, his unusual thoroughness in the higher manner of writing and his own extraordinary command of the instrument he writes for unquestionably assure him of his rank among the best keyboard composers and performers of our time. His abundance of ideas, which a striving genius usually is unable to constrain as soon as it seizes upon a subject suitable for representation, too often still causes him to pile up ideas without restraint and to arrange them by means of a bizarre manner so as to bring about an obscure artificiality or an artificial obscurity, which is disadvantageous rather than advantageous to the effect of the entire piece.

Fantasy such as Beethoven possesses in no common degree, supported especially by such excellent knowledge, is something very valuable and indeed indispensable for a composer who feels within himself the dedication to become a greater artist and who disdains superficial and conventional composition. Rather, he wants to put forth something that has an inner, powerful vitality, which entices the connoisseur to a more frequent repetition of his work. However, in all arts there is an overabundance that derives from a too great and frequent craving for effect and learnedness, just as there is a clarity and charm that can well exist in conjunction with any thoroughness and diversity of composition (this word is used entirely in the general artistic sense).

This reviewer, who after having attempted gradually to accustom himself to Beethoven's manner, is beginning to value him more than before and cannot therefore suppress the wish that it might please this fanciful composer to allow himself to be guided throughout his works by a certain economy, which is, of course, more advantageous than the opposite. Indeed, this wish is intensified even more by the present work, which is clearer and therefore more beautiful than many of his other sonatas and remaining fortepiano pieces, although they do not thereby lose any of their thoroughness.

There are undoubtedly few artists to whom one must exclaim: save your treasures and be thrifty with them! For not many artists abound in ideas and are skilled in their combinations. It is therefore less a direct censure of Mr. v. B. here than a well-meant acclamation, which retains something honorable even if it does censure.

Therefore, as stated, this tenth collection seems to the reviewer to be worthy of much praise.[2] Good invention, earnest, manly style, well-ordered and connected thoughts, well-maintained character in every part, difficulties not carried to excess, and an entertaining treatment of harmony lift these sonatas very high above many others.[3] In regard to the fundamentals of feeling from which it usually emanates, this manly style bears a certain similarity to the characteristics of Phil. Em. *Bach's* style, taking into consideration our present manner of writing, which departs much from *Bach's* choppy style.[4]

Mr. v. B. must be on guard against his occasionally too liberal style of composing, entrances of unprepared intervals and the frequent harshness of transition notes (such as appear, for example, on pp. 3 and 43, and which only a quick tempo can make bearable);[5] and from time to time he ought to remind us less of organ style.

In return, the reviewer is obliged to present the readers with a nice idea that brought him much joy. In the last, completely characteristic rondo, after the bass has accompanied a fixed passage with thundering sixteenth notes, the passage stops on a seventh chord on A. The bass canonically takes up the echo of the preceding theme

OP. 10
No. 3, Rondo, mm. 99–101

and now runs through the following important harmony in syncopated motion most delightfully in all brevity and calm (for the sake of clarity let the key of C be indicated here)

OP. 10
No. 3, Rondo, harmonic reduction of mm. 101–06

whereupon the conclusion is carried through with somewhat austere power in chromatic runs of sixteenth notes, up- and downward, and in other ornamentations, while the bass still continues the previous short themes with which the rondo began.

NOTES

1. The reviewer is writing about the first edition of the sonatas, which was published in September 1798 by Joseph Eder in Vienna.

2. Although many eighteenth-century composers used one opus number for a set of works, Beethoven's opus numbers contain both single works and sets through 1815 (after that date only songs and bagatelles were grouped together in a single opus number). The reviewer obviously assumed that "opus 10" was the "tenth collection" of Beethoven's works, although ops. 3, 4, 6, 7, and 8 contain only one work each.

3. This gendered description of Beethoven's music as "manly" is one of the first in a long line of criticism continuing through the twentieth century that directly associates Beethoven's music with masculinity. This association was so well established that Robert Schumann likened Schubert to a "maidenly character" in comparison to Beethoven's alleged masculine qualities (see his review of Schubert's Impromptus, op. 142, *Music and Musicians,* trans. Fanny Ritter [London: Reeves, 1877], 296–97).

4. C. P. E. Bach's influence on and relation to Beethoven's style has been frequently discussed. In his chapter on "C. P. E. Bach and the Viennese Classical Composers," Hans-Günter Ottenberg compares Beethoven's piano sonatas, songs, and piano concertos to Bach's (see his *Carl Philip Emmanuel Bach,* trans. P. J. Whitmore [Oxford: Oxford University Press, 1987], 185–98).

5. On p. 3 of the first edition the development section of the first movement of op. 10, no. 1, appears (mm. 115–69). On p. 43 of the first edition, the first episode of the rondo of op. 10, no. 3, appears (mm. 27–55). In the former case, the author may be referring to the retransition that begins in m. 136, which contains a fair amount of harshness in its combination of accents and dissonance. In the latter case, the author may be referring to the unprepared key change from D major to B♭ major at m. 33 (enforced by Beethoven with *sforzando* marks) or the striking chromatic passage at mm. 49–55. The first edition also contains an egregious mistake in m. 41, where the left hand is printed with a *fortissimo* E♮ against the right hand syncopated *fortissimo* E♭; while such a mistake would have been recognized as a misprint by any music critic, such a dissonance would only fuel the fire of anyone who chastened Beethoven for the harshness of his transition passages.

≈

OP. 11
TRIO FOR PIANO, CLARINET, AND CELLO IN B♭ MAJOR.

See also entry no. 57

64.
"Reviews," *Allgemeine musikalische Zeitung* 1 (22 May 1799): 541–42.

This trio, which here and there is not exactly easy but is, nevertheless, more flowing than many other pieces by the author, makes quite a good ensemble on the fortepiano with its keyboard accompaniment.[1] With his unusual harmonic knowledge and love for more serious composition, this same author would provide us with many good things that would leave our insipid hurdy-gurdy pieces, not infrequently by famous men, far behind if he would always write more *naturally* than artificially.

NOTE

1. This review refers to the first edition of the Trio published by T. Mollo in Vienna in October 1798 (it had been announced in the WZ on 3 October 1798). The edition is titled "Grand Trio pour le Piano-Forte avec un Clarinette ou Violon, et Violoncelle"; four parts were included in the edition. According to Czerny, Beethoven himself was responsible for the arrangement of the violin part; this alternate orchestration undoubtedly improved the marketability of the Trio.

~

OP. 12
THREE SONATAS FOR PIANO AND VIOLIN IN D MAJOR, A MAJOR, AND E♭ MAJOR

65.
"Reviews," *Allgemeine musikalische Zeitung* 1 (5 June 1799): 570–71.

Until now, this reviewer wasn't familiar with the keyboard pieces of the author.[1] After having arduously worked his way through these quite peculiar sonatas, overladen with strange difficulties, he must admit that while playing them with real diligence and exertion he felt like a man who had thought he was going to promenade with an ingenious friend through an inviting forest, was detained every moment by hostile entanglements, and finally emerged, weary, exhausted, and without enjoyment. It is undeniable that Mr. van *Beethoven* goes his own way. But what a bizarre, laborious way! Studied, studied, and perpetually studied, and no nature, no song. Indeed, to put it precisely, there is only a mass of learning here, without good method. There is obstinacy for which we feel little interest, a striving for rare modulations, a repugnance against customary associations, a piling on of difficulty upon difficulty so that one loses all patience and enjoyment. Another reviewer (M. Z. no. 23)[2] has already said almost the same thing, and this reviewer must agree with him completely.

Nevertheless, this work shouldn't be thrown away because of these complaints. It has its value and can be of great use, particularly as a study for experienced keyboard players. There are always many who love excessive difficulties in invention and composition, that which one could call perverse, and if they play these sonatas with great precision, they will always experience pleasure in the music itself in addition to a pleasant personal feeling.

If Mr. v. B. would only deny himself more and follow the path of nature, he could, with his talent and industry, certainly provide us with quite a few good things for an instrument over which he seems to have extraordinary control.

NOTES

1. This review refers to the first edition of the sonatas published by Artaria in Vienna in December 1798 or January 1799; the edition was announced in the WZ on 12 January 1799.

2. See the review of the Twelve Variations for Piano and Cello on "Ein Mädchen oder Weibchen," op. 66, and "Mich brennt ein heißes Fieber," WoO 72. Mary Sue Morrow points out that "particularly in the area of modulation, *AmZ* reviewers showed a definite preference for restraint, favoring compositions that 'did not stray much into distant keys' "; given Beethoven's chromatic modulations (see especially the first movement of op. 12, no. 2), she argues that this reviewer was justified in feeling that "the young composer was trying too hard to be new and different" (see Morrow, *German Music Criticism in the Late Eighteenth Century: Aesthetic Issues in Instrumental Music* [Cambridge: Cambridge University Press, 1997], 154–55).

∼

66.

"Pieces for Two Violins, Alto, and Violoncello," *Allgemeine Musikzeitung zur Beförderung der theoretischen und praktischen Tonkunst, für Musiker und Freunde der Musik überhaupt* (Offenbach), 1 (August 1827): 79.

Arrangement for String Quartet by P. W. Heinzius[1]

Whoever is familiar with Beethoven's music and knows how it often surprises most strikingly through its quite characteristic melodies and harmonies and how it is listened to by connoisseurs with particular attentiveness knows what awaits him here. Mr. Heinzius proves through his arrangement of these sonatas as quartets that he is equal to his task. To be sure, the opus is not altogether easy, but it doesn't have great difficulties either. For those who are not yet familiar with these sonatas, which have been reworked into quartets here, we will indicate here what they contain.

The first quartet consists first of an Allegro in $\frac{4}{4}$ time in D major, then an Andante in $\frac{2}{4}$ time in A major with variations (one of the variations, the third, is in A minor); finally, a Rondo, Allegro, in $\frac{6}{8}$ time in D major follows.

The second quartet consists of an Allegro assai [*sic,* Allegro vivace] in $\frac{6}{8}$ time in A major, then an Andante in $\frac{2}{4}$ time in A minor, and finally an Allegro piacevole in $\frac{3}{4}$ time in A major.

The third quartet consists of an Allegro moderato [*sic, Allegro con spirito*] in $\frac{4}{4}$ time in E♭ major, then an Adagio in $\frac{2}{4}$ time in C major, and finally a Rondo allegro in $\frac{2}{4}$ time in E♭ major.

NOTE

1. This arrangement was published by Simrock at Bonn in 1827.

~

OP. 13
PIANO SONATA IN C MINOR ("PATHÉTIQUE")

67.
"Reviews," *Allgemeine musikalische Zeitung* 2 (19 February 1800): 373–74.

This well-written sonata is not unjustly called pathetic, for it really does have a definitely passionate character.[1] Noble melancholy is announced in the effective, well, and flowingly modulated Grave in C minor, which occasionally interrupts the fiery Allegro theme that gives much expression to the very vigorous agitation of an earnest soul.[2]

In the Adagio in A♭ major, which, however, must not be taken slowly and which has a beautiful and flowing melody as well as modulations and good motion, the soul is rocked into a state of repose and a feeling of solace from which it is awakened again by the rondo on the first *tone* of the Allegro, in both meanings of the word.[3] In this way the chief emotion forming the basis of the sonata is carried out; by this means the sonata itself gains unity and inner life and thus real aesthetic value. To be able to say something like that about a sonata—assuming, as is the case here, that every other requisite of musical art has not been left unfilled—is obviously proof of its beauty. The only thing with which the reviewer would like to charge *Beethoven*, who indeed can be inventive and novel when he wishes, not as a fault but only as a wish for more perfection, would be that the theme of the rondo contains too much of a reminiscence. From where? The reviewer himself cannot determine, but at any rate the idea is not new.[4]

It must indeed be a pleasant feeling for the Viennese music public, which as is well known expresses much enthusiasm for music and supports it with distinguished ardor, to have so many excellent artists. Mr. van *Beethoven* unquestionably belongs among them, and we will hope that he will often present us with products of his genius and diligence.

1. This refers to the first edition of the sonata published by Hoffmeister in Vienna by 1799; it was announced in the WZ on 18 December. As Richard Hill and Alan Tyson have shown, Kinsky-Halm incorrectly attributes the first edition to Eder. See Richard Hill, review of Alexander Weinman, *Wiener Musikverleger und Musikalienhändler von Mozarts Zeit gegen 1860* in *Notes* 15 (1958): 396–97; and Alan Tyson, "Notes on Five of Beethoven's Copyists," *Journal of the American Musicological Society* 23 (1970): 439–71.

2. On Beethoven's use of the adjective "pathétique" in relation to rhetoric and the pathetic and sublime styles in eighteenth-century music, see Elaine Sisman, "Pathos and the *Pathétique:* Rhetorical Stance in Beethoven's C-Minor Sonata, Op. 13," *Beethoven Forum,* vol. 3 (1994), 81–105.

3. The word "Allegro" was used in music criticism to refer generally to movements in quick tempos, but it also retained its Italian meaning of "lively or merry." Unlike previous reviewers, this author mentions without censure Beethoven's irregular modulations in the Adagio to E major, the enharmonic equivalent of F♭ major, in an A♭-major movement, perhaps because he recognized the affective importance of the gesture.

4. The reviewer may have had Mozart's Fantasy and the Sonata in C Minor, K. 475 and K. 457 (published in Vienna by Artaria in 1785), in mind. For a discussion of the similarities, see Theodore von Frimmel, "Bemerkungen zur Sonate pathétique," in *Beethoven-Forschung,* no. 2 (Vienna: Kommissionsverlag Gerold, 1911), 33–42.

≈

68.

M . . . s, "Grande Sonate pathétique pour le clavecin ou piano-forte comp. et ded. S. A Msgr. le Prince Charl. de Lichnowsky par L. van Beethoven. O XIII. Pr. 16 gr.," *Zeitung für die elegante Welt* 7 (6 August 1807): 997–98.

This sonata is in C minor. It begins with a Grave of sublime character, which fades away into an excitingly fiery Allegro di molto. The Grave returns twice for only a few beats, but the heroic effect maintains the upper hand.[1] The following Adagio cantabile (in A♭ major) flows over into milder sentiments. But in the Rondo allegro, which concludes the work, the high-mindedness of a resolved heart is announced again in a powerful and beautiful expression, uniting tender feeling and energy within itself. Friends of alluring and imposing melodies will admire this sonata no less than connoisseurs of harmonic art, the most interesting examples of which are to be found especially in the two Allegros. However, as little as it belongs to the easier sonatas, it still contains fewer difficulties for the experienced hand than the sonata indicated above[2] and various others of B's sonatas, excepting perhaps the quick crossing of the hands.

A single engraving error in this otherwise very correct edition is easy to report, namely, p. 14 in the second measure of the third note system, where the half note G in the descant should be changed to A♭.

NOTES

1. Material from the Grave introduction reappears at the beginning of the development section and before the short coda. Beethoven's recall of material from slow introductions or earlier movements in his sonata-form works for the purpose of dramatic effect is one of the rhetorical fingerprints of his style through the works of the late period, although it represented a departure from normal Classical period procedures. Remarkably, the earliest example appears in the first movement of the Piano Sonata in F Minor, WoO 47, no. 2, written when Beethoven was eleven or twelve, published in 1783.

2. The reviewer refers to the Piano Sonata in B♭, op. 22.

~

OP. 15
PIANO CONCERTO NO. 1 IN C MAJOR

See also entry nos. 56 and 85

69.
"News: Berlin Concert Music," *Allgemeine musikalische Zeitung* 7
(26 December 1804): 197–98.

A new fortepiano concerto by Beethoven, provided with chromatic passages and enharmonic changes, occasionally to the point of bizarrerie, concluded the first part. The solo part was very difficult and was performed by Mr. Wustrow with much skill. The very strong accompaniment was extremely exact. The first movement was splendidly worked out, but the modulations were far too excessive; the Adagio in A♭ major was an extremely pleasant piece, richly melodic, and was greatly embellished by the obbligato clarinet.[1] The last movement, All' Inglese, distinguished itself only by its unusual rhythms and also was well executed.[2]

NOTES

1. The reference to "far too excessive" modulations in the first movement may apply to mm. 47–82 (and the corresponding measures in the recapitulation), in which Beethoven moves from the minor dominant into the major flattened submediant to the minor subdominant with intermediate chromatic motion. The remoteness of the modulation was still being pointed out in the twentieth century by Donald F. Tovey, who remarked that "a fragment of the second subject appears in a remote key, and is carried through other keys in rising sequence" (see his *Concertos and Choral Works* [rpt. Oxford: Oxford University Press, 1989; in series Essays in Musical Analysis], 48).

2. The description of the rondo as an "All' Inglese" is explained in Daniel Türk's *Klavierschule* of 1789 (p. 399), in which he writes "The Anglaise (English dance, contredanse, *Country-dances*) is for the most part of a very spirited character which often borders on the moderately comic. It can be in $\frac{2}{4}$, $\frac{3}{4}$, and sometimes also in $\frac{6}{8}$ meter and is

played in a very lively, almost skipping manner. The first note of every measure is strongly accented. Although the tempo is fast, it is not always of the same degree of speed" (see his *School of Clavier Playing,* trans. Raymond Haggh [Lincoln: University of Nebraska Press, 1982], 393).

∼

OP. 16
QUINTET FOR PIANO AND WIND INSTRUMENTS IN E♭ MAJOR

70.
"Vienna," *Der Freymüthige* 1, no. 58 (12 April 1803): n.p.

Mentioned: Quintet for Strings, op. 29, and *Christus am Ölberg,* op. 85

There is so much news from this remarkable Imperial city buried among the stock of manuscripts of *Der Freymüthige* that the editor sees himself forced to dedicate an entire folio to it so that none of it becomes old.

Amusements of the Viennese after Carnival [*sic*].

Spring is still not here, and the magnificent surroundings of Vienna still do not offer pleasure. Theater and social gatherings are thus the only delights. Games or music are the soul of social occasions. The dominating games are Whist, Boston, Ombre, Tarots, and Preference. Games of chance are partly forbidden and partly not appropriate to the spirit of the nation that severely gets carried away with heated passions. There are frequently amateur concerts at which unceremonious amenities prevail. They usually begin with a quartet by *Haydn* or *Mozart,* then an air by *Salieri* or *Paer,* for example, then a fortepiano piece with or without accompaniment, and then the concert usually closes with a chorus or something like that from a popular opera.[1] The most excellent fortepiano pieces that were admired at the last carnival were a new quintet by *Beethoven,* brilliant, serious, full of deep meaning and character, but now and then too harsh, here and there sublime leaps in the manner of this composer. Then follows a quartet by *Anton Eberl,* dedicated to the Empress, lighter in character and full of refined but profound feeling, originality, fire and strength, brilliant and impressive.[2] Among all the musical compositions that have appeared for some time, these are certainly two of the best. Recently *Beethoven* has been engaged by the Theater-an-der-Wien at a considerable salary, and there he will soon produce an oratorio of his work *Christus am Ölberg.* Among the artists on the violin the most distinguished are *Clement, Schuppanzigh* (the producer of Augarten concerts in the summer), and *Luigi Tomasini.*[3] *Clement* (director of the orchestra an-der-Wien) is an excellent concert player; *Schuppanzigh,* on the other hand, performs quartets very agreeably. Good dilettanti are *Epplinger, Molitor,* and others. Great artists on the pianoforte are *Beethoven, Hummel, Madam Aurnhammer,* and more.[4] The famous Abbé Vogler is also here now and plays fugues in particular with great precision, although his very heavy touch betrays the organist. Among the dilettanti, Baroness Ertmann plays with astonishing precision, clarity, and delicacy, and Miss Kurzbeck brings great understanding and deep feeling to the keys.[5] Mesdames von Frank and Von Natorp, formerly Gerhardi and Sessi, are excellent singers.[6]

NOTES

1. "In Vienna these concerts therefore do not last nearly as long as in Berlin, where enjoyment is exhausted. The Editor."

Ferdinando Paer (1771–1839) was particularly well known for his operas. He worked in Vienna from 1797–1802 and became concertmaster at Dresden in 1802 where he composed *Leonore, ossia l'amore conjugale,* based on the same plot Beethoven later used in *Fidelio.* A copy of Paer's score was found among Beethoven's papers.

2. Anton Eberl (1765 or 66–1807) was an Austrian pianist, composer, and concert master. His style was close enough to that of Mozart that several of his works were published under Mozart's name. A biographical sketch of Eberl appears in AMZ 9 (1807): 423–30.

3. Beethoven's friend Franz Clement (1780–1842) was one of the outstanding violinists of his time. He idolized Beethoven, who apparently wrote his Violin Concerto, op. 61, specifically for him. He also conducted numerous works by Beethoven at the Theater-an-der-Wien. See Robert Haas, "The Viennese Violinist, Franz Clement," *Musical Quarterly* 34 (1948): 15–27.

Ignaz Schuppanzigh (1776–1830) was a prominent violinist and a close friend of Beethoven. As the leader of Count Razumovsky's quartet, he gave first performances of several Beethoven quartets. Details of the changing membership of the "Schuppanzigh Quartet" are given in connection with several pertinent reviews in vol. 2 of this work.

Luigi Tomasini (1741–1808) was a close associate of Haydn in the service of the Esterházy family. He directed major performances of Haydn's chamber music and composed a large amount of chamber music and some orchestral works.

4. There are several extensive studies of Beethoven's piano playing; three of note are William S. Newman, *Beethoven on Beethoven,* 45–82; Franz Kullak, *Beethoven's Piano Playing,* trans. Theodor Baker (New York: Da Capo, 1973); and Walther Nohl, "Beethoven als Klavierspieler," in *Ludwig van Beethoven als Mensch und Musiker im Täglichen Leben* (Stuttgart: C. Gruninger, 1927), 12–61.

See entry no. 4 for the female pianists Au[e]rnhammer and Kurzbeck.

5. Baroness Dorothea von Ertmann (1781–1849) was an outstanding performer of Beethoven's music. (See Anderson, letter no. 764 of 23 February 1817; see also entry no. 42, n. 10.)

6. Christine Frank-Gerhardi was the daughter of an official at the court of Emperor Leopold II. Although she was a dilettante, Beethoven regarded her highly enough to accompany her frequently in musical soirées at her father's house. The soprano part in *Die Schöpfung* by Haydn is believed to have been written for her.

Marianna Sessi-Natorp (1776–1847) came from a large Italian family that produced several prominent singers; her sister, Anna Maria Neumann-Sessi (1790–1864), is also mentioned in these reviews. A diagram showing the relationship between various members of this family appears in Kutsch and Riemens, *Großes Sängerlexikon,* col. 975–76.

The remainder of the article deals with nonrelated theater events in Vienna.

71.

"Correspondence and Notes: From Magdeburg, 6 April,"
Zeitung für die elegante Welt 23 (6 April 1823): 732.

Mentioned: Overture to Goethe's *Egmont*, op. 84

In the first three of these collections, we heard as never before:

> 2 Haydn quartets
> 3 of the same by B. Romberg
> 1—by Spohr
> 2—by Fesca, and
> 1 Mozart quintet—

Instead of the last four, however, a concert took place yesterday in which Mr. C. Müller performed a Mayseder concerto with great virtuosity; Mr. Gerke, a budding virtuoso and student of Spohr, displayed in a potpourri of [works by] his great master a cultivated talent that is admirable for his age; Beethoven's Quintet in E♭ (originally a sextet)[1] was performed consummately in all of its peculiarities; the Overture to *Egmont* by Beethoven as well as the *Cantemire* by Fesca, however, were given a performance that left absolutely nothing else to desire.

What grandly exquisite accomplishments Beethoven has made in all genres of instrumental music (including quartets and quintets) is known and is possible only for a mighty, abundantly rich genius. It is also known what melodic charm and cheerful originality are unique to Haydn's creations, and also how B. Romberg through his composition enriched the most splendid things there are for his instrument, the violoncello. However, it has by far not been sufficiently recognized (and therefore it is our duty to mention this) what a rare artistic talent and rich artistic soul is expressed in the now existing fourteen quartets and four quintets of our highly honored countryman, the concertmaster Fesca, in Karlsruhe.[2]

NOTES

1. There is no evidence that op. 16 originated as a sextet or that it appeared in an arrangement for sextet during Beethoven's lifetime. There may have been some confusion about the form given the alternative part included in the first edition: "Grand Quintetto pour le Piano-Forte avec Oboë, Clarinette, Basson, et Cor ou Violon Alto, et Violoncelle."

2. Friedrich Fesca (1789–1826) was first violinist in the chapel of the Grand Duke of Baden at Karlsruhe. He eventually wrote sixteen string quartets, as well as two operas, three symphonies, a violin concerto, and a number of sacred vocal works.

~

OP. 17
SONATA FOR PIANO AND HORN
see entry no. 57

OP. 18
SIX STRING QUARTETS IN F MAJOR, G MAJOR, D MAJOR, C MINOR, A MAJOR, AND B♭ MAJOR

72.
"News: Vienna," *Allgemeine musikalische Zeitung* 3 (26 August 1801): 800.

Distinguished among the recent works appearing here are splendid pieces by Beethoven (Mollo and Co.). Three quartets offer valid proof of his art, but they must be played frequently and well since they are very difficult to perform and are by no means popular.[1]

NOTE

1. Opus 18, like many groups of six quartets, was originally released in two parts consisting of three works each. The publisher T. Mollo issued the first edition in two books in June and October 1801. This report must refer to the June publication of op. 18, nos. 1–3.

~

73.
"Brief Notices," *Allgemeine musikalische Zeitung* 8 (16 July 1806): 670–71.

Op. 18, nos. 1 and 2 only; arrangement for piano, violin, and cello

Six new, large sonatas all at once, cried the reviewer while reaching for these first two, full of joyful expectation.[1] He had hardly turned the page, however, when he found that these sonatas are B.'s famously known violin quartets arranged for the keyboard.[2] Now let's not make a fuss about that, even though it should have been indicated in the title, because the arrangement is made so reasonably that one willingly desires to hear these ingenious products again, notwithstanding that they cannot possibly be performed and be as exceptional as in the original version and on the original instruments. And in spite of their austere and unmanageable nature, one can hardly get enough of listening to them, assuming of course that one manages to understand and to reproduce them.

Keyboard players who want to dazzle and please themselves by performing ornamentations and the like will want to leave these works alone. Whoever is concerned with hearing an ingenious composition and making it available for others to hear, let him acquire them, particularly no. 1 (F major), which in the original is also one of the reviewer's favorites of these quartets and which can also be played on the pianoforte much better than no. 2 (G major). The engraving and the entire outward appearance are quite excellent, as one is accustomed to seeing from this publisher. Also, while playing them through twice, the reviewer found no errors, something that is not a trifle in such music!

NOTES

1. Although the term *sonata* acquired its meaning as a "solo or chamber instrumental cycle of aesthetic or diversional purpose" during the Baroque period, writers continued to use the term during the Classical period to refer to any instrumental piece. See William S. Newman, *The Sonata in the Classic Era,* 3rd edn. (New York: Norton, 1983), 19ff.

2. Ferdinand Ries's arrangement of the String Quartets, op. 18, as piano trios was published by Simrock in Bonn in 1806 with the opus number 60. The title of the arrangement on the title page reads "Six grandes Sonates pour le piano Forte, Violon obligé et Violoncelle ad lib."

〜

74.
"Brief Notice," *Allgemeine musikalische Zeitung* 22 (15 November 1820): 784.

C minor; arrangement for piano four-hands

The Quartet in C Minor and C Major, splendid in every regard, is the one out of the six earlier ones (still the dearest of all for not just a few people) for which we owe this master our gratitude.[1] That precisely Beethoven's quartets, as well arranged as they are, must lose more on the pianoforte than those of many other masters, especially even Mozart's, is due to the subject and the style. Dilettanti presume this as a matter of course. Following this presumption, however, they will find in this, as in the other B. quartets arranged in this manner, diverse instruction, ingenious entertainment, and fine enjoyment. The piece is arranged with diligence and skill. The engraving and paper are very good.

NOTE

1. The fourth string quartet in op. 18 contains three movements in C minor and one (the Scherzo) in C major. Mockwitz's four-hand arrangement of Quartets Nos. 1–3 appeared

in January 1817 and of Quartet No. 5 in February 1821. The four-hand arrangement of No. 6, prepared by J. P. Schmidt, appeared in September 1826. Quartets Nos. 1–3 were issued in January 1817, No. 5 in February 1821, and No. 6 (arranged by J. P. Schmidt) in September 1826.

≈

75.
"Music," *Zeitung für Theater und Musik zur Unterhaltung gebildeter, unbefangener Leser: Eine Begleiterin des Freymüthigen* 1 (1821): 208.

Op. 18, no. 5

Concertmaster *Möser*[1] concluded the quartet entertainment for this year with an outstandingly beautiful performance of a Haydn quartet full of humor and grace in D major, one of the more recent, highly genial quartets by Andreas Romberg in E♭ major—containing a brilliant Allegro movement, an excellent Adagio cantabile, a minuet along with a trio and concluding rondo full of originality and artistic work—and finally a genial performance of one of the most magnificent quartets by Beethoven, in A major, with the beautiful variations in D major and a rondo that is truly a new invention. The *new* year too promises us a renewal of similar enjoyment of art.

NOTE

1. Karl Möser (1774–1851) studied music in Berlin under the concertmaster Karl Haack and became a leading figure in Berlin's music life with his frequent chamber music soirées. He directed a number of premieres of Beethoven's music, including the first Berlin performance of the Ninth Symphony in 1826.

≈

76.
"Concert in Berlin," *Der Freymüthige* 21 (10 February 1824): 120.

Op. 18, no. 6

The quartet subscription sessions of concertmaster Möser have found a delightful continuation. At the seventh session on 4 February, a quartet by Andreas Romberg was performed for the first time; the previous evenings had been dedicated exclusively to Mozart, Beethoven, and Haydn. The Romberg quartet (F major) is soundly and most diligently composed, and for the first violin in particular it is very advantageous and brilliant. Nevertheless, the ideas occasionally seemed to us somewhat obsolete and flat and without any particular trace of genius. Regrettably we missed a Mozart quartet and we wished Romberg would have been put in Haydn's place.—The highest pleasure was afforded by Beethoven's magnificent Quartet in B♭ Major, which, having already been offered in the sixth session, was repeated today "at the request of many." The genius of Beethoven flowed here in the most sumptuous abundance, not like a mountain stream bursting through ravines and rocks, but rather like a friendly brook through a blooming meadow. In this work, the maestro has achieved a rare control over himself. Contrary to his custom, he has been brief and clear, has avoided the baroque and bizarre, and still has not given up his originality for one moment. In the last movement, a gloomy Adagio, which exhausts all harmonic devices, is followed by a friendly, cheerful scherzo in $\frac{3}{4}$ time.[1] This movement is the crown of the entire piece and leaves the listener with an extremely beneficent impression, which one can submit to all the more readily since fewer means and strong effort are employed to bring it about.

NOTE

1. The last movement is titled "La Malincolia" and precedes the final Allegretto quasi allegro. For a discussion of this movement as it relates to eighteenth-century aesthetic descriptions of contemplative music, see Carl Dahlhaus, "La Malincolia," in *Ludwig van Beethoven,* ed. Ludwig Finscher (Darmstadt: Wissenschaftliche Buchgesellschaft, 1983), 200–11.

$\approx$

77.
J. P. S. "News: Berlin, 16 November 1826: Quartet Music," *Berliner allgemeine musikalische Zeitung* 3 (22 November 1826): 382.

String Quartet No. 1; mentioned: Symphony No. 9, op. 125

The first of the six older Mozart quartets, in G major, followed and was performed by the players in a way that was as finely nuanced as it was expressive of the music's character. Beethoven showed himself worthy of his forerunners in the first quartet in F major with that genius that we admire in astonishment from his oldest up to his most recent artistic creations, even if we cannot always grasp them and discover the context for the ideas. These older quartets are nevertheless quite clear, grand, and new in invention, as in the combination of harmonies. What beautiful melancholy and elegiac depth animate the fantasy-like Adagio in D minor, and how impudently and teasingly does the rondo, in contrast, bubble forth with jovial humor!

Music Director Möser's ability to comprehend the spirit of compositions and to reproduce them with his violin playing is too well recognized to make any discussion about it necessary. Haydn's humor, Mozart's soul, and Beethoven's sublime genius are accurately perceived by this ingenious virtuoso and presented clearly to the listener. Also, Messr. Ries, Lenss and

Kranz accomplished what was required, individually and together, in order to create as perfect a totality as possible.

This fine artistic enjoyment will soon be increased even more by the forthcoming Möser concert, in which we will have the pleasure of hearing an excellent bassoonist, Mr. Ohmann from Kassel, and the colossal work of Beethoven's most recent symphony, with Schiller's "Ode to Joy" marvelously coordinated with orchestra, solo, and chorus.[1] Such music is a pillar for the vacillating tastes of the times, and to help firm up its buttress let every true friend of art do his part as best he can.

NOTE

1. For information on this performance, see Alfred Kalischer, "Beethoven und der preußische Königshof unter Friedrich Wilhelm III," in *Beethoven und Berlin* (Berlin: Schuster & Loeffler, 1908–10), 327–88.

~

78.
"Berlin, Friday, 7 May: Overview of the Productions of 1830,"
Iris im Gebiete der Tonkunst 1 (7 May 1830): n.p.

It cannot be the task here to discuss these six quartets themselves, which are known to the art world as six glittering jewels and which have appeared in the above-mentioned edition.[1] We are concerned only with the *edition* of these unsurpassable works, which appear for the first time in full score. It is worthy of the content. In its large, permanent octavo format it joins the similar editions of Haydn's and Mozart's quartets and even excels them perhaps in external elegance and more correct and distinct engraving. It is a highly meritorious undertaking of publishing houses when they bring about editions of this kind, for the pure study of music cannot be promoted better by any means than by full scores of masterpieces, which are still very rare in poor Germany. It is to be hoped that the other quartets, quintets, the Septet, etc. will follow in a similar manner. The low price of one fl. for each quartet, which accordingly is much more expensive in the fortepiano arrangement, should cause every musician who is serious about his artistic training to purchase this edition and others similar to it. We wish this from our hearts for the publisher, the artists, and—*for art!* The latter would gain most from this since superficial and empty pieces of inferiority will have to stand ashamed next to such works.

NOTE

1. "Bibliothek musicale. Partitiens des six premiers Quatuors L. v. Beethoven."

The first score edition of the Quartets, op. 18, was published by Jean André in Offenbach in 1829 in what we would today recognize as a miniature score format, although the reviewer describes it as a "large, permanent octavo format." As the reviewer states clearly, these early score editions were designed solely for study purposes and marked a milestone in Beethoven reception history.

~

OP. 19
PIANO CONCERTO NO. 2 IN B♭ MAJOR
Also see entry no. 56, n. 6

———————

79.
"New Music Publications," *Zeitung für die elegante Welt* 2 (13 March 1802): 256.

The Bureau de Musique in Vienna and Leipzig has recently published in a splendid engraving:

A beautiful but also rather difficult fortepiano concerto in B♭ major, written with much art, which is the most recent by this ingenious composer and great fortepianist in Vienna, Louis van Beethoven (price 2 Tlr. 12 Gr.).[1]

NOTE

1. The first edition of op. 19 was published four months earlier in December 1801 by Hoffmeister in Vienna and the Bureau de Musique in Leipzig.

~

80.
"Music Publications," *Zeitung für die elegante Welt* 3 (8 February 1803): 136.

With Symphony No. 1, op. 21

As splendid, recent music publications, the following need only to be named without further proof of judgment:

1. Concert pour le Piano F. par Beethoven Oeuv. 19. in the Bur. de Mus. 2 Rthr. 12 Gr. This concerto is very brilliant, diligently composed, and full of beautiful, original ideas.

2. Collection des Quatuors comp. p. I.[1] Haydn, 6 Cahiers,[2] each can be obtained ibidem especially for the prepayment price of 1 Rthlr. 4 Gr. Pleyel also has in his collection some arranged pieces; here only the

real originals are to be found. Moreover, in the Paris edition there are innumerable errors; also the most recent quartets are missing.

3. Grande Sinfonie par Beethoven, Oeuv. 21 ibidem. 2 Rthlr. 12 Gr. A very originally composed, beautiful symphony that is very effective.[3]

NOTES

1. p. I. = par J[oseph].

2. "Cahier" generally means "paper book," "scholar's exercise book," or "six manuscript leaves."

3. The first edition of Symphony No. 1 was published in December 1801 by Hoffmeister in Vienna and by the Bureau de Musique in Leipzig. It is described as a "Grande Simphonie" on the title page.

~

OP. 20
SEPTET FOR VIOLIN, VIOLA, CLARINET, FRENCH HORN, BASSOON, VIOLONCELLO, AND DOUBLE BASS IN E♭ MAJOR

Also see entry nos. 23, 46, 48, 85, 86, and 138

81.
"News: Linz, 10 November," *Musikalische Zeitung für die österreichischen Staaten* 2 (15 November 1812): 117.

Arrangement for string quintet by Franz Anton Hoffmeister;[1] mentioned: several other works

Van Beethoven has left our city again without fulfilling our most ardent wishes to hear him play in a public concert. Only a small circle was fortunate enough to hear him at Count v. *Dönhof's,* a liberal patron of the arts who in his own way understood how to honor this great artist.[2] First Mr. v. Beethoven played a sonata from his earlier compositions, then a short improvisation. When his Septet, arranged as a quintet by Hoffmeister, was played for him by a few dilettantes, he again took his place at the fortepiano and to the amazement of all present improvised on the theme of the first minuet almost an entire hour. Only the promise he left us, from a man who steadfastly keeps his word, will console us in our present loss of enjoyment. He departed with the respect of all who became closely acquainted with him.

NOTES

1. The first edition of Franz Anton Hoffmeister's (1754–1812) arrangement of Beethoven's Septet was published in August 1802 (as noted in an advertisement in the WZ on 18 August). The first edition of the original had appeared only one or two months earlier

in Vienna with Hoffmeister. The publication of the arrangement prompted Beethoven to publish a notice in the wz on 20 October 1802, in which he stated that the arrangement was not an original work, but a transcription. He added, "The making of these transcriptions is on the whole a thing against which nowadays (in our prolific age of transcriptions) a composer would merely struggle in vain; but at least he is entitled to demand that the publishers shall mention the fact on the title page, so that his honor as a composer may not be infringed nor the public deceived—" (see Anderson, app. H, notice 1). The Septet's popularity was attested to by the extraordinary number of arrangements that appeared during his lifetime; for a partial list, see Kinsky-Halm, 50–51.

2. Count Ludwig Nikolaus Dönhoff (1769–1838) gave several soirées in Linz in Beethoven's honor during the composer's visit there in 1812. A somewhat different account of Beethoven's performance at one of these events, based on a personal communication from the Linz concertmaster Franz Glöggl, appears in Thayer-Forbes, 541.

∾

82.
"Brief Notice," *Allgemeine musikalische Zeitung* 18 (31 July 1816): 536.

Arrangement for piano four-hands

This particularly beloved, exquisite work—known as one of the most richly melodic, cheerful, and comprehensible among B's works—also looks quite good in this arrangement.[1] Indeed, the first Allegro looks as if it originally had been written this way. (In the variations, where particular consideration is given to the specific *timbre* of the instruments, that is least of all the case.) Also, everything can be played easily and comfortably, and it shows in general that whoever arranged it understood what he was doing and worked diligently. Whoever likes such arrangements in general will certainly find joy and pleasure here.

NOTE

1. This review concerns the first four-hand arrangement by Fr. Mockwitz of the Septet published in April 1815 by Breitkopf & Härtel in Leipzig. Several other four-hand arrangements (including ones by Czerny, G. E. Griffin, G. W. Marks, and unnamed arrangers) appeared during Beethoven's lifetime in arrangements for one or two pianos.

∾

83.
Allgemeiner musikalischer Anzeiger (Frankfurt) 1 (15 July 1826): 17.

Arrangement for flute, clarinets, horns, bassoon, trumpet, serpent, and trombone by Bernhard Henrick Crusell;[1] mentioned: Piano Sonata, op. 106

This famous, richly melodic work, which by itself could suffice to characterize the earlier period of our admirable Beethoven, has been arranged with taste and experience for flute, one (small) E♭ and two B♭ clarinets, two horns, two bassoons, a trumpet, serpent, and trombone, and in this form it also creates an exquisite effect.[2] It is odd that Beethoven is supposed to have declared precisely this work as one of his least successful, for although its design is somewhat expansive, it is nevertheless infinitely richer in true beauty than many of his later works, for example, the "Grand Sonata," op. 106.[3]

NOTES

1. Bernhard Henrick Crusell (1775–1838), Finnish composer, conductor, and clarinet virtuoso. Crusell also translated French, German, and Italian operas for the Swedish stage.

2. This review concerns the arrangement for eleven wind instruments published by Peters in Leipzig in 1825. Included in this unusual arrangement was the serpent, a wind instrument constructed out of an undulating shape of wood covered with leather; it had six finger holes, a short brass mouth pipe, and an ivory or wood mouthpiece. Although the instrument appeared in France in the late sixteenth century, it was still in use in orchestras and military bands in the late eighteenth century. In the early nineteenth century, three or four keys were added, but the instrument lost favor by the mid-nineteenth century. See Robert Eliason, "Serpent," *New Harvard Dictionary of Music,* ed. Don Randel (Cambridge MA: Belknap, 1986).

3. Beethoven's dissatisfaction with the Septet was recorded in a conversation with Charles Neate in the summer of 1815. Neate mentioned that the Septet was very much admired in London, and Beethoven is supposed to have replied: "That damned stuff! [or "a damned thing"] I wish it were burned!" (Thayer-Forbes, 620). Undoubtedly Beethoven's reaction owed much to the fact that the Septet is one of his most conventional works and that critics, such as the one who wrote this review, frequently praised it by castigating his more innovative compositions. It is also true, however, that Beethoven chafed when a particular work was extremely popular regardless of its innovations.

The title page of the first edition of the *Hammerklavier* describes it as a "Grande Sonate," a term Beethoven had used earlier for four sonatas written on a larger scale: ops. 7, 13 (*Pathétique*), 22, and 53 ("Waldstein").

∾

84.
"News: Berlin," *Allgemeine musikalische Zeitung* 30 (28 May 1828): 363–64.

With Symphony No. 6, op. 68; Symphony No. 7, op. 92; and String Quartet, op. 132

Above all, Mr. M. D. Möser delighted us in his last soirées with Spohr's Overture to *Faust,*[1] and a new septet by Lenss,[2] which manifested less peculiarity of invention than taste, diligence, and knowledge of instruments, in addition to considerable skill in modulation. We were delighted further by Beethoven's truly romantic *Pastoral Symphony,* which reminded us of the joys of country life at a befitting time. Then in the sixth session of the second Möser quartet cycle we heard, in addition to a very humorous quartet by the eternally youthful and fresh and jovial Haydn, a quartet by L. Spohr (in E♭ major), less perfectly executed than the very difficult, new Quartet by Beethoven in A Minor, op. 132, which despite all of the individual qualities of beauty of its ideas, did not manage to appeal in its total effect. This was most likely the fault of the exhausting length of the movements and rhapsodic development. The scherzo was understood the most and was received with approval.

At the conclusion of his sessions for this year, Mr. M. D. Möser organized one of the most first-rate instrumental concerts of the past winter. An unknown but effective overture by Fesca began the entertainment. This was followed with the Quintet in G Minor by Mozart with the beautiful, cheerful Adagio in E♭ major whose effect is heightened by mutes.

Haydn's jubilant Symphony in E♭ Major with the initial timpani tremolo found general approval. A new octet by Spohr (which is being engraved by Schlesinger) was promised, but instead, however, we heard three movements of Beethoven's beloved Septet performed excellently. Beethoven's marvelously grand Symphony in A Major concluded this ingenious and very well-attended entertainment.

NOTES

1. This is a reference not to the most famous work of this name in German literature, Goethe's *Faust,* but to a literary text for Louis Spohr's opera *Faust,* which was written in 1813 by Joseph Karl Bernard and premiered in Prague on 1 September 1816. A vocal score of the first edition had been published in Leipzig in 1822. Bernard (1780–1850) moved to Vienna in 1800 and became editor of the wz in 1819. He was acquainted with Beethoven by 1814 and became one of his closest friends during the composer's last decade. In 1823 he completed the libretto for an oratorio titled "Der Sieg des Kreuzes" to be composed by Beethoven; the work was sketched, but not completed, by Beethoven.

2. Heinrich K. Lenss (1793–1856) was a composer of chamber music and played in the Karl Möser quartet soirées (see entry nos. 76 and 77 and entry no. 75, n. 1).

∾

OP. 21
SYMPHONY NO. 1 IN C MAJOR
Also see entry nos. 29, 80, and 119

85.
"News: Musical Events,"[1] *Allgemeine musikalische Zeitung* 3 (15 October 1800): 49.

Mentioned: Piano Concerto No. 1, op. 15, and Septet, op. 20

Finally Mr. Beethoven did indeed obtain the theater once, and this was probably the most interesting public concert for a long time.[2] He played a new concerto of his own composition, which has very many beautiful qualities—especially the first two movements.[3] Then a septet by him was played, which is written with very much taste and feeling. He then improvised in a masterly way, and at the end a symphony of his composition was performed in which there was very much art, novelty, and a wealth of ideas. However, the wind instruments were used far too much so that there was more music for wind instruments than for a full orchestra.[4]

Perhaps we might do well to make note of the following things about this concert. The orchestra of the Italian opera performed to its own disadvantage. First—quarrels about who should direct. Beethoven rightfully thought that he could not entrust the direction to Mr. Contini and could entrust it to no one better than Mr. Wranitsky.[5] The gentlemen did not want to play under him. The faults of the orchestra, as criticized above, thus became all the more striking since B's compositions are difficult to execute. While they were accompanying, the players did not make any effort to pay attention to the soloist. As a result there was no trace of delicacy in the accompaniment, no yielding to the flow of the soloist's feelings, etc. In the second part of the symphony, they became so lax that in spite of all efforts, no fire could any longer be brought forth in their playing, particularly not in the wind instruments. With such behavior what use is any amount of skill,—which cannot at the least be denied to most members of this organization? How effective then can even the most splendid composition be? Who will invent and teach us the great magic word that will expel such customs and personal and other petty considerations and instill life, spirit, and fire for art itself. It may be that it is not better in many other large towns. However, when one considers how much—in every respect, how very much—could be here, in this wealthy Imperial City, with so much love for music, with so much skill, if we only truly *wanted it,* we must be offended, and we cannot cease complaining, wishing, and accusing those who bear the blame.

NOTES

1. The original article uses the word *Akademien.* In Germany this term is used in the sense of "academy" or "learned society," but in Austria it also referred to a literary or musical event or performance.

2. On the serious difficulties that artists faced when they wished to reserve theaters in Vienna for concerts, see Mary Sue Morrow, *Concert Life in Haydn's Vienna* (Stuyvesant NY: Pendragon, 1989), and her "Making It in the Big City: Beethoven's First Decade in Vienna," *Beethoven Journal* 10 (1995): 46–52.

3. Beethoven originally planned to perform the Third Concerto at this concert, which was his first benefit concert. Unfortunately, the concerto was not ready on time and he revised the First Concerto in C Major instead (this second version survives in a complete score in Berlin, Mus. ms. autogr. Beethoven 12). See Hans-Werner Küthen, preface to *Beethoven Konzert für Klavier und Orchester Nr. 1, C-Dur* (Munich: G. Henle, 1990), v.

4. The statement "Nur waren die Blasinstrumente gar zu viel angewendet" has traditionally been taken as a criticism of Beethoven's scoring. In view of the writer's comments in the next paragraph, however, it might be taken to apply to the performance itself.

5. Paul Wranitsky (1758–1808) was a Czech musician whose conducting talents were highly valued by both Haydn and Beethoven.

~

86.
"Music," *Historisches Taschenbuch: Mit besonderer Rücksicht auf die Österreichischen Staaten* (Geschichte des Jahres 1802) (Vienna, 1806): 201.

With Septet, op. 20; Sonata for Piano and Violin, op. 23; Piano Sonata, op. 26; Piano Sonata, op. 27; and String Quintet, op. 29; mentioned: String Quintet, op. 4

Beethoven wrote his First Symphony in C Major, a masterpiece that does equal honor to his inventiveness and his musical knowledge. Being just as beautiful and distinguished in its design as its execution, there prevails in it such a clear and lucid order, such a flow of the most pleasant melodies, and such a rich, but at the same time never wearisome, instrumentation that this symphony can justly be placed next to Mozart's and Haydn's. Also a Violin Quintet[1] and a Septet with Horn and Clarinet (op. 20) are beautifully conceived and splendidly written. Impartial connoisseurs were not as pleased with Beethoven's most recent fortepiano works that, they perceived, conspicuously strove to be unusual and original, only too often at the cost of beauty. This peculiarity, which verges on the fantastic, was found particularly in Beethoven's op. 23 and in a few movements of ops. 26 and 27, which, to be sure, offer many a brilliant and significant example of beauty as compensation.

NOTE

1. Opus 4.

~

87.
F——b——t, "Public Concerts in Vienna: Vienna, 7 April 1803," *Zeitung für die elegante Welt* 3 (7 April 1803): 362.

With Symphony No. 2, op. 36; Piano Concerto No. 3, op. 37; and *Christus am Ölberg*, op. 85

The *Zeitung f. d. e. W.* is universally read here and is valued according to the merit it deserves. However, one also regrets just as universally that for a considerable time so little news of Vienna has appeared in it.[1] Since I, as a mere observer without any connections of any kind, am in a position to report news perhaps more impartially than many others, I will try to provide your journal with news more frequently in the future.

The most significant thing I can report to you now are concerts and events, of which there are very many in this musical city and, of course, of varying worth. The choicest ones up to now have been the event put on by Mad. Auernhammer in the Hoftheater, then the cantatas by Messrs. Paer and Beethoven, the first of which was *Das heilige Grab,* and the second *Christus am Ölberg.*

Mr. van Beethoven had raised the prices of the seats for his cantata and announced with great pomp several days previously that all pieces to be performed would be of his composition. Since he is, as is well known, employed as composer at the Theater-an-der-Wien, the management turned over the receipts for his benefit. The pieces performed consisted of two symphonies of which the first had more worth than the second because it was performed with unforced ease, while in the second a striving for novel and striking effects is more visible. Moreover, it goes without saying that neither was lacking striking and brilliant qualities of beauty. Less successful was the next concerto, in C minor, which Mr. v. B., who otherwise is known as a first-rate fortepianist, also performed not to the complete satisfaction of the public.

The cantata, *Christus am Ölberg,* was authored by *Franz Xaver Huber,*[2] who to be sure has perhaps enough theatrical knowledge for a tolerable opera, but indeed little poetic talent for a cantata.[3] The following chorus of mercenaries who want to capture Jesus can serve as an example:

> We have seen him
> > Go toward that mountain,
> Just take a left,
> > He must be quite near!-

And the rest is also written in this poetic spirit.

On the whole, B's music was good and contains a few first-rate passages. An aria by the seraph with trumpet accompaniment had a splendid effect, and in the chorus mentioned above, Mr. v B. showed that a composer of genius is capable of making something great from the worst material. A number of ideas from Haydn's *Creation* seem to have found their way into the final chorus.

NOTES

1. "That is true. But the blame for that is borne by the good Viennese themselves who indulge so much in the abundant pleasures of art and entertainment and become so lackadaisical that, in spite of all the challenges, they would rather leave it at that than write about it afterwards. That has a valuable side. Having become accustomed to too many good and splendid things in the area of the arts, one doesn't consider it worth the effort to make a lot of talk about many things. But nevertheless, one should really be more

patriotic and let foreigners take more interest in the noteworthy events in Vienna. Perhaps this observation will rouse one or another good mind and observer to voluntarily join the *Z. f. d. e. W.* We would most humbly be forced to decline entirely too specific theater reports of which enough pour in anyway and are put aside. Rather, these can benefit *Der Freymüthige* of Mr. v. Kotzebue more. The editor."

2. Franz Xaver Huber (1755–1814) was a political journalist who was frequently at odds with the Habsburgs because of satire on Austrian political conditions. He was married to the sister of the singer Magdalena Willmann, who was admired by Beethoven. See Thayer-Forbes, 232, for Beethoven's proposal of marriage to Magdalena.

3. Beethoven claimed in a letter from 23 January 1824 that he had helped Huber write the text to *Christus am Ölberg;* writing about the deficiencies of Bernard's oratorio text *Der Sieg des Kreuzes,* Beethoven noted that "although the subject is very well thought out and the poetry has some merit, yet it just cannot remain *as it is at present. Christus am Ölberg* was completed by myself and the *poet* in a fortnight. But the poet was musical and had already written several works to be set to music" (see Anderson, letter no. 1260, and Brandenburg, letter no. 1773). Barry Cooper has hypothesized that "Beethoven himself wrote the scenarios and decided the emotional content of the various episodes in the work, deriving many of the ideas from paraphrases of his earlier writings. . . . Huber then expressed these ideas in verse in a more poetic form" (see his "Beethoven's Oratorio and the Heiligenstadt Testament," *Beethoven Journal* 10 [1995]: 22). Such a process might account for the pedestrian literary quality of Huber's verses.

~

88.

"Continued Detailed News on Concerts in Berlin," *Allgemeine musikalische Zeitung* 7 (5 December 1804): 157–58.

The third concert, from 15 November, began with the excellent Symphony by Beethoven in C Major, which was received with so much well-deserved applause in last year's concerts. Every connoisseur noticed again with true joy the excellent artist, Mr. Westenholz, on the oboe. Thanks be to Asclepius and the muses who gave him back to art after a nearly fatal illness. We hope that with Mr. W.'s not very strong constitution he will spare himself for the time being when practicing his very difficult and exhausting instrument and that he will remain among us for a long time yet. Mr. Barmann played first bassoon today, and with respect to the wind instruments one could not wish for a more perfect orchestra. The aforementioned grand symphony, this exquisite, clear, harmonious, and, nevertheless, not bizarrely composed masterpiece by B. in the genre of the most recent grand instrumental compositions, was performed with energy and taste. How magnificently the first Allegro surged back and forth in the tempests of feeling and affects! How pleasantly the quasi-allegretto calmed our excited senses! How superbly and beautifully the wind instruments performed the melody in the trio of the minuet where the two violins play the continuous passages completely even! This wasn't quite the case with the beginning of the finale, which, to be sure, is very difficult with such a large orchestra when the most precise evenness is required in stroke and expression. The entire piece, however, was excellent.

~

89.

Johann Friedrich Reichardt, "Grand Concert Performance in the Royal Opera House for the Benefit of the Widows of Musicians of the Royal Orchestra on 16, 23, and 30 December 1804," *Berlinische musikalische Zeitung* 1 (1805): 7.

In order to draw attention to how much the arrangement of such a large concert depends on the selection of all the individual parts, let it just be noted here that the selection of the two symphonies that opened the concerts was not exactly fortunate. At the moment that an eager public awaited the first powerful symphonic sound of a numerically large orchestra, the first symphony by Beethoven began on a short upbeat with the chord of the seventh above the dominant of the principal key.[1] No one will censure an ingenious artist like Beethoven for such liberties and peculiarities, but such a beginning is not suitable for the opening of a grand concert in a spacious opera house.

NOTE

1. Beethoven's First Symphony opens in the "wrong key" with a C-major chord with a flatted seventh that resolves to the subdominant chord, F major. Both the Second and Third Symphonies open with the kind of grand rhetorical gesture Reichardt described here.

~

90.

"Vienna, 28 January," *Allgemeine musikalische Zeitung* 7 (13 February 1805): 321–22.

With Symphony No. 3, op. 55

At the residence of Mr. von Würth, the Beethoven Symphony in C Major was performed with precision and ease. A magnificent artistic creation. All instruments are used exquisitely, and an uncommon wealth of beautiful ideas is magnificently and charmingly displayed in it. Nevertheless, cohesion, order, and light dominate everywhere.

An entirely new symphony by Beethoven (which should be differentiated from the second that appeared some time ago in the local Kunst-

und Industrie-Comptoir) is written in an entirely different style.[1] This long composition, exceedingly difficult to perform, is actually a very broadly expanded, bold, and wild fantasia. It is not at all lacking in startling and beautiful passages in which the energetic and talented spirit of its creator must be recognized; however, very often it seems to lose itself in irregularity. The symphony begins with a very strongly scored Allegro in E♭, followed by a funeral march in C minor, which subsequently is developed fugally. After this comes an Allegro scherzo and a finale, both in E♭. The reviewer certainly belongs to Mr. v. Beethoven's most sincere admirers. However, in this work he must confess to finding much too much that is strident and bizarre, so that an overview of the whole is obscured and the unity is almost completely lost.

NOTE

1. The first edition of the Second Symphony was published by the Bureau d'Arts et d'Industrie in Vienna in March 1804. They published the first edition of the *Eroica* in October 1806. The first public performance of the *Eroica* was given on 7 April 1805 at the Theater-an-der-Wien. Although one might assume from this review that the reviewer had heard the *Eroica* at one of the banker Würth's concerts, it is more probable that he heard it at one of Prince Lobkowitz's private concerts. The Würth musicales featured an orchestra of amateur musicians; although they did perform Beethoven's First Symphony and the Third Piano Concerto in their 1804–05 season, the *Eroica* may have been too difficult. Furthermore, it is unlikely that Lobkowitz would have allowed it to be performed elsewhere in a private concert, as he had purchased the rights to perform it from Beethoven. For a discussion of early rehearsals and performances of the Symphony prior to its first publication, see Tomislav Volek and Jaroslav Macek, "Beethoven's Rehearsals at the Lobkowitz's," *Musical Times* 127 (1986): 75–80. For information on Würth's concerts, see Morrow, *Concert Life in Haydn's Vienna*.

∼

91.
Johann Friedrich Reichardt, "Miscellaneous news," *Berlinische musikalische Zeitung* 1 (1805): 386.

Mr. Westenholz, our first-rate oboist from the Royal Orchestra, gave a public concert yesterday in the beautiful concert hall of our national theater in which we got to hear the following musical compositions.[1] It commenced with Beethoven's well-known Symphony in C Major. Although often heard, its originality and excellent performance were listened to with pleasure. Then Mr. Fischer sang a nice German Romance.

NOTE

1. Friedrich Westenholz (1778–1840) was an oboe player at the royal Kapelle in Berlin until his retirement in 1828. It is difficult to determine whether the Mr. Fischer cited here

is Ludwig Franz Josef Fischer (1745–1825), who created the role of Osmin in Mozart's opera *Die Entführung aus dem Serail*, or his son Josef Fischer, who sang at the Berlin Hofoper from 1810 to 1818 and later became an impresario in Palermo. See Kutsch and Riemens, *Großes Sängerlexikon*, supplementary volume, col. 316.

~

92.

J. F. R.[1] "Concerts by the Royal Orchestra for Widows and Orphans," *Berlinische musikalische Zeitung* 2 (1806): 19.

For the opening of these concerts, a different symphony could have been selected than the one by Beethoven in C with which last year's concerts also began and which we already heard performed so often and so splendidly in the Schick and Borer [*sic*] concerts.[2] One of the two Mozart symphonies with their gorgeous unison, which we heard in the second concert, would have opened the first concert better than the ambiguous though ingenious beginning of this Beethoven symphony. Thus, the magnificent, artistic work in both Mozart works would have been shared, enjoyed, and admired twice with greater attentiveness.

NOTES

1. The initials undoubtedly refer to Johann Friedrich Reichardt. This entry is an excerpt from a general report three columns in length.

2. Ernst Schick (1756–1815) was a violinist from Holland who was active in the musical life of Berlin. Together with Bohrer (first name unknown; ca. 1771–1805), a chamber musician in the private orchestra of the Queen of Prussia, he organized a series of subscription concerts at which Beethoven's First and Second Symphonies were both performed.

~

93.

"News: Vienna, 27 February," *Allgemeine musikalische Zeitung* 9 (18 March 1807): 400.

With Symphony No. 2, op. 36; Symphony No. 3, op. 55; three String Quartets, op. 59; and Symphony No. 4, op. 60

Beethoven's Grand Symphony in E♭, which was reviewed in your paper with so much impartiality and propriety, will be performed very soon along with two other symphonies by this composer (in C and D) and a fourth, still completely unknown symphony by him, in a very select society that has subscribed quite considerable contributions for the benefit of the composer.[1]

Also three new, very long and difficult Beethoven Violin Quartets, dedicated to the Russian Ambassador, Count Razumovsky,[2] are drawing the attention of all connoisseurs.[3] They are profoundly conceived and exquisitely composed, but not generally comprehensible—excepting perhaps the third in C major, which will win every educated friend of music with its ingenuity, melody, and harmonic power.

NOTES

1. The author probably refers here to the "Liebhaber Konzerte," a series of twenty concerts given in the 1807–08 season to a carefully chosen audience. The seventy members could give tickets to friends, but none were to be sold to the public; 1,309 places were available. The *Eroica* was performed on 6 December 1807 (with Beethoven conducting) and 2 February 1808; the First Symphony on 17 January 1808 and 20 March 1808; the Second Symphony on 25 November 1807 and 22 February 1808; and the Fourth Symphony on 27 December 1807. See Morrow, *Concert Life,* 345–48.

2. Count Andreas Razumovsky (1752–1836), Russian Ambassador to Vienna, married Countess Elizabeth Thun, the sister of Prince Karl Lichnowsky of Vienna, in 1788 and was sent to Vienna in 1792. Both Prince Lichnowsky and Count Razumovsky were among Beethoven's early admirers and supporters in Vienna. An accomplished violinist, Razumovsky formed a string quartet in 1808 in which he played second violin to Schuppanzigh's first. Razumovsky commissioned the three quartets of op. 59, which are commonly known as the "Razumovsky" Quartets.

3. According to an entry in the diary of the Munich court painter, Joseph Stieler, Schuppanzigh's quartet had played op. 59, no. 2, around 9 April 1807 (see *Beiträge zur Beethoven-Bibliographie,* ed. Kurt Dorfmüller [Munich: Henle, 1978], 316); for further information on the op. 59 Quartets' first performances and reception, see Alexander Wheelock Thayer, *Ludwig van Beethovens Leben,* continued by Hermann Dieters, completed by Hugo Riemann, vol. II (Leipzig: Breitkopf & Härtel, 1910), 536–37; henceforth Thayer-Dieters-Riemann.

~

94.
"News: Munich," *Allgemeine musikalische Zeitung* 14 (6 May 1812): 315.

Seventh concert. Symphony by Beethoven in C Major (No. 1), more pleasing and melodic than one expects from this artist.

~

95.
"Music: Première symphonie pour le pianoforte, à quatre mains, arrangée par Charl. Zulehner, comp. p. L v. Beethoven: Ibidem: Price 1 Thaler and 6 Groschen,"[1] *Zeitung für die elegante Welt* 13 (14 January 1813): 79.

This is the famous Grand Symphony in C Major that begins with the seventh chord. It must be very welcome to the friends of this ingenious Beethoven composition to perform such a work on the pianoforte and achieve every effect that is possible in an appropriate keyboard reduction.[2]

NOTES

1. "Symphony No. 1 for Pianoforte, for four hands, arranged by Charl. Zulehner, composed by L. v. Beethoven. Ibidem. Price 1 Thaler and 6 Groschen."

Karl Zulehner (ca. 1770–1830) studied music under J. F. X. Sterkel (see entry no. 45, n. 1) and was well known for his piano redactions of excerpts from operas. He also composed some piano sonatas. His involvement with Beethoven's music began quite early; in the WZ of 22 October 1803, Beethoven took the extraordinary step of warning the public against a prospective complete edition of his music that Zulehner intended to publish. The statement is reprinted in Anderson, *Letters,* vol. 3, app. H, p. 4. Zulehner's transcription of the First Symphony was reprinted from his own original edition by Kühnel in Leipzig in 1813. See AMZ 15 (1813), Intelligenz-Blatt XC, col. 66.

2. Zulehner's transcription of the First Symphony was published by Kühnel in Leipzig in 1813.

~

96.
Kühn, "Concert in Berlin," *Zeitung für Theater und Musik zur Unterhaltung gebildeter, unbefangener Leser: Eine Begleiterin des Freymüthigen* 1 (25 September 1821): 147.

The magnificent, splendid Symphony in C Major by *L. van Beethoven*— one of his older, more comprehensible instrumental compositions—was performed quite splendidly, the rondo in a very fast tempo but nevertheless quite successfully. Nothing but applause of the selected gathering of listeners rewarded the effort of the artists.

~

97.
"Grand Sinfonie en Ut majeur (C major) de Louis van Beethoven," *Allgemeine musikalische Zeitung* 24 (13 November 1822): 756.

We are familiar with the beautiful Paris edition of Haydn's symphonies engraved by Pleyel in full score. Beethoven's first symphony appears here in the same format, in the same arrangement, and engraved just as beautifully; we hope that the others will follow gradually.[1] There is no need to discuss the work here. Since its first appearance, it has been a favorite piece of all full orchestras, all connoisseurs, and all not completely wretched music lovers and therefore is renowned and sufficiently recommended. It goes without saying that the publication of symphonies in full score promotes learning and facilitates precise conducting a great deal.[2] Indeed, practically only then does it become possible, for the higher this genre of instrumental music is now developed, the less sufficient the direction by the performing concertmaster from the first violin part becomes. And thus we need only wish the undertaking good progress.

NOTES

1. This notice refers to the first German score edition of the Symphony, published in early 1822 by Simrock in Bonn. The very first score edition had been published in January–February 1809 by Cianchettini & Sperati, London. On Simrock's plan to publish six symphonies in score, detailed in a letter of 13 May 1822 to Beethoven, see Kinsky-Halm, 54–55, for a portion of the relevant German text, and Albrecht, letter no. 285, for an English translation of the complete letter.

2. The first six symphonies were initially published in parts only; full-score editions followed at a distance of four to fifteen years after the publication of the parts (First Symphony: parts in 1801, full score in 1809; Second: parts in 1804, score in 1808; Third: parts in 1806, score in 1809; Fourth: parts in 1808, score in 1823; Fifth: parts in 1809, score in 1826; Sixth: parts in 1809, score in 1826). The first editions of Symphonies Nos. 7–9 were published concurrently in full score and parts. Prior to their publication in score, the first six symphonies were conducted either from manuscript copies of the full score (sometimes borrowed from lending libraries, such as the one run by Breitkopf & Härtel in Leipzig) or from the first violin part alone. The latter practice is criticized here.

～

98.
"Correspondence: Berlin, 13 January 1824," *Berliner allgemeine musikalische Zeitung* 1 (21 January 1824): 31–32.

Mentioned: Symphony No. 3, op. 55

The *Medea* overture I didn't know, the Requiem by Cherubini just as little. I collected my thoughts in order to comprehend such a great work as much as possible. But—right after that: "grand symphony by Beethoven." What anxiety! What joy! Where was I to obtain the strength to endure another grand symphony after a grand Mass? Nevertheless! Finally, I did indeed hear a symphony by my Beethoven. In the last two years, I had heard one here only once: the *Eroica*. Another time, a "grand symphony by Beethoven" was announced again. Nothing could have kept me from hearing it. It was the C-Major Symphony, Beethoven's smallest one to be sure, but always beloved and welcome. After the first movement, my ear was already listening carefully to the dancing of the spirits in the moonlight. I heard how the breezes lead them here and there, how remnants of fragrance flutter strangely between the clouds, as it resounds harshly but softly from the oak trees, as the breezes and the high leaves sing sweet-solemn melodies and the thunder sends its greeting from a passing cloud on the distant horizon. No!—There followed a viola concerto or an aria by Rossini. I departed, and to this hour I do not know whether another piece by Beethoven was served up. But that was a virtuoso concert. . . .

Will you believe it, Dear Editor, that no symphony was performed? I repeat, a symphony by Beethoven was promised and not performed, whatever my concert companion may report about it. The grand symphony had become a small overture.

~

OP. 22

PIANO SONATA IN B♭ MAJOR

See also entry no. 68, n. 2

99.

M . . . s, "Music," *Zeitung für die elegante Welt* 7 (6 August 1807): 997.[1]

Beethoven's inexhaustible genius gives each of his works such an entirely unique character, one cannot easily be compared with the other. In a similar manner, this sonata, in its beautifully contrasting and associated movements, unites in a very original way brilliant and vigorous qualities, qualities that are solemn and moving, cheerful, pleasing and turbulently grand or sublime. It is in B♭ major. The first movement, Allegro con brio, is full of powerful motion and proclaims the restless effects of an energetic heart in all the traces of a now rising, now falling passion. In the following expressive Adagio (in E♭ major),[2] a calming effect begins, more tender sensations and even a solemn, serious mood take possession of the deeply feeling but assuaged heart. In the adjoining menuetto, it begins to open itself to more joyful feelings and returns to them soon again from restless ebullitions (in the trio). The Rondo allegretto with which the Sonata concludes has as its major characteristic something pleasing, something ingratiating and asserts itself here in spite of the power of a few wild outbursts, which in this music are in contrast to the beautiful, lovely song of the theme.

After this weak attempt to describe the aesthetic spirit of the present work, let me briefly add the following on its technical content. It belongs to Beethoven's more difficult sonatas, which demand a very skilled and powerful hand for many brilliant passages. Besides the many beautiful qualities of the melody, it is distinguished, as the products of this master usually are, by an artistic treatment of harmony and modulation to the most interesting degree.

NOTES

1. The first edition of op. 22 was published in March 1802 by Hoffmeister in Vienna and the Bureau de Musique in Leipzig. In 1807 a *Titelauflage* of the edition was published

at A. Kühnel in Leipzig at the Bureau de Musique, which probably was the occasion for this review.

2. Actually, Adagio con molto espressione.

∾

OP. 23

SONATA FOR PIANO AND VIOLIN IN A MINOR

See also entry no. 86

100.

"Reviews," *Allgemeine musikalische Zeitung* 4 (26 May 1802): 569–70.

With Sonata for Piano and Violin, op. 24

It is a great joy to go through a number of *recently published* keyboard pieces, finding again and again the same thing in most, occasionally spiced with a fleeting new idea, and then, finally, to come upon something *newly invented* like these two sonatas by Beethoven.[1] The reviewer considers them among the best that Beethoven has written. The original, fiery, and bold spirit of this composer, which even in his earlier works could not escape the more attentive mind but which for that reason did not find the friendliest reception everywhere because it occasionally stormed about in an unfriendly, wild, gloomy, and dreary manner, is now becoming more and more clear, begins more and more to disdain all excess, and emerges more and more pleasant without losing anything of his character. And to be sure, the stricter an artist like B. proceeds against himself in his own training, the less he strives to impress and glorify himself, and the more certainly he will work for the satisfaction of the better people and at the same time for his own permanent fame.

In addition to strict order, clarity, and working out that is true to their nature, these two sonatas are distinguished (among the others known to the reviewer by this composer) by their cheerful but by no means dull scherzos, which are placed very appropriately in the middle. Finally, both, and particularly the first (op. 23, A minor), are by far not so difficult to play and therefore can be recommended to a larger public than many earlier works by Beethoven. Nevertheless, they need to be performed with character and precision, and not hurried through.

NOTE

1. The two Sonatas, ops. 23 and 24, were first published with a title page that reads "Deux Sonates pour le Piano Forte avec un Violon." In Vienna, T. Mollo published the first

editions in October 1801. The sonatas were also published separately with an altered title page (see Kinsky-Halm and Dorfmüller, *Beiträge*). The critic's description of the works as "newly invented" in this article is noteworthy. Later that year, on 18 October 1802, Beethoven wrote to Breitkopf & Härtel to offer them the variation sets, ops. 34 and 35; in the letter he writes: "*Each theme is treated in its own way and in a different way from the other one*. Usually I have to wait for other people to tell me when I have new ideas, because I never know this myself. But this time—I myself can assure you that in both these works *the method is quite new so far as I am concerned*" (see Anderson, letter no. 62, and Brandenburg, letter no. 108).

∾

101.

V. d. O . . . r, "Brief Reviews," *Berliner allgemeine musikalische Zeitung* 4 (1 August 1827): 251.

Arrangement by A. Brand for Trio[1]

This ingenious piece of music by the great, immortalized composer is arranged for the indicated three instruments with the requisite skill, and since we do not have an abundance of original trios for three string instruments, it can be most highly recommended. Occasionally a quartet player fails to appear or comes too late, etc.; for such situations every careful organization must have a few good trios in addition to the famous Mozart trios. For that reason, the present piece might be desirable to many.

NOTE

1. Alexander Brand's arrangement of the sonata for string trio was published by Schott in Mainz in 1826. It was advertised in the "Intell.-Bl.," *Cäcilia* 18 (1826): 19. One earlier string trio arrangement had been published by André in Offenbach in 1818 (arranged by A. Uber).

∾

OP. 24
SONATA FOR PIANO AND VIOLIN

See entry no. 100

———————————

OP. 25
SERENADE FOR FLUTE, VIOLIN, AND VIOLA

See op. 41

———————————

OP. 26
PIANO SONATA IN A♭ MAJOR

See also entry no. 86

102.
"Reviews," *Allgemeine musikalische Zeitung* 4 (30 June 1802): 650–53.

With Piano Sonata No. 1 in E♭ Major, and No. 2 in C♯ Minor, "Moonlight," op. 27

These are the three compositions for pianoforte with which Mr. v. B. recently enriched the selected company of educated musicians and skilled keyboard players.[1] Enriched—for they are true enrichment and belong among the few products of the present year that will hardly ever become obsolete; certainly No. 3 can never become obsolete. The reviewer does not wish to repeat what has been said on different occasions by others in these pages in praise of B.'s more recent compositions. It applies entirely to these works and is familiar to *the* class of friends of music for whom B. writes and who follow him and are capable of enjoying him. To the less educated or those who *want* nothing more than easy amusement from music, these works would be recommended in vain. Therefore there remains nothing left for the reviewer but to make a few short remarks.

Sonata No. 1 is probably composed far too artificially in places. By no means, however, should that be said of the truly great, gloomy, and magnificent work of *harmony*, which the composer calls "Marcia funebre sulla morte d'un Eroe" in order to lift the player directly to the correct point of view.[2] Here, everything difficult and artistic is part of the expression and therefore the essential point. Whoever complains here, as well as in various places in No. 2 or almost entirely in No. 3, about the difficulty of the ideas or the execution is like *those* popular philosophers who insist on presenting any profound treatise in the language of polite conversation at tea. In No. 2 the reviewer especially liked the first three movements up to p. 5.[3] The short Presto at the very end did not have a good effect on him and was approximately the same as the usual thundering conclusion in Italian opera arias that are written for grandiose effects.[4] Absolutely nothing in particular can be singled out in No. 3. This fantasia is one solid whole from beginning to end; it arises all at once from an undivided, profound, and intimately excited heart and is cut, as it were, from one block of marble. It is probably not possible that any human being to whom nature has not denied inner music should not be stirred by the first Adagio (to which the author appropriately added "Si deve suonare tutto questo pezzo delicatissimamente e senza sordino")[5] and be guided higher and higher, and then as intimately moved and as highly elevated by the Presto agitato as free-composed keyboard music can elevate him.[6] These two principal movements are written in the terrifying key of C♯ minor with consummate reason.[7] As far as something like this can be expressed with conventional signs, the composer has indicated everywhere how it is to be played and how to handle the peculiarities and superior qualities of the pianoforte. These notations and, more visibly, the entire arrangement and the presentation of his ideas, show that Beethoven understands the handling of the pianoforte like hardly any other composer for *this* instrument and as Ph. Em. Bach understood how to handle the clavichord. However, one must have a very, very good instrument if one wants to be satisfied to some extent with one's performance of many of his movements,—for example, the entire first movement of No. 5.[8] That the reviewer does not complain about difficulties of execution when they are necessary for the representation of a significant idea has already been mentioned. And one must admit to Mr. v. B. that the passages in his compositions of this *kind,* which are difficult to execute, and especially in the present pieces, are not without effect, as Clementi's are occasionally. However, Mr. v. B. should not so often expect the admirers of his compositions to play movements that can only be played properly with an extraordinarily large hand. A composer can justifiably demand study, diligence, and effect if he knows how to compensate for them. But as it is written, who can add a cubit to his stature by worrying?[9]

NOTES

1. The first editions of ops. 26 and 27, which occasioned this review, appeared in March 1802 from Jean Cappi in Vienna. Opus 27, nos. 1 and 2, were printed separately with plate numbers 878 and 879.

2. The third movement of op. 26, the funeral march, was quite popular as an independent work. Cappi, the publisher of the first edition of the complete sonata, released it as an independent piece already in 1802 (the same year as the complete sonata). Kuhn in Berlin, Simrock in Bonn, and Bureau de Musique in Leipzig also published it in that manner in 1802. Beethoven himself arranged it for orchestra in 1815 (WoO 96), and Tobias Haslinger published a vocal arrangement of it by Seyfried, with a text by Jeitteles, the author of *An die ferne Geliebte,* following the composer's death in 1827 as "Beethoven's Begräbniss!" (Beethoven's funeral).

3. The first five pages of the first edition include only the first two movements of op. 27, no. 1.

4. The critic here refers to the concluding measures of the final movement, marked "Presto" and covering the last line of music in the first edition.

5. "Si deve suonare tutto questo pezzo delicatissimamente e senza sordino" = "One must play this whole piece very delicately without the damper [i.e., with pedal]."

6. The three movements are labeled "Adagio sostenuto," "Allegretto," and "Presto agitato."

7. During the Baroque and Classical periods of music history, the different keys came to symbolize and be used to express different emotional states. The history of these symbolic associations is outlined in Rita Steblin, *A History of Key Characteristics in the Eighteenth and Early Nineteenth Centuries* (Ann Arbor MI: UMI Research, 1983). The key of C♯ minor was a rare key during the Classical period (in part because it was out of tune due to the tuning systems of the day); according to the aesthetician, poet, and musician C.

F. D. Schubart (whose views on this matter Beethoven respected), it was reserved for the depiction of "penitential lamentation, intimate conversation with God, the friend and help-mate of life: sighs of disappointed friendship and love lie in its radius" (Steblin, *History of Key Characteristics,* 123).

8. Opus 27, no. 2. It is not clear why this is referred to here as no. 5 and above as no. 3. At the beginning of the review, however, the three works, in order, are clearly labeled 1, 2, and 5!

9. Matt. 6:27. Also Luke 12:25.

∼

103.
M . . . s, *Zeitung für die elegante Welt* 7 (1807): 941–42.

With Rondo for Piano in G Major, op. 51, no. 2

This sonata by Beethoven in A♭ major is without doubt one of his most perfect masterpieces of this kind. Its character is noble, grand, and sublime. A certain solidity and calm, which express dignity, are dominant in its development and in the way it expresses high effects and passions. Even the theme for the variations, with which it begins, makes the profound impression of a noble, feeling heart by combining masculine energy with soft intimacy. Often the sentiment inclines toward dark gruesome gravity, but soon it is dissolved in milder tones. The scherzo Allegro molto is full of enchanting fire and has a romantic blend of wildness and tender rapture that can hardly be described. Then the exceedingly original funeral march on the death of a hero resounds solemnly in A♭ minor. An equally original, fiery Allegro forms the conclusion.

The *Rondo* in G Major belongs to the less difficult and particularly pleasing compositions by the great Beethoven. It consists of an Andante Grazioso e Cantabile in $\frac{2}{4}$ time, which alternates in the middle with a very lovely Allegretto in $\frac{6}{8}$ time in E♭ major.

∼

104.
"Review: *Für Freunde der Tonkunst,* by Friedrich Rochlitz," *Allgemeine musikalische Zeitung* 27 (29 June 1825): 443–44.

"Commentatiuncula in usum Delphini."[1] A joke that has seriousness as its background. Grétry had maintained in his essays on music that many Haydn symphonies had such a definite expression that one could provide the text for them.[2] Spazier, his translator, tried to make that ridiculous;[3] Apel defended it and carried out the idea—in his own way.[4] And now, many things, in part very strange things, were written about attempts to reduce instrumental music to concepts and accordingly to express music in distinct words. R.

wants to demonstrate the entirely inadmissible nature of this idea—that is to say, not in Grétry's sense but others—without becoming involved directly in the dispute or in extensive theorizing. Therefore he makes up a man who joyfully embraces the idea with both arms and carries it out with discernment and obstinacy. And, on the basis of what he logically derives from a false principle, he unsuspectingly exposes its inadmissibility. This honest eccentric interprets exegetically from a series of Beethoven variations nothing less than his entire inner and outer life. He does this in such a manner that he believes that it would have to be clear as day to everyone. He does this step by step, from birth to the hour where he writes his strange commentary. It is understood what is meant by that: every single person who searches that way finds what he wants, and everyone finds something different. Thus it is and cannot be otherwise. But the man deals with this unfortunate matter so well, and besides is also such a good-natured, trusting, not at all foolish and, in his own way, charming person that there is concern that he will prejudice many readers in favor of what he is there to oppose. At least we have just found in a different notice of this book that the author now quietly withdraws with a few pleasantries that can have any and no meaning, as though he did not know what to think.

With that we take our leave from the author for now and in parting still want to shake his hand with gratitude and kindness as a friend who has brought us a pleasant and useful present.

NOTES

1. This review (an excerpt from an extended review, cols. 433–44) deals with a chapter in the second volume of Friedrich Rochlitz's book *Für Freunde der Tonkunst,* with the title "Commentatiuncula in usum Delphini" (Little Commentaries for the Use of Delphinus [a name] [398–427]), which attempts to satirize the theory that certain forms of music can be reduced to concepts expressed in words and thus elicit structural narrative affects in the listener, an extension of the eighteenth-century doctrine of affects. By the time Rochlitz's book appeared in 1825, this idea had begun to be widely adopted by progressive music critics. Rochlitz was still sufficiently conservative to find the idea distasteful and expressed his disdain by presenting in a first-person narrative a hapless listener who finds the history of his own life expressed in considerable detail in a Beethoven piano sonata. The reviewer is concerned that the narrative style of the satire will have the opposite effect on the reader and will create support for this doctrine. For further reading on this particular dispute, see Wallace, *Beethoven's Critics,* 79–82.

The following offers a sample of Rochlitz's satirical narrative affect as subjective fantasizing related to the "theme" of op. 26 in A♭ major. "Theme: the known quantity, the foundation, which afterwards is developed further: Andante, A♭ major, three eighth beats, more serious than cheerful, but gentle, friendly, and pleasing. At the same time, not at all without strength and, in all modesty, of great promise. Look, Bernhard, I said to myself, your known quantity was exactly like that—your foundation was from God the Lord, which afterwards was to be developed further. It was exactly like that according to the little you remember from your earliest child- and boyhood, and according to much that others have told you about it. However sad it may make you, put it together once more: a boy, more serious than cheerful, but gentle, friendly, and pleasing, and at the same time not at all without strength and, in all modesty, of great promise! Yes indeed, your Creator made you like that, and how graciously. Thus your father maintained you, your pious mother nourished you, bodily and spiritually, and how lovingly!"

2. André-Erneste-Modeste Grétry (1742–1813), a Belgian composer, wrote some fifty operas and numerous treatises on music. For the source of this debate, see his *Mémoires ou essais sur la musique* (Paris, 1789), 414, in which he advanced the ideal that instrumental works like Haydn's symphonies would benefit from being set to texts. Beethoven's Variations for Piano (WoO 72) are based on a theme from Grétry's opera *Richard, Cœur de Lion.*

3. Johann Gottlieb Karl Spazier (1761–1805), author and composer, served as editor for the music journals *Berlinische musikalische Zeitung* and *Zeitung für die elegante Welt,* both of which were important to the critical reception of Beethoven's music. In his translation of Grétry's *Mémoires,* published as *Grétrys Versuche über die Musik* (Leipzig: Breitkopf & Härtel, 1800), he held Grétry's ideas on texts in instrumental music up for ridicule.

4. Johann August Apel's (see entry no. 27, n. 5) article "Musik und Poesie" (AMZ 8 [16 and 23 April 1806]: 449–57, 465–70) was the immediate object of Rochlitz's parody.

~

OP. 27
PIANO SONATAS

See entry nos. 86 and 102 [nos. 1 and 2]

OP. 28
PIANO SONATA IN D MAJOR ("PASTORAL")

105.
"Reviews," *Allgemeine musikalische Zeitung* 5 (8 December 1802): 188–90.

With Seven Variations, WoO 46

Beethoven remains faithful to his character and manner, if one can say this in order to describe a certain, definite way of representing one's ideas. And an artist like B. can really do nothing better than remain faithful to himself. This character and manner have been stated in these pages so precisely, and the composer already has such a respectable public throughout the entire musical world, that little remains for the advertiser of new works to say than, they are there. And it would be very nice if one had nothing further to say about the works of a great many artists, excluding those for whom a public had yet to be developed or identified. For, in the end, what is the result if one praises or censures individual things in works of art, using the word in its true, higher meaning? Or can one justifiably attribute that honorable name to those products that present material for the many individual details, even praiseworthy ones? In art, as it should be, details do not remotely make up the total work. They can constitute an interesting product, but they never constitute a complete work, which must exist in the meaning of the total work, which those who enjoy it must also find.

Number 1 [WoO 46] is accompanied throughout by an obbligato violoncello, which with such a long title should have been the last thing to pass unnoticed.[1] Whoever wants to perform this violoncello part must be in full command of his instrument. The variations are not among the most excellent ones we owe to this master.

Number 2 [op. 28] is on a very large scale and is peculiar to the extent of being strange and adventurous, particularly the first and third movements (the sonata has four).[2]

NOTES

1. The "long title" is "Variations pour le Clavecin sur le Thème Bey Männer [sic] welche Liebe fühlen de l'Opera die Zauberflöte de Mr. Mozart Composées et dediées son Excellence Monsieur Le Comte de Browne Brigadier au Service de SM. L'Empereur de Russie par Louis van Beethoven à Vienne chez T. Mollo et Comp. Le Ier Jenvrier 1802."

2. Although the reviewer does not specify what he found "strange and adventurous" about the first and third movements, both depart from the conventions of the day (the first movement, for instance, in the character of the first theme; the third in its registral and harmonic surprises).

~

OP. 29
STRING QUINTET IN C MAJOR

Also see entry nos. 70 and 86

———————

106.
"Rondeau tiré du grand quintuor de L. van Beethoven,"[1] *Musikalische Eilpost* 1 (1826): 108.

Arrangement for piano four-hands by J. P. Schmidt[2]

No longer is there anything more unfortunate than arranging Mozart's difficult fugue with its many small and artistic motives for four hands.[3] Nor can there be a more unskilled arranger than J. P. Schmidt. Whoever does not want to take us at our word should play both works; each page will provide him with the proof.

NOTES

1. "A Rondo from the Grand Quintet by L. van Beethoven."

2. J. P. Schmidt's arrangement of the Rondo of op. 29 was published by Trautwein in Berlin in 1826. His arrangement of the complete work was published by Breitkopf & Härtel in Leipzig in May 1828.

3. The word "both" in entry no. 106 refers to the unidentified Mozart fugue mentioned here. The fugue was probably the one published by Trautwein in Berlin in 1826. It is listed as a four-hand arrangement of a Mozart piece listed as "la Fugue (Quatour de Violon)" in the 1826 volume of Whistling, *Handbuch der musikalischen Literatur* (Leipzig: C. F. Whistling, 1826), 25. It may be the Fugue for Two Pianos in C Minor, K. 426 (also arranged by Mozart for string quartet, K. 546). This fugue was popular during Beethoven's lifetime, as evidenced by the number of editions that appeared. Beethoven himself made a copy of mm. 42–77 with some alterations; the manuscript is at the Beethoven-Haus, BH 604 (see Willy Hess, *Beethoven-Studien* [Bonn: Beethoven-Haus, 1972], 37). For a discussion of the Mozart fugues and Beethoven's transcription, see Kirkendale, *Fugue and Fugato, in Rococo and Classical Chamber Music*, 152–81, 218.

~

107.
"Review," *Berliner allgemeine musikalische Zeitung* 3 (15 February 1826): 51.

Arrangement for piano four-hands by J. P. Schmidt

The rondo from the Quintet (one of the most charming compositions in all of music) has not yet appeared in a four-hand arrangement. Both arrangements are very useful and as easy to play as can be wished for in such compositions. Therefore, they can be recommended to all friends of music, but especially to those who don't have the opportunity to get acquainted with them and practice them in their original form.

~

108.
"Brief Reviews," *Berliner allgemeine musikalische Zeitung* 5 (19 November 1828): 445–46.

The publication of the scores of Beethoven's quartet music is one of the most desirable and honorable undertakings of the publishing business. In this genre, Germany possesses an artistic treasure that has to be all the more precious since nothing even remotely worthy of comparison is found in any other country. In itself, it is evidence of a profound and rich appreciation of art and a thoroughly perfected artistic training to undertake an artistic creation with such limited means.

Undoubtedly the reason why our greatest masters always show a delightful preference for quartet music and entrust to it the most delicate, spirited, and mature artistic faculties is, in particular, the simplicity and ease of the material. Thus, whoever doesn't know the quartet compositions of Haydn,

Mozart, and Beethoven must regard his knowledge of music as basically incomplete.

The most customary way of publishing parts is only useful for practicing. Even the fortepiano arrangements for two and four hands appear only as an insufficient makeshift and are all the less adequate the richer and more singular the original is. Nevertheless, this kind of surrogate has done a great service for the broader dissemination of works. For that reason, the most perfect way of dissemination remains the full-score edition. Its usefulness will become all the more universal the more that music instruction and fortepiano playing are perfected and contribute to the ability to read and play scores. This is unquestionably a more noble goal than that of manual dexterity, which is overvalued at the cost of all intellectual content.

The publication of precisely this quintet, the most ingenious and artistically most mature by our great maestro and at the same time one of his simplest and therefore now generally beloved works, is undoubtedly as desirable to friends of art as it is useful to the larger public.[1] Whatever the sensuous excitation in listening, it is excelled by the peacefulness of enjoyment and intellectual absorption in reading the score. Thus, those who have often heard the quintet will joyfully receive it anew and with a different feeling in the form of a score. Here one can peacefully observe, as it were, the genesis of the work. In this regard, it is even desirable to add that the origin of such a work is not to be found in a higher idea that calls forth an edifice structure like a command from God. Rather, it is found in general, even more in the indefinite artistic desire to create, that is, in the intention to make music. That much and no more is revealed to us in the first theme

OP. 29
Allegro moderato, mm. 1–9

and the motive

OP. 29
Allegro moderato, mm. 17–19

is intended to do nothing more after the repetition of the theme than continue until the first principal movement has been played to the end and the sweetly innocent second movement follows.

OP. 29
Allegro moderato, mm. 41–48

This movement soon rises above the first, and one sees the composer more profoundly stirred by the work itself. And in the elaboration of the first movement, for example, on p. 11,

OP. 29
Allegro moderato, mm. 111–15

we hear the fluttering approach of more ominous sounds, into which the soul thinks it is submerging like a gaze into a quiet mountain lake. Nevertheless, they are only sounds passing by and do not interrupt the more lightly woven melody for long. Now, just as the first part was elevated higher than the beginning, the composition rises in a similar way in each of the following parts: in the sensitive and noble Adagio, in the light scherzo, which tonally is animated more warmly in a charming sweep until the finale, full of grace, fluttering ease, sparkling life, and sweet satisfaction, thunders to a close with increasing urgency. Thus the entire work is shown in its intensified beauty, in the glory of its conclusion, as a triumph of *the art* of the composer. As such it will be recognized all the more clearly, the less a deeper stimulus appears to be necessary to this work as it is to so many other works.

1. The first score edition of op. 29 was published by Adolph Martin Schlesinger in Berlin in 1828. Schlesinger's firm in Berlin and its branch in Paris published several of Beethoven's late works (including the last three piano sonatas, which they commissioned).

~

OP. 30
THREE SONATAS FOR PIANO AND VIOLIN IN A MAJOR, C MINOR, AND G MAJOR

109.
"Reviews," *Allgemeine musikalische Zeitung* 6 (2 November 1803): 77–79.

No. 1

If something pedestrian ever escapes men of intellect, from whom one usually hears something witty, one is easily inclined to believe that they weren't entirely understood or that somewhere in their words there must be a subtly hidden point. The reviewer had approximately the same experience with this sonata.[1] Although he only rarely discovered in this sonata a trace of this composer of so many original and excellent things, nevertheless, he continued to mistrust his judgment until finally he had played it through several times and his expectations still remained unsatisfied. By no means does it follow that this sonata is pedestrian. Indeed, such a thing cannot flow from Mr. v. B's. pen. However, the reviewer is confident in saying that it is not entirely worthy of him, and he appeals to Mr. v. B.'s own sense of feeling for corroboration. Thus the first movement does not have the beautiful flow of thoughts that one meets with (especially in his later works). For that reason it quite naturally lacks a definite character, which otherwise distinguishes all of Beethoven's works to such a great advantage. Also, the third movement, an Allegretto with variations, is not entirely successful. At the very least, it should have been easy for Mr. v. B. to create even more valuable ideas from the theme. The fifth variation proves this sufficiently, although it contrasts with its sisters a little *too much* because of its contrapuntal gravity. The reviewer was least satisfied with the unworthy tricks Beethoven plays with the small or diminished seventh and the augmented-sixth for thirteen measures on the last page. In the opinion of the reviewer, something like that could only happen to Mr. B while writing in great haste or, at best, when he was in an entirely unfortunate mood and was indulging himself while improvising.

As a sincere admirer of Mr. B.'s works, the vast majority of which are excellent, the reviewer would regret it greatly if he couldn't add to these remarks his assurance that in spite of the faults reproved here, the sonata distinguishes itself very favorably from an unfortunately large number of new keyboard sonatas. It deserves to be known particularly *for the sake of its second movement,* a very beautiful Adagio, solidly sustained by a melancholic quality that is quite worthy of the best Beethoven Adagios. Beyond this, the sonata is also by far not as difficult to perform as most of his works.

The engraving would be good if the sharps, flats, and natural signs weren't in such varying positions, and if they made a better visual impression through a more suitable relationship to the note heads.

NOTE

1. The first edition of op. 30 was published in May and June 1803 by the Bureau d'Arts et d'Industrie in Vienna.

⌁

110.
By the O . . . r, "Brief Reviews," *Berliner allgemeine musikalische Zeitung* 4 (22 August 1827): 272.

Sonata No. 2, arrangement for two violins, viola, and cello by Ferdinand Ries[1]

PRO

The laudable quartet composer, Mr. Ries, presents to quartet societies the exquisite C-Minor Sonata:

OP. 30
No. 2, Allegro con brio, mm. 1–2

for the purpose of becoming more closely acquainted with it as a quartet. It is faultlessly and skillfully arranged with a good treatment of the string instruments.

CONTRA

Why didn't this ingenious composer use the time he dedicated to this arrangement to compose a quartet himself? Then there would be one quartet more to stimulate quartet societies. Those advantages listed above would not be lost, and, besides, then ideas never heard before hopefully would have appeared. Instead, some keyboard player belonging to some quartet society will only hear something familiar in a different form that is not at all pleasing. The light rounding of the fortepiano passages will always simply be clumsily played with a bow, and only a few places will gain, especially in the Adagio.—However, the piece has lost more than it gained in the other three movements, especially the first and last. An arrangement by someone else, even though less skillful, would, nevertheless, be a more excusable work; but Mr. Ries!

NOTE

1. The three Violin Sonatas, op. 30, were published in arrangements for string quartet by Simrock in Bonn: no. 1, arranged by P. W. Heinzius, appeared in January–February 1831; no. 2, arranged by Ries, in 1827; no. 3, again by Heinzius, in March 1829.

〜

OP. 31
THREE PIANO SONATAS IN G MAJOR, D MINOR, AND Eb MAJOR

111.
Johann Spazier,[1] "Repertory of a Keyboard Player," *Zeitung für die elegante Welt* 3 (28 June 1803): 612.

G-Major and D-Minor Sonatas

The following is the content of the five cahiers[2] according to the order in which they appeared.

1. *van Beethoven.* Two highly original sonatas that (as most of the other composers do as well) one can regard as fortepiano solos in a grand style, for they deviate entirely from the usual sonata form.[3] As in symphonies and concertos, a certain routine has been maintained, according to which some themes are brought forth without any connection. Thus, instead of one totality, they contain three to four totalities that have either a ridiculous or no relationship at all to each other.—The first sonata is the most original, but both are a little too long (fifty pages of notes) and occasionally *bizarre*.

NOTES

1. See entry no. 104, n. 3.
2. See entry no. 80, n. 2.
3. The first edition of op. 31, nos. 1–2, appeared in April 1803 from the publisher Hans Georg Nägeli in Zurich. Opus 31, no. 3, appeared in May–June 1804. Because of the many errors found in the print, Simrock in Bonn issued an "Editiou [*sic*] très correcte" of nos. 1–2 already in the fall of 1803 and a complete set in 1804. Cappi in Vienna also issued an edition of the sonatas (nos. 1–2 in 1803 and no. 3 in 1804–05).

~

OP. 32
SONG *AN DIE HOFFNUNG*[1]

112.
"Brief Notes," *Allgemeine musikalische Zeitung* 8 (17 September 1806): 815–16.

A trifle that should not be overlooked! The song was taken up with feeling and given back in the same way in all simplicity.[2] Also, only a few trifling exceptions could be taken to the treatment of the words in regard to declamation and rhythm. For example, the meaning of the words "O Hoffnung," in the first strophe, needs to be connected more closely to the preceding text.

NOTES

1. *An die Hoffnung* was written by the minor poet Christoph August Tiedge (1752–1841). Strongly influenced by the poet Friedrich Schiller, Tiedge gained popularity during his life with his *Urania über Gott, Unsterblichkeit und Freiheit* (1803, *Urania on God, Immortality, and Freedom*—Urania was the Greek Muse of Astronomy), which was one of the most widely read works of the times. Beethoven was on friendly terms with Tiedge.

2. The first edition of op. 32 was published by the Kunst- und Industrie-Comptoir in Vienna in September 1805.

~

OP. 34
SIX VARIATIONS FOR PIANO ON AN ORIGINAL THEME, IN F MAJOR

113.
"Reviews," *Allgemeine musikalische Zeitung* 5 (11 May 1803): 556–57.

A favorable prejudice for these variations is aroused by the fact that this famous composer who so far has not included small pieces of this genre among his works with opus numbers has done so with the present work.[1] And this prejudice is completely justified. The variations are very beautiful and are handled in a particular manner that is also different from *this* composer's earlier variations. An excellent theme and these variations contain whatever occurred to this richly inventive mind about the main ideas of this theme as it was being given free reign. One can get an idea of the latter just by indicating the content: Theme: gentle, but meaningful, F major, Adagio cantabile, $\frac{2}{4}$ time; Variation 1, playing out completely free and graceful, D major, the same time, same tempo; Variation 2, B♭ major, earnest, Allegro ma non troppo, $\frac{6}{8}$ meter; Variation 3, happy G major, Allegretto, c time; Variation 4, E♭ major, clear, Tempo di minuetto, $\frac{3}{4}$ time; Variation 5, C minor, dignified and powerful, Marcia, $\frac{2}{4}$ time; transition to the return of F major, Variation 6, F major, Allegretto, $\frac{6}{8}$ time, happy, at times dallying; worked-out conclusion in free Adagio molto.[2] Everything thus comes together and makes a beautiful, well-rounded entirety. The variations are not forbiddingly difficult to perform: one must simply not allow oneself to be frightened at the abundance of short notes. The overly wide reaches, which have also been complained about in these pages, are not found here.

NOTES

1. According to Breitkopf & Härtel's printing register, the work was first published in April 1803. It is fitting of the reviewer to note that this is the first of Beethoven's variation sets to which he gave an opus number. In a letter written around 18 December 1802, Beethoven requested that the publisher print the following "short introductory statement" on the first edition: "As these variations are distinctly different from my earlier ones, instead of indicating them like my *previous ones* by means of a number (such as, for instance, Nos. 1, 2, 3, and so on) I have included them in the proper numerical series of *my greater musical works,* the more so as the themes have been composed by me" (Anderson, letter no. 67, and Brandenburg, letter no. 123).

2. This review is particularly striking because the author comments only indirectly on what the majority of modern critics see as the revolutionary musical idea behind op. 34: the downward spiraling tonality, which descends by thirds through the variations until the piece returns to the tonic.

∾

114.
Der Freimüthige 4 (January–June 1806): 166.

Difficult, but not awkward, here and there somewhat affected, but more often well chosen, and on the whole quite worthy of the ingenious musical artist, who makes one wonder whether one should marvel more at his audacious, brilliant ideas, or at his striving to make the baroque eccentricities, which are peculiar to them, nevertheless pleasing and sentimental and rich in art.[1]

NOTE

1. See entry no. 6 and note 1 to that entry for the special meaning of "sentimental" in the early nineteenth century.

~

Op. 35
FIFTEEN VARIATIONS AND A FUGUE IN E♭
ON AN ORIGINAL THEME FROM THE BALLET
DIE GESCHÖPFE DES PROMETHEUS.[1]

Prometheus Variations; see op. 55

115.
"Reviews," *Allgemeine musikalische Zeitung* 6 (22 February 1804):
338–45.[2]

Inexhaustible imagination, original humor, and deep, intimate, even passionate feeling are the particular features, as it were, from which arises the ingenious physiognomy that distinguishes nearly all of Mr. v. B's works. This earns him one of the highest places among instrumental composers of first rank, since particularly his latest works show unmistakably the care that he takes to maintain a chosen character and to combine the greatest freedom with purity of phrasing and, I would like to say, with contrapuntal elegance.

All of the peculiarities of this composer just cited can be found to a very distinct degree in the work named above. Even the form of the whole, which deviates so far from what is customary, bears witness to unmistakable genius. Before the actual theme begins (a melody from the composer's ballet *Gli uomini di Prometeo,*[3] which has also appeared as a keyboard reduction published by Hoffmeister and Kühnel on separate sheets)[4] and after a full chord of E♭-major harmony as the key of the entire piece, the simple bass of the theme in threefold intensification appears as an introduction. Immediately thereafter it appears as bass with *one melody,* then as the middle voice embraced by *two* countermelodies, and finally as the upper voice with *three* new ones—now, therefore, as a four-voice setting. Each emerges from the other beautifully and naturally. The reviewer just cannot suppress his wish that the bass of the second clausula[5] of the theme, where it appears completely unadorned at the beginning, might have been made a bit more meaningful.[6] Certainly, though, as easy as a slight change would have been without damaging the beautiful arrangement indicated above, he probably disdained doing so, in order to be able to present the theme entirely in the way that a large public was accustomed to hearing in the ballet.[7] After this introduction, with its gradually fuller and fuller settings, the theme itself now steps forward powerfully, and from it Mr. v. B. develops, with his accustomed agility, fifteen excellent variations, to which are added a fugal finale with yet two more beautiful variations and an excursus.[8]

In order that the review of this extremely significant little work (certainly not according to the number of pages; but how many operas are there about which there is not half as much to be said at all!) does not become a book, the reviewer must be satisfied to mention only the most important things, individual recollections of which will follow. Everyone who is acquainted with Mr. v. B.'s work, even if only superficially, will be convinced in advance, even without assurance from the reviewer, that here he is being offered neither shopworn figurations nor threadbare harmonies in the accompaniment. But scarcely could there be anyone among his admirers (to *their* honor I will believe that their number is quite large) who, even with very high expectations, would not nevertheless be very pleasantly surprised by the very ingenious figurations, arpeggiations, and the rhythm of the third variation. Nor would the unexpected, unpretentious return to E♭ major in the last three measures of the sixth variation and, most of all, the amusing peculiarity of the tenth variation fail to surprise them. Likewise, the twelfth variation is created out of a beautiful, new, and truly significant figuration. But the most outstandingly successful are, in the reviewer's opinion, the minore Variation, no. 14, the Largo Variation, no. 15, and the fugato finale. In the minore, the bass of the theme is first the upper voice, then, in the repetition, the lower voice. Through this inversion and with the addition of a small ligature, the harmonic progressions in m. 7, already beautiful and new in themselves, attain, among other places, a completely individual charm. Likewise, the entire minore, through its so deeply gripping melancholic character, so consistently maintained, can by itself, as a self-contained small piece, be certain of the most beautiful effect. The Largo, with a treasure of excellent new ideas, will surely provide splendid enjoyment to everyone who is able to conquer its completely individual difficulties, so that one no longer observes any strain in their performance. And incidentally, *this* variation will indeed not bear any uneven, awkward touch at all in its performance. Everything must flow by as easily and evenly as though it were a jest. It goes without saying that we are speaking here only of finger technique: one may still discern the gravity in the actual expression. Traces of solid *contrapuntal* knowledge, refined by educated taste, are found primarily in the fugato finale. Here, too, this knowledge will offer the most pleasure to the connoisseur, and likewise to the educated amateur, as they may rightfully expect it at just this point. The fugal fragment of the theme consists only of the few bass notes:

OP. 35
Finale. Alla Fuga, mm. 1–7

which, however, the composer's inexhaustible humor didn't make *just a little of*. One of the particularly successful ideas (not to mention the interesting play of twisting and turning harmonies, inversions, and the like) seems to the reviewer to be the spot where, after appearing now as a middle voice, now as an upper voice, always correctly supported by its countersubject, or at least by a very similar figure, the theme appears *al rovescio*. It is the last measure of the third system on p. 17. Also, the succession of ideas leading up to the entry in B♭, at the end of the same page, deserves, among so much that is worthy of distinction, a special distinction. But may it suffice that what has been said here will be enough to excite the curiosity of all connoisseurs and educated amateurs for the work itself. I would call these variations the variations par excellence among the *more recent* fruits of this species.

Now a few more observations for the composer.

Instead of the first four measures of the second clausula of the fifth variation, the reviewer would have liked to have heard something else from Mr. v. B.'s rich inventive gift since the three imitations in the octave, as they appear *here,* on one and the same instrument, turn out a bit too uniform.[9]

The canon in the octave of Variation no. 7 is certainly quite strict and correct throughout. The canonic form is interchanged with the *galant* style only once,[10] albeit intentionally, but the canonic form is also somewhat *stiff*.[11] Beethoven should have disdained taking up this affectation (for it is *nothing more* than that) here in this variation. Whatever in a work of art speaks *only* to the intellect is at the very least an hors d'oeuvre. And Mr. v. B. must affirm through his own feelings that our feelings come away from this canon empty-handed. If the next-to-last sixteenth note in the second measure of the Largo were based on the F-major chord, it would be more correct and certainly better.[12] The strict analogy between this and the fourth measure, where the upper voices also move together in thirds, cannot mollify the harshness that is so perceptible in the passage just mentioned. This is even more noticeable when this particular spot returns in a different arpeggiation. On p. 20 Mr. v. B. overlooked yet another slight carelessness. The bass of the last eighth note of the twelfth measure must read

OP. 35
Finale. Alla Fuga, m. 172

and the following quarter note.

OP. 35
Finale. Alla Fuga, m. 173

The progression of the bass from the fifth to the sixth measure on p. 21 is also incorrect; at least, speaking kindly, it is less good than if it read:

OP. 35
Finale. Alla Fuga, mm. 186–87

The same applies, with a slight modification, when a similar spot thereafter soon occurs, which is based on the same harmony.

To those who wish to learn to perform these variations, the reviewer, in order to arouse their courage to be persistent, can provide them with the assurance that, if they succeed in executing all the difficulties with facility, and in incorporating all the expressive markings precisely into their performance so that they sound as if they are being felt for the first time, there will surely be no keyboard composition that they will need to set aside as too difficult for their abilities.

I say *none,* since there is enough opportunity here to practice one's fingers even for the performance of Sebastian Bach's fugues. In short, whoever performs these variations exactly as they are written, without visible strain, belongs in the first rank of keyboard players. If he remains *loyal* to the composer not just in terms of expression, but is able to add on something of his own into the bargain, that is, something *good* and *ingenious, quantum satis,*[13] he will take a place among the true keyboard *virtuosos* with all due honors. A few hints concerning the practice of these variations may perhaps be of some use to some people. It goes without saying that I am speaking here neither to the virtuoso nor at all to the genius. The outstanding talent, and likewise those who neither are nor wish to become keyboard players, may skip over the following.

In the third variation, care should be taken that the hand is already in position above the keys a moment before striking the full chord. Otherwise the result will be an awkward performance that does not conform to the unusual rhythm—a shifting least of all to be tolerated here.

The success of the tenth variation will likewise be facilitated by remembering to observe this same principle; the left hand must simply be particularly precise in striking the keys, and the finger on the first note will, so to speak, be cast to that on the following note. For example, begin with the fifth finger and then shift over alternately to the fourth, third, and second. The twelfth variation demands that both hands be exceptionally calm and, I would say, somewhat limp. Otherwise it might be difficult to perform the slur that binds two sixteenth notes at a time. Any other interpretation, however, would be unsatisfactory for this figuration at this point. The thirteenth variation is an excellent exercise in dealing with passages including leaps and can serve very well to give solidity and power to the fourth finger of the right hand and the fifth finger of the left hand. Both must strike the key with proper force, the first on the appoggiaturas above, the other on the supporting notes in the bass; in this manner, the hands themselves will also attain the necessary release for the chords in the middle. I will say nothing about the minore, since it does not really contain any fingering difficulties; the only correct performance is one that is strict and true to the instructions, and thus one will find confirmation of what has been said above. The observation made earlier that the many notes must be performed as relaxed and with as much fluency as however possible, and without any visible effort, applies to the fifteenth variation. *Here* in particular, the reviewer cautions against tempo rubato, which unfortunately is now used all too frequently, and which all too often just tries to hide, in vain, the lack of a true feeling for meter. The practiced eye cannot be deceived by window dressing.

Here, in the fifteenth variation, the slow tempo and the many full chordal figurations and arpeggios do cover up the theme a little. All the same, it must always be heard as much as possible. Thus, *no* arbitrary wavering of the tempo *here;* good taste cannot do otherwise than disapprove. For the fugal finale the same thing is applicable that must be observed in general for all fugal passages. Namely, one must make every entry of the theme stand out, particularly when it is in the middle, and make the characteristic qualities of the surrounding figurations noticeable. In this connection, the reviewer also draws attention to the fact that the hands from time to time must alternate with one another, not by regarding the direction of the note stems, but simply whatever is most comfortable, always, however, without in the least compromising the value of the notes. What has been said here about the hands applies to the fingers on p. 19, system 2, m. 2, where the trill, which had previously been played by the second and third fingers, must now be continued without any break by the thumb and index finger. However, let this be sufficient.

Paper and engraving are very good; nevertheless *a few* small errors have slipped in.[14]

NOTES

1. This work is known both as the "Eroica" Variations (since Beethoven reused some of the material from the piano variations in the last movement of the Symphony) and as the "Prometheus" Variations (since the theme of the variations came from the ballet). Beethoven himself unequivocally wished the set to be associated with the *Prometheus* ballet music; in a letter to the publisher, he protested: "In the grand variations you have forgotten to mention that the theme has been taken from an allegorical ballet for which I composed the music, namely: Prometheus, or, in Italian, Prometeo. This should have been stated on the title page" (see Anderson, letter no. 79, and Brandenburg, letter no. 140).

2. This review is the first of three (the other two are of the Third Piano Concerto [AMZ 7 (10 April 1805): 445–57] and the *Eroica* Symphony [AMZ 9 (18 February 1807): 319–34]), which began a dramatic change in the tone of the AMZ's Beethoven reviews. The composer himself objected to the disparaging tone of some of the early reviews in a letter to Breitkopf & Härtel, the AMZ's publisher, dated 22 April 1801. See Anderson, letter no. 48, and Brandenburg, letter no. 59.

The editor of the AMZ apparently felt this review to be so significant that he placed Beethoven's portrait at the beginning of the issue in which it appeared: no. 21 of vol. 6. Prior to this time, composers' portraits had appeared only at the beginning of an entire volume of the journal.

3. The reviewer gives an Italian translation of the title *Geschöpfe des Prometheus*.

4. Beethoven actually used this theme four times, beginning with the seventh of a set of Twelve German Dances for orchestra, WoO 8. The final, and most famous, appearance was in the finale of the *Eroica* Symphony, op. 55, which, however, was not published until five years after these variations. At the time this review appeared, *Die Geschöpfe des Prometheus,* although written in 1800–01, had just appeared as op. 43. The four-hand arrangement to which the author refers was probably based on the original piano reduction published in 1801 by Artaria-Cappi in Vienna. See Kinsky-Halm, 102–04.

5. Here the author uses the term "Klausel," which derives from Latin and can mean either a cadence or a grammatical clause. In music history, "clausula" and its German equivalent are used in the latter sense to designate a section of early polyphonic music, but it is doubtful whether the author was aware of this meaning.

6. The reviewer here refers to the odd four measures that begin the second half of the bass of the theme: a measure of silence followed by three pounding *fortissimo* eighth notes in three octaves followed by another measure of silence and a unison B♭ marked *piano* and with a fermata.

7. Actually, the passing-note A♭ was added in the fourth measure of the second half, which was not present in the ballet.

8. The author resorts to a Latin term to express "coda." It underscores a style representative of the university jargon of his times.

9. These are the same four measures of the bass of the theme that the reviewer criticizes the first time they appear.

10. The French word "galant" was still in common use at this time to designate a style that was free of contrapuntal complications, making use of melodies with simple harmonic accompaniment. The term does not, strictly speaking, apply to the style of these variations, which are quite varied and sophisticated even in the sections that, as cited here, are not contrapuntal. The use of the term here may correspond to the distinction between a "connoisseur" and an "amateur"; the fugal and canonic sections of the piece would appeal more to a "connoisseur," whereas the "galant" might be pleasing to an "amateur."

11. The reviewer probably considers the final four measures of the "Canone all' ottava" to be the ones that borrow a galant sensibility. "Intellectual" contrapuntal writing was often criticized by the aesthetic critics of the Classical period.

12. The critic is complaining about the second chord in the following progression: $V7/ii$–$vii7$–V/ii–ii (which he argues should resolve to the supertonic chord). He recommends that the right hand d^2 on the third from the last thirty-second note in m. 2 be changed to a c^2, so as to agree with the prevailing harmony and eliminate the passing dissonance that Beethoven created in this passage.

13. "Quantum satis": "however sufficient" or "whatever is enough."

14. The review concludes with a list of printing errors.

Op. 36
SYMPHONY NO. 2 IN D MAJOR

See also entry nos. 29, 87, and 93

116.
"News: Leipzig," *Allgemeine musikalische Zeitung* 6 (9 May 1804):
542–43.

Of the completely new or as yet almost unknown music from the other weekly concerts, the following pieces can be singled out in particular. . . .

It cannot be a matter of indifference to any society of musicians and friends of art that at last a second symphony by Beethoven has just now appeared (engraved in Vienna, in the Kunst- und Industrie-Comtoir [sic]).[1] It is a noteworthy, colossal work, of a depth, power, and artistic knowledge like *very few*. It has a level of difficulty, both from the point of view of the composer and in regard to its performance by a large orchestra (which it certainly demands), quite certainly unlike *any* symphony that has ever been made known. It demands to be played again and yet again by even the most accomplished orchestra, until the astonishing number of original and sometimes very strangely arranged ideas become closely enough connected, rounded out, and emerge like a great unity, just as the composer had in mind. It must also be heard again and yet again before the listener, even a knowledgeable one, is in a position to follow the details in the entire piece and the entire piece in the details and to enjoy it with enthusiasm in the necessary repose. It goes without saying that *everyone* must first accustom him- or herself a little to something as completely unusual as practically everything here is. What we say applies not only to others, but also to ourselves, and therefore we are as little concerned with rendering a more definite judgment as we are with making a fuss that the first performance, for which only a short rehearsal was possible, was not completely successful.[2] It is to be hoped that it will not be necessary to recommend this work to all orchestras of intelligence, skill, and persevering diligence, and to all listeners to whom music is more than a short-lived amusement.

NOTES

1. The first edition of the Second Symphony was published in March 1804 by the Bureau d'Arts et d'Industrie (Kunst- und Industrie-Comptoir) in Vienna. The First Symphony had been published more than two years earlier in December 1801.

2. The premiere was given on 3 April 1803 by Beethoven in the Theater-an-der-Wien; the Third Piano Concerto and *Christus am Ölberg* were also performed for the first time on this occasion. The difficulties surrounding the rehearsal and performance are discussed in Thayer-Forbes, 328–31.

117.
"News: Vienna the 1st of August," *Allgemeine musikalische Zeitung 6* (15 August 1804): 776–77.

With Piano Concerto in C Minor, op. 37

The second subscription series of our Augarten concerts opened very brilliantly. I will name for you the pieces performed, because from this one can to some extent infer the overall effort of this institute, and this deserves to be kept in mind even by foreigners. The concert began with Beethoven's Grand Symphony in D Major, a work full of new, original ideas, of great power, effective instrumentation and learned development, which however would benefit from the shortening of some passages and by the sacrifice of many modulations that are far too strange. This symphony was followed by a concerto by Beethoven in C minor, the themes of the first and last movements of which I will set down for you:

OP. 37
Allegro con brio, mm. 1–4

Rondo allegro.

OP. 37
Rondo. Allegro, mm. 1–8

This concerto belongs incontestably among Beethoven's most beautiful compositions. It was masterfully performed. Mr. Ries,[1] who had the solo part, is presently Beethoven's only pupil, and his passionate admirer. He practiced the work entirely under the guidance of his teacher and gave a very restrained, expressive performance, as well as showing uncommon skill and assurance in easily overcoming extraordinary difficulties.

NOTE

1. Ferdinand Ries (1784–1838) was the son of Franz Anton Ries, with whom Beethoven had studied during his childhood in Bonn. See also entry no. 30, n. 2. In *Biographische Notizen* (1838), Ries gave the following account of this performance: "I had asked Beethoven to write a cadenza for me, but he refused and told me to write one myself and he would correct it. Beethoven was satisfied with my composition and made a few changes; but there was an extremely brilliant and very difficult passage in it, which, though he liked it, seemed to him too venturesome, wherefore he told me to write another in its place. . . . When the cadenza was reached in the public concert Beethoven quietly sat down. I could not persuade myself to choose the easier one. When I boldly began the more difficult one, Beethoven violently jerked his chair; but the cadenza went through all right and Beethoven was so delighted that he shouted 'Bravo!' loudly. This electrified the entire audience and at once gave me a standing among the artists" (Wegeler-Ries, 101–02).

~

118

"Details on Concert Music in Berlin," *Allgemeine musikalische Zeitung* 7
(28 November 1804): 145–46.

After these general remarks,[1] I return to my real purpose, which is to give some details of the first concert of the year. It was opened with a new Grand Symphony by Beethoven in D (Vienna, Industrie-Comptoir). This symphony was, in fact, the most difficult problem that can be posed for an orchestra that has not constantly practiced together, and the problem was solved famously. The violins were quite uniform and the various figures were performed precisely and with fire. The modulations, often shrill, were also clean and correct. The violas and basses were powerful and prompt. The wind instruments, played by Messrs. Schröch, Grosse, Bliesener, Kreuzwatis, Böttcher, Schneider, and several others, joined in correctly, and the frequent solo passages were performed with taste. Flute and horns were particularly distinguished, the bassoon was somewhat too strong, and as for the oboe we missed the beautiful tone of our Mr. Westenholz (unfortunately he is ill). In regard to the composition of this piece, there is much originality, richness, and often a surplus of harmony and occasionally, however, bizarrerie. The symphony begins impressively with a short Largo, alternating with cantabile solo phrases by the winds, and then proceeds to a modulated Allegro. The Andante quasi allegretto in A♭ has a very pleasant melody and a broad working out. The minuet with trio is entirely new, and even small features such as the short horn solo, which enters in the middle, have a special effect. The last Presto occasionally becomes wild, but it is worked out exquisitely. In general, this symphony didn't create such a sensation as symphonies by Mozart and Haydn. The applause by the connoisseurs expressed gratitude to the musicians for surmounting the difficulties well and for performing them for nearly three-quarters of an hour.

NOTE

1. This entry represents an excerpt from the article. The entire report (cols. 143–48) contains descriptions of music by Domenico Cimarosa (1749–1801), Rodolphe Kreutzer (1766–1831), to whom Beethoven dedicated the "Kreutzer" Sonata, op. 47, Johann Mayr (1763–1843), and Cherubini (*Lodoiska*, 1791).

~

119.
"Music in Leipzig: Michael through Christmas 1804,"
Allgemeine musikalische Zeitung 7 (2 January 1805): 215–16.

Mentioned: Symphony No. 1, op. 21

Concerning symphonies, several of the best by Haydn and Mozart were repeated, but some were not as well performed this winter as the previous year. What is the reason for this? Should we shy away from rehearsals? Or should we become indifferent toward the honorable calling to put together one of the foremost among those orchestras *not* financed by the aristocracy? The newest symphony by Beethoven (D major), despite its great difficulties, was given twice in such a way that one could enjoy it *completely*. As has been observed in Vienna and Berlin, we also find the entire piece too long and some details overworked. We would also like to add that the all too frequent use of all the wind instruments impedes the effect of many beautiful passages, and the finale strikes us, even now after closer acquaintance, as all too bizarre, wild, and shrill. But all of this is so far outweighed by the powerful, fiery spirit that breathes in this colossal work, by the wealth of new ideas and their almost totally original treatment, as well as by the depth of artistic knowledge, that one can cast the work's horoscope and find that it will remain and be heard with ever new satisfaction when a thousand currently celebrated fashionable pieces have long since been dead and buried. Beethoven's earlier and friendlier symphony (C major), which was performed very beautifully, is a favorite work of the local concertgoing public. That more gloomy symphony, however, was also heard with attention, unmistakable engagement, and much applause. The first Allegro and the thoroughly original minuet were particularly enjoyed by the public.[1]

NOTE

1. Two additional performances of op. 36 during 1805 are noted briefly in the article "News: Frankfurt am Main" (AMZ 8 [22 May 1805]: 544–52). The first (col. 549) reports that on 6 March the Symphony was "not performed very well, the main cause of which may have been that too many dilettantes took part in the performance who had not properly participated in the rehearsals." Later, on 3 April (col. 551), the Symphony "was given again, and again, in my judgment, it was not given the way it should be performed and as I certainly will still get to hear it performed by the local theater orchestra."

~

"Review," *Allgemeine musikalische Zeitung* 9 (1 October 1806): 8–11.

Arrangement for a piano trio by Beethoven, with Symphony No. 3, op. 55

Beethoven's rightly celebrated Symphony in D, which has been frequently and thoroughly discussed in these pages, appears here as an arrangement.[1] We may well presume it is for those who do not entirely hear this *very* difficult work completely, or who, amid the abundance of artistically interwoven ideas and perhaps also amid the all too frequent use of the shrillest instruments, cannot understand it well enough. Finally, it is also for those who through recollection want to repeat the pleasure of the complete performance and look over and examine more calmly whatever was not entirely clear or particularly to their liking. Therefore, this reduction should in many respects be received with thanks, however much one may be opposed to the arrangement of *such* works in general, which on the whole is indeed completely justified. The reviewer, who has heard the entire symphony often, but who certainly did not consider it in terms of an arrangement, would hardly have believed that, in regard to the major points, one so satisfactory and yet so well suited to all three instruments could be made from it as is actually given here. In fact, one receives a not unworthy picture of the entire piece that is as complete as possible. In some parts, however, this was impossible. The beautiful Andante, for example, loses very much, since the masterful division among the various instruments, in particular the *opposition* of string and wind instruments, is missing. Also, several passages where the composer intended a beautiful effect based directly upon the charm or the distinctive characteristics of specific instruments here must leave us rather indifferent. Compare, for example, p. 13, system 4f.; p. 14, the two last systems and what follows; p. 16, the three first systems, and the return of these passages. Indeed, even the entire, original scherzando could be brought forward as proof, although even here it still remains an interesting piece. The last movement, in its tumultuous, wild adventurousness, could not be arranged as satisfactorily. It is also *very* difficult to play, even though it does not appear so at first glance, so that in this form as well one will only seldom hear it perfectly performed. In this form, the reviewer finds it to be by far the most inferior. The work is, in accordance with its inner worth, beautiful and also engraved practically without error.

Permit me to add at this point something that does not immediately pertain to this context. Two years ago Beethoven wrote a third great symphony, approximately in the same style as the second, but *yet* richer in ideas and artistic development, and certainly even broader, deeper, and more drawn out, so that it takes an hour to perform.[2] Now this is certainly overdone, since everything must have its limits. If a true, great genius may demand that criticism not set these limits for him according to caprice or custom, he must also respect *those* limits that are not dictated to him by this or that public, but by the ability of people in general to comprehend and enjoy. And certainly the musician needs to take these limits more into account than, say, the painter or the poet—most of all, however, the instrumental composer, since he loses all the advantages of auxiliary arts and accessory charms. He cannot say, as, if necessary, the poet can: either perform my—*Wallenstein* in its eleven acts over three days, or do not perform it at all, but simply read it![3] All the same, this work is simply written this way and is certainly (all the connoisseurs' voices that the reviewer has heard are in agreement upon this, even if the correspondents of certain tabloids are not!), I say, it is certainly one of the most original, sublime, and deepest products that this entire genre of music has to show. Would it then not truly be a shame if, perhaps because of lack of support or the confidence of a publisher, it were to remain in the dark and not be imparted to the world?[4] For a long time it has been said that it is going to be published in Vienna, but as yet we have seen nothing of this. The reviewer wishes nothing more through this apostrophe than to stir up, shake, and excite a bit.

NOTES

1. Beethoven's arrangement of the Second Symphony for a trio of piano, violin, and cello was published in 1805 by the Bureau des Arts et d'Industrie.

2. The first public performance of the *Eroica* took place on 7 April 1805 in the Theater-an-der-Wien at a performance conducted by Franz Clement. The Symphony was actually composed in 1803, three years earlier than this review.

3. The author is referring to Friedrich Schiller's classical trilogy *Wallenstein* (*Wallensteins Lager, Die Piccolomini,* and *Wallensteins Tod*), which was published in 1800.

4. The first edition of the *Eroica* was announced in the wz on 19 October 1806, the same month as this review.

≈

121.
"Remarks by a Traveler on the Condition of Music in Amsterdam," *Allgemeine musikalische Zeitung* 10 (2 March 1808): 366–67.[1]

The sixth concert began with the Symphony in D by Beethoven. The first movement in particular was played with strength and in the right tempo, but to my great annoyance, I had to do without the very beautiful Andante of this symphony. If the fault is to be attributed to the director, probably the only thing that can excuse him is the fact that usually many of the listeners chat during the most beautiful Andantes in symphonies by Haydn, Mozart, etc., and in general during most slow and solemn movements. They are only attentive when a fast movement is performed with somewhat shrill music (e.g., Turkish) and when at the same time there is particularly a lot of banging on the triangle, or when someone performs a solo with many difficulties and ornamentations or endless variations on some known theme (e.g., "O du lieber Augustin").

NOTE

1. The entire article comprises cols. 366–68 and 375–81.

~

122.
"News: Munich," *Allgemeine musikalische Zeitung* 14
(19 February 1812): 124.[1]

A Grand Symphony in D by Beethoven opened the first concert, given on 9 December. The works of this artist, unique in his own way, are as yet not well enough known here. People are accustomed to Haydn's and Mozart's works and should not be surprised if these rare products of Beethoven, which diverge so greatly from what is customary, don't always produce their effect upon the listener. This is not the place to evaluate this manner of composition. However, that a glowing fantasy, a high flight of powerful and ingenious harmonies prevails in it throughout, is admitted even by those who hold clarity and songfulness to be the highest degree of art. Incidentally, the Andante of this symphony nevertheless leaves nothing left to be desired in this respect. Certainly, the minuet and the final Allegro have a very bizarre quality. However, when the humor of so many of our writers attracts us, why do we want to expect the composer, who lays claim to the entire as yet so little charted domain of music, to stick only to customary forms? Why do we expect him always only to flatter the ear, never to unsettle us, and raise us above the customary, even if somewhat forcefully?

NOTE

1. A year earlier, AMZ had reported that "the weekly concert contained in two evenings several excellent pieces. Beethoven's ingenious and outstanding Symphony in D Major (No. 2) was performed with general and completely deserved approval" (13 [29 May 1811]: 379).

~

123.

"News," *Allgemeine musikalische Zeitung* 22 (19 July 1820): 492.[1]

From Switzerland in June. Of the recent gathering of the Swiss Music Society in Basel, I can relate to you the following. The friendly reception of the members of the society itself intensified their enthusiasm and contributed not just a little to the successful performance of their selected pieces of music. Beethoven's symphony (in D major) was given with great precision by a very large orchestra under the very good direction of Mr. Tollmann. The magnificent effect that his direction brought forth gave proof that B's symphonies must be performed by such a large orchestra in order to unfold properly the greatness inherent in them and proclaim the power of music with an irresistible rush.

NOTE

1. The entire article consists of cols. 485–503.

~

124.

"Brief Notices," *Allgemeine musikalische Zeitung* 25 (18 June 1823): 408.

Mentioned: Symphony No. 3, op. 55

The speedy progress of this beautiful edition of the complete Beethoven symphonies in score[1] (the first number appeared just half a year ago) must bring not just a little joy to every friend of the most inspired, original, brilliant, and magnificent products of recent instrumental music, and among which Beethoven's symphonies obviously and by general agreement belong. For it is a proof of the great acceptance these works have found and of how they continue to be held in honor. Nothing further needs to be said here about this, for it would be useless to speak not only about these two mighty symphonies, but also about the edition itself, since the format of the latter has only recently been discussed in these pages, and the continuation, Nos. 2 and 3, resembles the first. The price, although certainly not small, is nevertheless by no means too high, considering the length and full scoring of the works: No. 2 has 162 and No. 3, 231 pages, and that with the most efficient use of space possible.

NOTE

1. "By Simrock." The first German score editions of the First, Second, and Third Symphonies were published at Bonn and Cologne by Simrock in early 1822. Apparently

the projected complete edition didn't get beyond the Fourth Symphony, which appeared the following year; the first score editions of the Fifth and Sixth Symphonies were published by Breitkopf & Härtel in 1826.

~

125.
Musikalische Eilpost 1 (1826): 76.

Arrangement for piano, flute, violin, and cello by J. N. Hummel

Beethoven's magnificent Symphony in D is known. We also know how exceptionally well Hummel understands how to write and arrange for the pianoforte.[1] Thus, it only needs to be said that the work has appeared in this new form, that the pianoforte part certainly presents difficulties in the present-day sense of the word. Also, it certainly does require a capable player, and the parts for the three accompanying instruments are relatively easy. The outward appearance is very good, and the price very inexpensive.

NOTE

1. Hummel's popular arrangements of symphonies for piano, flute, violin, and violoncello were published and reprinted by Simrock in Bonn, Schott in Mainz, Schlesinger in Paris, and Chappell in London in the 1820s and 1830s. Hummel's arrangement of the Second Symphony was published by Schott in Mainz in 1826.

~

Op. 37
PIANO CONCERTO NO. 3 IN C MINOR

See also entry nos. 87 and 117

126.
"Review," *Allgemeine musikalische Zeitung* 7 (10 April 1805): 445–57.

The present grand concerto belongs to the most significant works that have appeared from this ingenious master for several years, and in several respects it might distinguish itself from all the rest to its advantage. In addition to such a total sum of beautiful and noble ideas, the reviewer finds, at the very least, in none of his newest works such a thorough working out, yet without becoming turgid or overly learned, a character so solidly maintained without excess, and such unity in workmanship. It will and must have the greatest and most beautiful effect everywhere that it can be well performed. This will be the case and has been so already, even where people are accustomed to hearing the greater Mozart concertos and observe them with impartial fondness, as in Leipzig. This work has already been discussed frequently and in detail—particularly in Vienna, and in Leipzig by the editor of this very journal. Inasmuch as the editor has entrusted me, a musician, with the further evaluation of this work, he indisputably has the well-considered intention that its artistic and technical parts be investigated in more detail. I, like everyone, must find this intention too laudable not to agree to it and, as far as I am able, will contribute to fulfilling it. Therefore, I will once again repeat briefly: in regard to its intended spirit and effect, this concerto is one of the most outstanding of all that have ever been written, and I will now try to clarify on the basis of the work itself where this effect comes from, insofar as it is achieved through the materials and their construction.

The string instruments begin the first movement, an Allegro con brio in C minor, with this idea in unison, which is then repeated by the oboes, bassoons, and horns on the basic dominant:[1]

OP. 37
Allegro con brio, mm. 1–4

OP. 37
Allegro con brio, mm. 5–8

In the course of the entire movement, this idea and this rhythm, sometimes completely, sometimes partly, are the basis of the various figurations and the like and are worked out. In a particularly fortunate way, B. inserted the few notes of the third measure

OP. 37
Allegro con brio, mm. 3–4

through nearly the entire movement, often very unexpectedly, and thus converged, combined, and blended the most heterogeneous material. All the various places where this happened with great success cannot be cited here.

OP. 37
Allegro con brio, mm. 199–202

Let just a few give proof to our claim and visually demonstrate the manner of the treatment.

OP. 37
Allegro con brio, mm. 211–22

A further exposition is as little necessary as is a suggestion of the effect that is produced thereby in attentive listeners. But I do want to mention yet one more spot like that in this movement, since it is so outstanding in yet another respect!

OP. 37
Allegro con brio, mm. 416–28

After the cadenza Beethoven makes a deceptive cadence, the (*inganno*)[2] moves from the dominant-seventh chord to the second inversion of the major-minor seventh chord on C and now lets the pianoforte continue to play solo until the final cadence. The effect of this conclusion is in itself very surprising and excites the spirit in an uncommonly agreeable way. It becomes even more so, however, through the excellent choice and treatment of the instruments, which extends through the entire work, but may be demonstrated here with a triviality. I mean the spot right in the first measures after the cadenza, where during the solo part of the pianoforte those few but significant notes, which are all the more forceful here, are heard from the timpani.

One principal means for reaching the intended effect in such a work is, furthermore, the purposeful *preparation* and gradual guidance of the listener to what is highest and most decisive. This purpose is served principally by the tuttis, in part when they are composed in the character of the whole and in part also when they are suggestive of the subsequent principal ideas. To be sure, they are suggestive in a way that is in accordance with that character, without, however, depriving the solos and their more extensive development of their salient and piquant qualities beforehand. This technique has also been used here by Beethoven in a masterful way; the principal ideas of the whole—as they had to be here—are stated simply and powerfully in the ritornellos and always seem to develop from this simple suggestion as if by themselves. No example can be given of this, for the whole work is example and proof.

Another means, particularly necessary in such a long and extensively developed piece of music, for drawing and intensifying the attention of the listeners again and again, is provided by modulations into distant keys. They are spices, but for this very reason they should be used only rarely and at the most outstanding points. Otherwise, as in most of the recent compositions, a too strong portion of spices brings about an *overstimulation,* which produces exhaustion instead of accomplishing its goal. B., who elsewhere has also sometimes been guilty of this, has successfully avoided it in this concerto. He offers modulations like that, but only rarely, and when he does use them, they are in the right place and precisely for this reason have the proper effect. I will likewise set down one of these spots here, although it only attains its significance in context.

OP. 37
Allegro con brio, mm. 188–98

The second movement is a Largo in E major with muted violins, which begins thus:

This is assuredly one of the most expressive and emotionally rich instrumental pieces that has ever been written, and if it is well performed by the soloist and the entire orchestra (which, however, is of no little significance here) and does not create a sensation, the fault can only lie with the audience.

One may call it the attempt at a portrait of the melancholic mood of a noble soul, depicted in the subtlest nuances. For that reason, it only *seems* to contrast sharply (as does the key—E major versus C minor). To the contrary, it is simply an exchange that is completely founded in the nature of the soul. This movement is woven out of so many details, which are, nevertheless, superbly connected, that I do not see how something can be excerpted for my purpose without either filling entire pages or greatly distorting it. Therefore, I will make only one observation: more than any previous composer for the pianoforte, B. has brought into play here all means that this instrument possesses for the expression of gentle feelings. To those who are still echoing each other on the basis of the old belief (founded perhaps on Bach's, Schwanberger's,[3] and such like keyboard concertos) that the pianoforte is lacking in a more tender expression, the proper performance of this piece is just as complete a refutation as a philosopher's walking was a refutation of the doubts of his colleagues who denied the existence of motion.

Following his instinct, which also guided him quite correctly, the composer let this Largo be followed by a truly passionate finale, which, in regard to its working out, deserves just as much attention as the first Allegro.

The very beginning of the theme:

where the chord is based on the dominant and is extended to the minor ninth, announces and indicates the real essence, and is very original. The withholding of the first full cadence in the tonic through thirty-two measures creates ever higher excitement and tension and captivates the listener irresistibly. B. also creates a similar effect quite perfectly at those places, among others, where he again leads into the theme, and then, usually through the chromatic scale, leads up through one or more octaves to the minor seventh or ninth, but does not yet let the listener come to rest. Instead, he holds him in suspense until the very end of the theme.

In the end, this tension could, however, go too far and would then provoke satiety and adverse feelings (as is the case of several other most recent composers who work out their good ideas to the point of death), if B. did not make use of means to alleviate it at the proper time—at least in high time. Among these belong the modulations to the major mode, which here are used with very prudent restraint and thus have a very beautiful effect. Even more peculiar, however, and leading back extremely well to the abandoned path, are the places where the composer begins the theme in major, but returns to minor with the minor ninth in the third measure. Also where he then goes into A♭ major, and the clarinet, as if in amiable invitation, plays the melody for the pianoforte, which subsequently repeats it with sixths in broken chords in the left hand. At the conclusion of this section in A♭ major, the composer agreeably surprises both connoisseurs and amateurs by letting the theme of the finale be developed fugally, *pianissimo,* by the string instruments, and then, since he is leading back toward C minor, goes from the dominant G, instead of back to C, up a minor second, letting this A♭ be taken up by the pianoforte and struck alternately by the two hands, and moves through an enharmonic alteration, whereby A♭ becomes G♯, to E major.

OP. 37
Rondo, mm. 252–68

At the point where the modulation returns to C minor, B. places the first three notes of the theme into the accompaniment, and lets the pianoforte step in between with arpeggiated diminished- seventh chords, which, as the string instruments are moving forward very weakly in eighth notes, creates a deep, strange impression.

OP. 37
Rondo, mm. 274–85

A Presto, ⅜ time in C major, forms the final conclusion of this movement, the theme of which is taken from what comes before:

OP. 37
Rondo, mm. 407–08

and the whole closes just as interestingly as it began, only somewhat more peacefully and amiably, as indeed is appropriate.

I conclude herewith this review, which is written only for those who can think and enjoy at the same time, or who wish to study the work themselves. These, particularly the latter, will certainly also discover small failings—although certainly very few of these. Precisely for this reason I can spare myself from enumerating them, which would be very hard for me to do with such a work, where excellence is so infinitely predominant.

The concerto demands an orchestra that is capable of much, wants the best, and, in order also to accomplish that truly, understands what it plays. It also demands a capable soloist, who, in addition to all that is customarily called virtuosity, also has knowledge in his head and a heart in his breast—otherwise, even with the most extraordinary skill and assurance, exactly that which is most excellent will be left behind. Such a true virtuoso, however, will still be able to shine in this concerto, for, as richly as it is scored and worked out through all the instruments, the solo part is just as outstanding and gratifying. The composer, by the way, prevented all arbitrary embellishment by writing out very precisely and carefully all the genuine ornaments, which is likewise to be praised. Whoever plays only notes will thus find many passages to be monstrously difficult; but, as has been said, this work is also not for them.[4]

NOTES

1. "Oboi, Corni e Fagotti," Italian for "oboes, horns, and bassoons."
2. "Inganno," Italian for "deceptive cadence."
3. Johann Gottfried Schwanberger (also Schwanenberger; ca. 1740–1804) was educated in Italy and composed in the Neapolitan style. He was also the author of four keyboard concertos. Like those of Bach, the concertos were originally performed on the harpsichord. This passage illustrates the semantic distinction, frequently made in these articles, between the German word *Klavier,* which at this point could still also mean harpsichord or clavichord, and the internationally current terms "fortepiano" and "pianoforte," which apparently were interchangeable and therefore referred to the instrument that led by a direct line of development to the modern piano. As the text reveals, the author of this

article uses the term "pianoforte." As indicated in entry no. 2, n. 2, the translations reflect the authors' own usages of "fortepiano" and "pianoforte."

4. A paragraph follows with corrections of a few printing errors.

≈

127.
"News: Leipzig," *Allgemeine musikalische Zeitung* 14 (13 May 1812): 333.[1]

Mr. Neudeck played Beethoven's magnificent Pianoforte Concerto in C minor, the dearest to us of all that this master has enriched the world with. It was played by everyone with love and joy and was received in the same way. Mr. Neudeck played with diligence, care, and skill: in the first movement his playing should have shown more smoothness and inner cohesion and in the second occasionally more soul and delicacy. He played the finale splendidly.

NOTE

1. This entry comprises a small part of a general article (cols. 331–36) on concerts in Leipzig.

≈

Op. 38
TRIO FOR PIANO, CLARINET OR VIOLIN, AND CELLO (ARRANGEMENT OF SEPTET FOR VIOLIN, VIOLA, CLARINET, FRENCH HORN, BASSOON, VIOLONCELLO, AND DOUBLE BASS IN E♭ MAJOR)

See entry no. 138

≈

Op. 41
SERENADE FOR PIANO AND FLUTE (ARRANGEMENT OF SERENADE FOR FLUTE, VIOLIN, AND VIOLA, OP. 25)

128.
M.——s, "Serenade p. le fortepiano et flute (ou Violon) par Louis van Beethoven, arrangée d'une serenade et revue par l'auteur. O. 41. Preis 1 Thlr.,"[1] *Zeitung für die elegante Welt* 7 (22 December 1807): 1628.

No. 3. Beethoven's name itself recommends this very beautiful serenade, which is not hard to play and which consists of seven major movements of a very agreeable romantic character, that is, it consists of an entrata (Allegro), a minuet with two trios, an Allegro molto, an Andante with three variations, an Allegro scherzando e vivace, a short Adagio, and an Allegro vivace.[2]

NOTES

1. English: "No. 3. Serenade for Fortepiano and Flute (or Violin) by Louis van Beethoven, arranged from a Serenade and proofed by the author, op. 41. Price 1 Thaler."

2. For the second movement, the score reads "Tempo ordinario d'un Menuetto"; for the fourth, "Andante con variazioni"; and the fifth "Adagio." A. Kühnel in Leipzig reprinted a *Titelauflage* of op. 41 in 1807. The first edition of op. 41 appeared in December 1803, published by Hoffmeister & Kühnel in Leipzig.

∾

Op. 43
BALLET *DIE GESCHÖPFE DES PROMETHEUS*

See also entry nos. 31, 46, and 135

———————

129.
"Die Geschöpfe des Prometheus," Zeitung für die elegante Welt 1
(April 1801): 485–87.

The presentations at our court theater before Easter concluded with a new heroic-allegorical ballet in two acts: *Die Geschöpfe des Prometheus,* invented and developed by Mr. *Salvatore Viganò* and set to music by Mr. *van Beethoven.*[1] The first time, it was given for the benefit of the famous dancer, Miss *Casentini.* Its content was announced in a very peculiar program, presumably by an Italian not very well versed in the German language.

Prometheus rescues the people of his time from their ignorance, improves them with knowledge and art, and elevates them to moral awareness. This is the subject in brief. As much dignity and artistic design as it had, and as masterfully as some dancers, most notably Mr. Viganò himself, distinguished themselves, it nevertheless was not liked in general. The least satisfying of all to our spectacle-loving public was the fact that the stage remained completely unchanged from the second scene of the first act until the very end. The action began with a thunderstorm. The theater presented a small grove in which there were two children of Prometheus. Suddenly their father entered with a burning torch. (Where, and with what fire he lighted it, the spectators did not get to see.) After he had placed the fire on the breast of each child, they began at once to toddle around stiffly without gesticulating. (This scene lasted rather too long and became boring.) Now Prometheus led them to Apollo. Parnassus with all its dwellers did not exactly make the most agreeable sight. The nine Muses remained like lifeless statues upon their assigned spot until it was their turn to dance, and Apollo himself sat upon the highest peak of the mountain, always motionless. Perhaps this very scene made too little impression upon the artistic spirit of our beloved *Casentini*, for she, introduced by her father to the god of the muses, expressed no interest at all and, with conspicuous indifference, immediately allowed her glance to wander to other things. One can certainly not convince oneself that she should have ignored the respect she owes to such a public, particularly in a ballet that brought her over 4,000 gulden in receipts, simply because of a bad mood. Assuredly, however, with just a little more effort—even though a *Casentini* can never dance poorly—she would have made the ballet much more attractive.

The music also did not entirely live up to expectations, even though it possesses more than *ordinary* merit. Whether Mr. *van Beethoven* can achieve what a public like ours demands in regard to unity—which is not to say uniformity—of treatment, I will leave undecided. However, that he wrote *too learnedly* for a ballet, and with too little regard for the dance, is certainly not subject to doubt. Everything is laid out too grandly for a diversion, which is what the ballet should actually be, and because of the lack of suitable situations, it had to remain more of a fragment than a whole. This begins already with the overture. In any more substantial opera, it would be in the proper place and would not fail to make a significant effect. Here, however, it is in the wrong place. The warlike dances and Miss *Casentini's* solo, on the other hand, were probably the most successful for the composer. In the *Dance of Pan,* some people claim to find various reminiscences from other ballets. However, it seems to me that this is doing Mr. van B. a disservice, especially since only those who envy him can deny him his totally extraordinary originality, through which he admittedly often denies his observers the charm of sweetly pleasing harmonies.

NOTE

1. Salvatore Viganò (1769–1821) was an Italian ballet dancer, choreographer, composer, and the author of the ballet book for *Prometheus*. He and his wife Maria made significant contributions to the art of ballet at the end of the last decade of the eighteenth century with their dramatic and natural performances.

130.
August Kuhn, "Concert in Berlin," *Der Freymüthige* 23 (January 1826): 28.

An Adagio and Rondo for the flute, composed and superbly performed by the Royal Chamber Musician Gabrielski, and a horn duet, played with much virtuosity by the talented Schunke brothers,[1] must be mentioned here, as will Beethoven's overture to the ballet *Prometheus,* which was undoubtedly performed for the ninety-ninth time on today's concert, as if, as it were, no other overture existed for this purpose. When "Overture" or even "Overture by Beethoven" is on the concert program, one can wager a hundred to one that the above-mentioned, and no other, will be played. It is very beautiful, but heard much, much too often.[2]

NOTES

1. Gottfried Schunke (1777–1840) and his younger brother Michael (died 1821) came from a large family of musicians and gained much recognition as hornists in the Kassel court orchestra.

2. Kuhn's complaint that the Overture was being overplayed is verified in the printing history of the work: the Overture to the ballet was published separately from the complete ballet music in four editions of the orchestral parts and in more than twenty arrangements before 1830. See Kinsky-Halm for a partial list.

131.

Adolf Bernard Marx, "Reviews," *Berliner allgemeine musikalische Zeitung* 3 (12 April 1826): 118–19.

"Musique de Ballet en forme d'une marche arrangé pour piano quatre mains par Ludwig van Beethoven."[1]

This reviewer knows no merrier music by Beethoven. It is a ballet for— tightrope walkers, the family Kolter. Why not? Courtesans, bacchants or tightrope walkers!

> Reach right into the fullness of human life!
> Every one lives it, it's not known to many,
> And wherever you seize it, it is interesting.[2]

That is to say (and that is the condition): only if you seize it right! And here Beethoven has done that successfully. He has his tightrope walkers march by so cheerfully and lively that we find ourselves in the circus among the jubilant crowd and would like to join in shouting with joy to the bright colored, juggling aerial artists swaying delightfully. Everything is in its best, truest order. The drum and trumpet call out vigorously and more and more emphatically and prepare for something important, God only knows what. What follows? A little march that one might call ordinary if it weren't so merry. Now they climb the rope, but not without peril and fear—indeed, it is the beginners, and in the process the trumpet blows quite foolishly and clumsily. Is the clown there too? Now the scene is soon over. The march entertains in the interlude, and forthwith graceful, airy leaps delight us. It is probably Madonna Serafina or Angeline. That indeed has a noisier ending. But now the tour de force comes after a repetition of the march—or is it a battle piece, soldiers and robbers, or something like that? Or, is it an unintentional parody of our spectacular show? Here things proceed wildly and heartily and then again merrily, and then the key shifts from D minor in the finale to F♯, but not without plenty of noise. And now it comes to a pleasant end with dainty and pretty flourishes, and a thunderous coda from the march sends us home satisfied in an elevated mood.

This is certainly nothing more than a tightrope walker evening, which we have experienced here. But for us the pleasure was pure and honest. Isn't that more sensible than those contrived, prettified and thereby unseemly, unsuitable, hollow amusements with which we superciliously deceive ourselves? In the circus, at garden parties, oh heavens! Everywhere those grand parade overtures pursue us; indeed, even the most tender, most deeply felt compositions arranged for large drums, etc. And the only effect is that they stupefy us and transport us to a condition similar to sleep, for with all the beer bottles, coffee cans, and cries from boys selling cigars, who can perceive more than distracting noise? It is truly the worst kind of affectation to drag the grand and profound everywhere, and this happy unassuming work discussed above diverts from that other kind to suitable and therefore truly delightful music. It can also be had for large orchestras (music for wind bands).

By the way, dissatisfaction is caused by the incorrectness, found even in the title (un marche, cette piece se trouvent danse),[3] of many passages in this arrangement.

NOTES

1. "Ballet music in the form of a march arranged for piano for four hands by Ludwig van Beethoven." This is a four-hand arrangement of the March (no. 8) from *Die Geschöpfe des Prometheus*, op. 43, arranged by C. F. Ebers and published in 1822 by Hoffmeister in Leipzig. See Kinsky-Halm, 103.

2. David Luke, translator of *Johann Wolfgang von Goethe, Faust: Part One* (Oxford: Oxford University Press, 1987), offers the following poetic translation of these lines spoken by the Clown in "Vorspiel auf dem Theater": "Use real life and its rich variety! / They're living it, but unreflectingly, / They'll notice this or that they don't know" (lines 167–70).

3. "A march, this piece should be called a dance."

∽

Op. 45
THREE MARCHES FOR PIANO FOUR-HANDS

132.
"Brief Notices," Allgemeine musikalische Zeitung 6 (20 June 1804): 643.
With Seven Variations on *God Save the King* in C Major, WoO 78

Both little works belong only among the easier occasional pieces by this master. In both, however, and particularly in the first, his original spirit and his powerful nature are unmistakably apparent. Since in regard to execution they belong among the simplest pieces written by B., and every quite average keyboard player will now want to attempt music by B., these works will not fail to be in everyone's hands shortly. Therefore we will let the matter rest with the announcement of their existence. The marches were conceived and born in a strange, somewhat bizarre mood.[1] Therefore, whoever does not find them to his taste after first playing them through, let him remember that this lies in the nature of the thing. Let him play them several more times, and he will be able to take more and more interest in them with pleasure. The variations stay more within the usual sphere. B.'s spirit nevertheless betrays itself in the first, fourth, and seventh, with the coda.

NOTE

1. The story behind the conception of the marches confirms the reviewer's supposition. Ries, in order to placate an old countess who "tormented Beethoven with her devotion," replied in the affirmative when the countess asked if a march he had just improvised was by Beethoven. To Ries's horror, at Count Browne's home the next evening the countess praised the new march in excess and demanded that it be played again by Ries with Beethoven present. Ries hurriedly explained the ruse to Beethoven, who reacted with good humor, then rage, then laughter. Count Browne immediately commissioned Beethoven to compose three marches for piano, four-hands, resulting in the present work. See Thayer-Forbes, 307.

❦

Op. 46
ADELAIDE, SONG
See also entry no. 46

133.
"Music," Zeitung für die elegante Welt 3 (19 June 1803): 685.

It can be questioned whether it was necessary to through-compose this song,[1] one of the most tender by Matthison.[2] Reichardt and Zelter[3] have not done so, and both have made excellent melodies out of it.[4] But if it ever had to happen, one has to admit that the music could not have turned out more successfully and eloquently than in this piece by Beethoven. It is completely incomparable, particularly if, as the Italianate character of this music almost requires, one sings the well-set Italian translation. In tenderness, in touching intimacy and sweetness of expression, hardly anything could surpass the first part, which comprises the first three strophes. It is not possible to play and sing this music only once. One must repeat it endlessly.

NOTES

1. As opposed, that is, to setting it strophically, which was often considered not simply adequate but highly desirable for texts with great expressive power. When Goethe,

for example, preferred C. F. Zelter's setting of *Der Erlkönig* to that by Schubert, he demonstrated the widespread belief that setting such a text to music that called attention to itself in its own right created a superfluity of expressive details and detracted from the effect of the whole.

2. Friedrich Matthison (1761–1831) was a minor lyrical poet, widely imitated but severely criticized by Friedrich Schiller for his verbose and mawkish style. Beethoven felt such gratitude to Matthison for his "beautiful poetry" that, in a letter dated 4 August 1800, he sent a copy of this composition to the poet with a request for "another poem of its kind" (see Anderson, letter no. 40, and Brandenburg, letter no. 47).

3. Carl Friedrich Zelter (1758–1832) was a well-known violinist and composer. He established a choral society that became the model for many nineteenth-century male choral clubs. Because of Zelter's broad education, Goethe accepted him as his major adviser on music. Zelter helped distance Goethe from Schubert and Beethoven, whom he could only "admire with horror." The reviewer suggests his own conservative training when he portrays Zelter, as well as Reichardt, as composers of a simpler, less developed strophic style. Together with Reichardt, Zelter is thought to epitomize the conservative German school of *Lied* composers against whom Schubert rebelled with his more elaborate settings. Although this impression is only partly justified, the reviewer's citation of Reichardt and Zelter as the proponents of a simpler, less musically developed style than that adopted by Beethoven shows that they were already perceived in this way, albeit admiringly, long before Schubert began to compose.

4. The first edition of op. 46 was published in February 1797 by Artaria, but without an opus number. The opus number was first mentioned in an Artaria catalog of 1819. Later prints of the song were issued by Simrock, Hoffmeister, & Kühnel, and perhaps Böhme in 1803. As Simrock's edition appeared in late 1803, one of the other two prints must have occasioned this review. The complicated publication history is discussed in Lisbeth Weinhold, "Erst- und Frühdrucke von Beethovens Werken," in *Beiträge zur Beethoven-Bibliographie,* ed. Kurt Dorfmüller (Munich: G. Henle, 1978), 265–69.

∾

134.
"Review," *Berlinische musikalische Zeitung* 1 (1805): 9–10.

With song, *Das Glück der Freundschaft,* op. 88

Both of these compositions are a nice demonstration of how the composer can and does deal with the forms of the poems that are given to him. From the first song Mr. B. made a great aria "da due carattere,"[1] as the Italians say, which could conclude the greatest modern theatrical scene. From the second song he made a little rondo. Choice and treatment are much more successful with the latter than with the first. To treat with such length and importance a song that is merely an Italianate play upon a beloved name cannot possibly be called good by criticism and taste. Apart from this bad choice, the composition is not only extremely agreeable, but also rich in striking expression in the vocal part and in unique, meaningful modulations. One could only wish that the composition, regarded only as a piece of music, would not present such a conspicuously sharp contrast between the first truly noble section and the second thoroughly cheerful one. After the thoroughly good-natured painting and exposition of the images in which the poet reveals his tenderness, the cheerful treatment of his wonderment

ADELAIDE

Once, oh marvel, there will blossom forth on my grave,
A flower from the ashes of my heart,
Clearly there will glitter on each tiny purple leaf.

almost makes it appear that the composer was making fun of that wonderment. The whole thus obtains almost the character of a parody.

In the second very lovely little rondo, the repetition of the final verses and their treatment is much more successful. In both compositions, however, there appears a fashionable vocal mannerism, which an artist like Mr. B. should not use. Rather, it should please him if fashionable singers did without such things in his expressive melodies. The reviewer means the wrong accent on *Nachtigallen* on p. 6 of the first composition, and on *geteilte Lust verdoppelt,* etc. on p. 7 of the second, where all the short syllables are sung high and the long ones are sung low. For the last words, the composer even added a *sforzando* on every high note, in order to ensure the effect of the reversed accents, which are so offensive to a refined ear and feeling. In completely through-composed poems such as these, one should not tolerate falsely applied cadential formulas, which one will indeed have to put up with in melodies to which several strophes are to be sung that begin and end differently. In the first composition on p. 3, one should take note of *zittert* and on p. 8 of *Grabe,* or in the second on p. 3 of *Geleit.*—the Italian translation could be much better at several points.

NOTE

1. "Da due carattere," Italian for "with two affections," that is, expressing two different emotional states.

⌁

135.
"Concerts," *Wiener allgemeine musikalische Zeitung* 1 (1813): 300–01.

Mentioned: *Die Geschöpfe des Prometheus,* op. 43

On 9 May Mr. Ignaz Moscheles, Imperial Theater Composer, gave a musical performance in the Imperial Royal Little Redouten-Saal. . . .[1]
The remaining pieces of music at this performance were: to begin with, the overture to *Die Tage der Gefahr* by Cherubini,[2] and, prior to the already

mentioned Fantasy, in place of an aria, which Mad. Harlas was prevented from singing by an indisposition, the overture to the ballet *Prometheus* by L. v. Beethoven, both excellently performed with exceptional power and fire by the Imperial Theater Orchestra under the direction of Mr. Wranitzky.[3] Then came Mathisson's *Adelaide,* set to music by *Mr. v. Beethoven,* sung by Mr. Wild,[4] and accompanied at the pianoforte by the conductor *Gyrowetz.* As unusual as the appearance of a German vocal piece is at a concert, this nevertheless did not fail to have an effect upon a public that, not prejudiced in favor of particular forms, possesses a general receptivity to everything that is truly beautiful. Text, music, and performance combined to guarantee a splendid artistic enjoyment. *Mr. Wild* correctly understood the spirit of the composition and perfectly achieved the goal of the deepest feeling through simple, expressive, tenderly nuanced singing. The attempt made thereby to promote German national singing is particularly praiseworthy, although it can be foreseen that *Mr. Wild* will find few imitators in this matter, for such songs presuppose a full, powerful, resonant voice, which only extremely few of today's singers possess, and the lack of which they try to hide through excessive ornamentations, which, however, are not compatible with German national singing at all.

NOTES

1. A portion of the text has been omitted; it deals exclusively with the performance by Ignaz Moscheles and a Mr. Giuliani of their own sonata for piano and guitar.

2. *Les deux journées* (1800) by Luigi Cherubini (1760–1842) was known in German primarily as *Der Wasserträger* but also occasionally under the title in the text.

3. The reference is to Anton Wranitzky (1761–1819), who was director of Prince Lobkowitz's orchestra. His brother Paul was music director of the Court Theater; he also provided the external source for Beethoven's Variations for Piano on a Russian Dance from Wranitzky's *Das Waldmädchen,* WoO 71.

4. Franz Wild (1792–1860) gave a famous description of Beethoven's conducting in his autobiography. He is also quoted in Thayer-Forbes as having the following to say about a later performance of *Adelaide:* "It would be as untruthful as absurd were I to deny that my vanity was flattered by the distinction which the gathered celebrities bestowed upon me; but this performance of 'Adelaide' had one result which was infinitely more gratifying to my artistic nature; it was the cause of my coming into closer contact with the greatest musical genius of all time, Beethoven. The master, rejoiced at my choice of his song, hunted me up and offered to accompany me. Satisfied with my singing he told me that he would orchestrate the song. He did not do this, but wrote for me the cantata 'An die Hoffnung' (words by Tiedge) with piano accompaniment, which, he playing for me, I sang at a matinée before a select audience" (Thayer-Forbes, 610).

Wild's reference to Beethoven's cantata is not to op. 32 but to op. 94. Forbes indicates in a footnote that, although this song was written in 1813, he believes Beethoven revised it for Wild before publishing it in April 1816.

136.

"Concerts," *Allgemeine musikalische Zeitung mit besonderer Rücksicht auf den österreichischen Kaiserstaat* 6 (30 March 1822): 207.

The intermediate pieces at this performance consisted of *Adelaide* by *Beethoven,* sung by Mr. *Titz.* This most highly finished, lofty, ingenious composition by Beethoven is eternally new and beautiful. Mr. *Titz* has a very graceful voice with a gentle, melodious sound, which despite his lack of *strict* artistic training is nevertheless very flexible and pliant. The performance of the singer was noble and full of feeling and excited the loud applause of those present. The final tempo nevertheless seemed to us to be a little too fast.

~

137.

7——, *Allgemeiner musikalischer Anzeiger* (Vienna), 1 (28 March 1829): 49–50.

To squander even one more tiny little word on this angelic song would have to be seen as a transgression. Beethoven would remain immortal if he had not written a single other note.

It was considered appropriate to set an Italian translation to the existing edition, and that was *good;* for where is it written that—vice versa—translations must always and ever be made from a foreign language into German, and why should our sub-Alpine neighbors not likewise gain access to such an exalted pleasure? The publishing firm, however, has by no means designed this "soi-disant"[1] *new edition* (with which the author's honorarium fell through), with taste and in a manner worthily commensurate with its intensity; and that was *not* good.[2]

NOTES

1. "Soi-disant," French for "so-called."
2. A *Titelauflage* of the 1805 Viennese edition by Cappi was reissued as a "Neue Auflage" and as "46. Werk" in the first months of 1829 by the successors to the Cappi firm; the edition was announced in April 1829 in BAMZ (appendix no. 5 of vol. 6).

Op. 47
SONATA FOR PIANO AND VIOLIN ("KREUTZER")

138.

"Review," *Allgemeine musikalische Zeitung* 7 (28 August 1805): 769–72.

With arrangement of op. 20 for Trio, op. 38, and Eight Songs with
Piano Accompaniment, op. 52

1. The appendix to the title: *scritta—conzerto,*[1] seems curious, presumptuous, and boastful. However, it speaks the truth, serves in place of a preface, and pretty much defines what the audience for this strange work can be. This strange work, I say, for it is in fact peculiar, and, precisely speaking, we do not yet have anything of this type—or rather, nothing that has extended the boundaries of the type so far and then also truly filled them in this manner. How? This is the other question. The reviewer believes, after becoming carefully acquainted with this composition, that one has to have limited one's love of art to just a certain realm of the more ordinary, or be strongly prejudiced against Beethoven if one does not recognize this piece of music, developed far and wide, as a new demonstration of the artist's great genius, his vivid, often glowing fantasy, and his broad knowledge of deeper harmonic art. Also, however, one must be possessed by a type of aesthetic or artistic terrorism or be won over to Beethoven to the point of blindness, if one does not find in this work a new, blatant proof of the fact that for some time now this artist has indeed been dead-set on using the most exquisite gifts of nature and his diligence not simply to shift toward the greatest arbitrariness, but above all else always to be entirely different from other people. One will also find proof that he does not thereby simply drive his great ability violently up into the unknown (which could certainly bring forth monsters, but always admirable ones), but at the same time holds to an earthly goal, whether clearly or not, whereby neither his works, nor the world, nor he himself stand to gain.

Thus, this sonata also belongs among the products of this mood of the ingenious man. To develop its inner essence and to characterize it definitely in words, is impossible for me, and "eris mihi magnus Apollo,"[2] who is capable of doing this satisfactorily, and truly accomplished it? Given the regard that one owes this composer and, in fact, also to his creation, I have attempted to illustrate the progression of ideas only somewhat satisfactorily in outline. I have written a full page just on the first Presto, but I will spare the readers of the *mus. Z.*[3] If a path is to be described, we must be able to determine where it comes from and where it is going. Accordingly, let the matter rest with the following general declaration. If there were two virtuosos, to whom nothing any longer is difficult, and who furthermore possess so much spirit and knowledge that, with sufficient training, they could perhaps write such works themselves; if these two, precisely because of this all-encompassing spirit, are not distracted by the strangest protuberances in detail and if they come together and study the work (for they would have to do this too), then they will obtain full and rich satisfaction from doing so. This presumes, however, that they wait and perform it with intelligence at the time when people are able and willing to enjoy the most grotesque things. At any rate, after two lines of introduction, the sonata consists of an emotion-filled Presto, the keyboard part of which alone fills twelve closely printed pages, an original, beautiful Andante, with four extremely odd variations, and then another Presto, the most bizarre movement of all. The work is very beautifully engraved.

2. First of all, this has a French dedication, which is noteworthy because of the odd phrase in which the composer states that he is giving precisely this work to his patron because it is easy to perform. As is well known, the composition itself is known to be one of the most beautiful, or at least one of the most agreeable and amiable by this master, and dates from the time when he had not yet set that particular goal for himself. As it goes without saying with this composer, the new arrangement is very good.[4] The violin part, as can likewise be taken for granted, is a different one from that for clarinet. If one alternates the two instruments, one can enjoy the trio with satisfaction all the more often, for through the small alterations in both, this interesting painting is illuminated in several more pleasant colors. Nevertheless, the reviewer feels that the clarinet is the superior choice, presuming it is played very well. The whole work emerges like an original and almost as well as it does on the seven instruments. The performance of the keyboard part is, for Beethoven's music, really very easy. The engraving is not entirely correct; correction of the errors, however, will be very easy and therefore doesn't need to be indicated.

3. Could these eight songs also be by this outstanding artist, often admirable even in his mistakes? Is it possible? But it must be since they really are! At the very least, his name is in large letters on the title page, the publisher is given, the songs came out in Vienna, the composer's dwelling place, they even bear the number of one of his newest works.—Let whoever can understand how something so completely commonplace, poor, dull, at times even ridiculous could not only come from such a man but actually be published by him! Only the first of these songs, because of a touch of the comical, and the seventh, because of something patriotic, which, however, could be learned from any inarticulate urchin, are bearable.[5] You don't believe it? Certainly not! but here you may see—not the worst, only one of the shortest, and you must! If you wish, however, to enjoy the following composition completely,

simply set the other verses of the well-known, excellent text, as it should be done,—for example the fourth!

OP. 52, no. 8

"THE LITTLE FLOWER WONDERFULLY FAIR," BY BÜRGER[6]

1. There blossoms a little flower somewhere
In a quiet valley,
Which flatters the eye and heart so gaily,
Like the beams of the evening sun.

That is much more precious than gold,
Than pearls and diamonds,
Thus the little flower is justly called
Wonderfully Fair.

4. Oh if you had only known her!
She who was once my treasure.
Death snatched her from my hand,
Shortly after the wedding altar.

Then you would understand,
What Wonderfully Fair can do,
And look into the light of truth,
As into the bright day.

NOTES

1. The first edition was published by Simrock in Bonn in April 1805. Originally the title read: SONATA / per il Pian-forte ed un Violino obligato, / scritta in uno stilo molto concertante, / quasi come d'un concerto (Kinsky-Halm, 111).

2. "Eris mihi magnus Apollo": "then for me you will be as great as Apollo."

3. The abbreviation refers to *Allgemeine musikalische Zeitung.*

4. The arrangement of the Septet for piano trio (with clarinet or violin and cello), made by Beethoven himself, was published as op. 38 in 1805 in Vienna by the Bureau d'Arts et d'Industrie. The dedication on the title page is given extravagantly as "à Monsieur Jean Adam Schmidt / Conseiller de Sa Majesté l'Empereur et Roi, / Chirurgien Major de Ses Armées, Professeur public à l'Académie de Médecine et Chirurgie fondée par feu S. M. l'Empereur Joseph II, Membre de plusieurs Sociétés & &."

5. The title of the song is *Marmotte,* which is from the second (1778) version of Goethe's short drama *Das Jahrmarktsfest zu Plundersweilern: Ein Schönbartsspiel.* The play portrays the hustle and bustle of the fair as a symbol of human life in general. The play had little success outside of Frankfurt and Weimar. The following is the first of four strophes sung by the street boy Marmotte to earn his day's bread. Because of the mixture of German and French, the original is also given here:

> Ich komme schon durch manches Land,
> avec que la marmotte,
> und immer was zu essen fand,
> avec que la marmotte,
> avec que si, avec que la,
> avec que la marmotte,
> avec que si, avec que la,
> avec que la marmotte.
>
> [I have come through many lands
> With whom, the urchin,
> And always I found something to eat,
> With whom, the urchin,
> With whom, so, with whom, so,
> With whom, the urchin,
> With whom, so, with whom, so,
> With whom, the urchin.]

6. Gottfried August Bürger (1747–94) was one of the major poets of the *Sturm und Drang* movement and gained lasting fame with his folk ballad *Leonore.* Among his poems that Beethoven set to music are *Mollys Abschied* (op. 52) and *Seufzer eines Ungeliebten* and *Gegenliebe* (WoO 118). The German title of the poem cited in the text is *Blümchen*

wunderhold. Bürger was severely castigated by Friedrich Schiller for his commonplace and banal sentimentalism in folk ballads.

~

Op. 48
SIX SONGS

See also entry no. 46

139.
"Six Songs by Gellert,[1] to be Sung with Keyboard Accompaniment,"
Allgemeine musikalische Zeitung 6 (6 June 1804): 608–12.

It cannot fail to seem not a little strange to the greatest part of our readers to see six songs by Gellert not only newly composed,[2] composed by Mr. B., but also removed from their proper vocation set in figural music,[3] and more or less freely worked out. It can be said that one of the primary merits of Gellert's songs, even by the pious poet's own admission, is the fact that most of them are so well suited to the best old chorale melodies that they cannot be separated from them without losing something. The others are all at the very least so sacred in spirit and style that none of them should be treated any more freely than perhaps [Carl Philipp Emanuel] Bach[4] has already done, or what might perhaps be further done in the same manner. Now all of this is certainly not entirely unfounded, so that it can probably also be assumed that an educated musician would scarcely have come up with that idea, except in circumstances where an ongoing acquaintanceship with more recent literature is made nearly impossible. Nevertheless, this little work is there, and the best thing to do is to stick to what it is and how it became that. It is nonetheless very good, and various things in the work are so outstanding that, in regard to music itself or to music as an expression of the feelings that exist in the poems as a whole, some of these songs are not surpassed by anything in the entire multitude of the most recent collections. This sense of the whole, a field that rightly and properly belongs to the musician, is always properly interpreted by the composer and beautifully given back, except where the content (as in no. 2—"So jemand spricht, ich liebe Gott"—) is almost only dogma—in which case the song should never have been chosen and is by far the least successful. For that reason we will not mention it further. But even the rhetorical portion is well handled by Mr. B. almost throughout. Musical reproduction of the structure of the poem in general and, in particular, declamation, accentuation, and such like are correct and appropriate, whether the composer achieved this deliberately or simply followed his genius. The proportion of music and working out assigned to each song is also a happy one, with the exception of no. 5—"Gott ist mein Lied"—which is the most trivial of the songs and which has received an almost meager musical setting, which nevertheless must be repeated *fifteen times,* and which is manifestly unsuited to several strophes, such as 8 and 9. It is a genuine pleasure for us, however, to dwell somewhat longer on the four remaining songs.

"Gott deine Güte reicht so weit" is, when well considered, simple, almost like a chorale in the melody. However, it is written with a fast-moving, significant bass line, and if this is well brought out without disturbing the ties, and if the long, continuous E in the voice [mm. 27–32], on p. 3, line 1, is sufficiently motivated with crescendo and decrescendo, it will have the intended effect. But no. 3, "Meine Lebenszeit verstreicht," written in F♯ minor, has greater energy and is also much more original. A spirit of genius truly breathes here and immediately cancels any objections that one might raise to small, secondary details. In place of any analysis, let us look at the following important passage. Who can mistake the greatness that is raised to a thrilling level, particularly through the force of the gradual, restrained rise of the melody and then of the bass, but even more through the fullness of the striking progression of harmonies and the measure of the strength of the tones? Who could wish for something more generalized or indefinite, even though this music is admittedly not entirely appropriate to some strophes?

OP. 48 [Ex47]
No. 3, "Vom Tode," mm. 18–41

An excellent companion piece to this song is "Die Himmel rühmen des Ewigen Ehre," and we would have to repeat about it everything favorable that was said about the previous one, only in reference to its cheerful character in its continuous pathos, if more were necessary for something so perfect in itself than simply calling attention to it. Whoever is not moved by music particularly like that from the passage "Wer trägt der Himmel unzählbare Sterne" until the end will hardly be moved by any music, except maybe by trumpets, timpani, and bass drum. Finally, in no. 6, every strophe has received its own music, but in such a way that the composer, with great care and firm insight, grasp, and tempo brings back the principal motives of the melody in other contexts where appropriate. However, when this sorrowful penitential song ("An dir allein hab' ich gesündigt") becomes a more trusting, gentle prayer ("Früh willst du mich mit deiner Gnade füllen"), and the humble heart dares to give itself up to reassuring images and refreshing feelings, the composer goes into major. After a very good introductory and preparatory prelude, he proceeds with new music, which becomes ever more joyous through the rich and figured accompaniment. For this, one would certainly wish less of the usual caliber of fortepiano variation, but rather the kind that is played "cum grano salis,"[5] with the meaning and dress of the whole not completely forsaken, so that a little something of the poet's intended impression still remained at the end. The engraving and external format of this valuable little work are very good.

NOTES

1. For Gellert, see entry no. 24, n. 7.

2. The first edition of the Gellert songs had been published around August 1803 by Artaria in Vienna. According to Kinsky-Halm, this review concerns the reprint by Simrock in Bonn later the same year.

3. The reviewer is referring to the fact that many of these songs (from Gellert's *Geistliche Oden und Lieder,* 1757) were written in a style that allowed them to be incorporated in traditional Lutheran hymnology. Since the Middle Ages, such settings, without polyphonic accompaniment, had been referred to as *cantus planus,* or plainsong, as opposed to *cantus figuralis,* or figural music, which allowed for polyphonic settings and a freer treatment of the text. For further information on the shift in the perspectives of spirituality embodied in Gellert's hymns, see Wayne M. Senner, "The Reception of Gellert's Poetry in Iceland" in *The Reception of German Literature in Iceland, 1775–1850* (Amsterdam: Rodopi, 1985), 35–56.

4. C. P. E. Bach's *Herrn Professor Gellerts geistliche Oden und Lieder mit Melodien* were published in Berlin in 1758.

5. "Cum grano salis" is a Latin expression that can be translated as "with a grain of salt," meaning not to be taken too seriously.

~

Op. 49
TWO PIANO SONATAS IN G MINOR AND G MAJOR

~

140.

C. F. M.[1] "Music," *Zeitung für die elegante Welt* 24 (30 October 1824): 1718.

The ability to write simply and yet interestingly is allotted to few composers, but for the present one, whose originality only too often involves difficulties, it has succeeded beyond expectation in these thoroughly pleasing and agreeable Sonatinas.[2] The first consists of an Andante in G minor, $\frac{2}{4}$, and a Rondo allegro in G major, $\frac{6}{8}$. The second contains an Allegro ma non troppo in G major, $\frac{4}{4}$, and a Tempo di Menuetto. These movements have a cheerful character [and] comfortable fingerings and offer sufficient opportunity to demonstrate a refined and agile manner of performance.

NOTES

1. Christian Friedrich Michaelis; see entry no. 7, n. 1.
2. Although these sonatas were written in 1795 or 1796, they were not published until 1805 by the Bureau d'Arts et d'Industrie in Vienna; by this time, Beethoven's growing reputation had created a demand for works, which he may have originally withheld due to their relative stylistic simplicity. That same simplicity, however, created an immediate demand for the works, and they were immediately reprinted by Simrock in Bonn, by Hummel in Berlin, and others. This review may have been occasioned by the edition of Böhme in Hamburg, issued in 1823.

~

Op. 51, no. 2
RONDO FOR PIANO IN G MAJOR

See entry no. 103

Op. 52
EIGHT SONGS

See also entry no. 138

141.

1. *Allgemeiner musikalischer Anzeiger* (Vienna), 2 (4 September 1830): 141–42.

Genius expresses itself even in little things, and the magnificent *Beethoven,* sensible like all great men, has marked every bagatelle with his own stamp.[1] Among the present eight songs, each has its own merits.[2] "Urians Reise um die Welt"[3] is a good joke, made to entertain a merry company. "Feuerfarb," to a poem by *Sophie Mereau,*[4] is heartfelt and meaningful. *Bürger's*[5] little song "Von der Ruhe" is so appealing, so strikingly and truly set to music, that we far prefer it to all other musical arrangements of the same text. How light, merry, cheerful, and characteristic, on the other hand, is the treatment of *Goethe's Maigesang!*[6] It is truly a great joy, as we have once already had the opportunity to note, to see *Beethoven* vie with Goethe and reanimate the words of the great poet through a fresh coloring of tones, bringing them closer to the listener. "Mollys Abschied" is, in accordance with its feeling, a simple, moving song and hence entirely in its place. Likewise the song by *Lessing,* which follows it.[7] The lay person, accustomed only to marvelling over the great masses of tones in Beethoven's symphonies and gasping laboriously at the bold flights of the great tone-poet, will be amazed that such simple melodies slipped from his pen. The initiated, however, will perceive in them a new demonstration of his high artistry and his far-reaching spirit. The same thing is true of the seventh little song, "La Marmotte," which is handled freshly and humorously. How simple is the treatment of the keystone of this delicate edifice, *Bürger's* "Blümchen Wunderhold," how simple and yet how moving, how true! The blind worship of we Viennese for *Beethoven* has been taken amiss for a long time, and even now cautious people shake their heads when they hear the enthusiastic praises raised by his admirers. Yet we can rightly be proud of the fact that we understood and valued early on the tone-poet who was ahead of his time, which admittedly may stem in part from the fact that we possessed orchestras that understood how to perform his works appropriately earlier than did other cities. Now foreign countries are following our example, and *Beethoven's* symphonies are now exciting the loudest enthusiasm in Paris.[8] So, despite many unavoidable anomalies and eclipses of the sun, Vienna deservedly retains the reputation of the musical city par excellence, even if this is only the fruit of individual strivings and of the generally expanded sensibility for music.

NOTES

1. The word "Bagatelle" is used in the sense of "trifle" and not "light music or verse."
2. According to Kinsky-Halm, this review is in response to the publication of a reprint by Haslinger in Vienna after 1826. The first edition appeared in June 1805 in Vienna by the Bureau d'Arts et d'Industrie.

3. The poem was written by Matthias Claudius (1740–1815), known for his popular national poetry written in a style of naive simplicity and pious intimacy.

4. Sophie Mereau (1770–1806) was a German writer of Romantic novels and lyrical poetry and the wife of Clemens Brentano (1778–1842). Her poetry shows traces of the style of Friedrich Schiller with whom she worked on his *Musenalmanach*.

5. Gottfried August Bürger, see entry no. 138, n. 6.

6. The Goethe poem mentioned was published in 1775 with the title *Maifest;* later Goethe gave it the title *Mailied,* which most editions use today.

7. *Die Liebe* by Gotthold Ephraim Lessing. While Lessing ranks as one of the outstanding writers of criticism, theory, and drama, his contributions to lyrical poetry have rarely received any recognition.

8. The reviewer refers here to the legendary performances of Beethoven's symphonies by the Conservatory in Paris, which were described in great detail by Berlioz. See his *Mémoires,* trans. David Cairns (New York: A. Knopf, 1969).

∾

Op. 53
PIANO SONATA IN C MAJOR ("WALDSTEIN")

———

142.
"Reviews," *Allgemeine musikalische Zeitung* 8 (22 January 1806): 261–63.

These two works[1] make up the two newest volumes (nos. 14 and 15) of the well-known and rightly treasured *Répertoire des Clavecinistes,* published by the firm of Mr. J. G. Nägeli in Zürich.[2] The Beethoven sonata has already been published by another publishing house[3] (first movement: Allegro con brio, ¢ time, C major; second movement: Adagio, introduzione,[4] $\frac{6}{8}$ time, F major; third movement: Rondo allegretto,[5] $\frac{2}{4}$ time, C major) and will therefore only be mentioned here. It will be sufficient to add that the first and last movements belong among the most brilliant and original pieces for which we are grateful to this master, but that they are also full of strange whims and are very difficult to perform. . . .[6]

The engraving of both works is very beautiful, but not completely without errors.

NOTES

1. The other work cited is a sonata by V. J. K. Tomaschek (1774–1850).

2. Hans Georg Nägeli (1773–1836), Swiss composer, publisher and essayist, issued both the "Waldstein" and the three Sonatas of op. 31 in his *Répertoire des Clavecinistes.*

3. Nägeli's edition appeared in 1805, the same year as the first edition published by the Bureau d'Arts et d'Industrie in May. Simrock's edition also appeared in 1805.

4. Actually Introduzione (Adagio molto).

5. Actually Rondo (Allegretto moderato).

6. The last part of the review, which deals with Tomaschek, has been omitted.

143.

v. d. O . . . r, "Grand Sonata in C Major," *Berliner allgemeine musikalische Zeitung* 3 (10 May 1826): 155.

Arrangement for piano four-hands by Franz Adolf Succo[1]

This magnificent work

OP. 53
Allegro con brio, mm. 1–3

has long been well known to all keyboard players, with its original power, loftiness, and loveliness of the first movement, the breath of spring of its second movement, which comes smilingly forth as though from the regions of the soul.

OP. 53
Rondo, mm. 1–2 (incorrectly printed in 4/4)

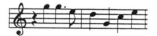

It has a theme like a drop of dew on a young rose, in which a small world is reflected. Gentle evening zephyrs move it and threaten to kiss it away; it extends itself, but pours forth all the more fully, and is replenished again and again, even *when* it slips away from us.

Unfortunately, the fact that this work has been arranged for four hands is deserving of censure.[2] Whoever knows it for two hands (and to what friend of music would it be unknown?) will not let half of it be taken away, since he can hold the whole work within his heart. Therefore this is not for such a person. It could thus only be recommended to two young friends, who understand each other well and do not yet know the work, but only under the condition that, after playing it through for the first time, each of them immediately sits down by himself at home and practices until he has learned it. Hic Rhodus, hic salta.[3] *Unfortunately,* we must once again predict that publishers will come off badly, precisely *because* the work is so beautiful. Everything that can be performed perfectly well with few resources and according to the composer's ideas may well be clothed in a larger garment by a beginning *musician*. A wise publishing house, however, must not engage in printing such efforts, however successful they may be. The reviewer does not except *those* efforts that have been made, for example, by Mr. Ritter von Seyfried[4] to arrange fortepiano compositions by Mozart and Beethoven for orchestra. The orchestra and the listeners certainly do not perceive these surrogates as complete, and fortepiano players also maintain firmly and rigidly that a sonata played on the fortepiano sounds better, more spiritual, more unified, and more suitable to the character of the work than when played by an orchestra. Painters will maintain that the expansion of a miniature painting, say, into an altarpiece, is an inappropriate undertaking. We therefore regret the beautiful printing job and the precious time consumed by this superfluous undertaking and advise Mr. Laue rather to allow the *three grand* new last quartets of the master to be arranged for the fortepiano; as far as we know, this has not yet taken place.[5] It may certainly sound strange enough if long, drawn-out bowings are sustained at the fortepiano. Nevertheless, it must therefore certainly be arranged, for without such an arrangement it will not sound right.[6]

NOTES

1. Franz Adolf Succo (1801–79), music director in Landsberg-an-der-Wien.

2. The four-hand arrangement was published by Laue in Berlin in 1826; its publication was announced in *Cäcilia* (vol. 14).

3. "Hic Rhodus, hic salta," is Latin for "Rhodes is here, leap here!" An admonition in an Aesop fable to the braggart on Rhodes to prove that he really can leap.

4. Ignaz Xaver, Ritter von Seyfried (1776–1841); see entry no. 32, n. 1.

5. It is difficult to identify the "three grand new last quartets" mentioned here. In May 1826 the three newest string quartets were op. 127 (first performed in March 1825), op. 132 (first performed in November 1825), and op. 130 (first performed in March 1826). None of these, however, had been published by May 1826. Given the difficult reception history of the late string quartets, it would be surprising for a reviewer to call for a piano arrangement prior to their publication as string quartets. The reviewer may have been referring to the three "Razumovsky" Quartets, op. 59. An arrangement for piano, four-hands, by C. D. Stegmann, however, had already been published by Simrock in Bonn in 1824 (interestingly, the title begins "Grand Quatuor").

6. The reviewer means that pianists will be tempted to play the quartets four-handed from score, but that compensation must be made from time to time for the limited sustaining power of the piano.

~

Op. 54
PIANO SONATA IN F MAJOR

144.
"Brief Notices," *Allgemeine musikalische Zeitung* 8 (2 July 1806): 639–40.

This sonata consists only of a Tempo di minuetto and a not particularly long Allegretto.[1] Both are difficult to perform, are written in an original spirit and with unmistakably mature harmonic art (particularly in as far as this leads to *expansion*), but both are also once again full of strange whims. Both kinds of B.'s peculiarities, those deserving of praise and those deserving of censure, have already been discussed often in these pages by others. Elsewhere, too, even the most fervent admirers of his truly deep spirit complain about them. Nevertheless, he demonstrates particularly how he holds all such observations in contempt by including completely ineffective peculiarities and affected difficulties even in his smaller pieces and not just where he tries to transform and exhaust his material completely and in every way possible. Thus, there is indeed nothing remaining for the reviewer to add apart from the observation that this new work again offers much material for the repetition of what has been said by others.

NOTE

1. The first edition of the Sonata, op. 54, was published in April 1806 by the Bureau d'Arts et d'Industrie in Vienna. It proved to be one of the least reprinted sonatas during Beethoven's lifetime.

Index of Names

Index of Periodicals

Index of Subjects

Unless otherwise specified, when a music genre such as symphonies is listed it refers to symphonies by composers other than Beethoven or to the symphony as a genre, without reference to particular works. Discussions of the meanings of Beethoven's music as interpreted by the critics are listed under either affective descriptions or program music.

Beethoven: birthdate and age of, 23–24, 48–49, 86, 99, 101; class status of, 128; copies of Mozart's music, 182; deafness of, 54, 59, 98–99, 103, 105, 110, 112, 120, 128, 131; death of, 99–101; dedications by, 137, 170, 225; early period, 63–64, 101–02, 105, 118–19, 132, 138–40, 154, 160, 171, 174; education (non-music), 102; estate of, 112–15; as eye-composer (rather than ear-composer), 97, 105, 131; fame of, 64, 77–79, 85, 88, 99, 101; family and family life, 23, 101–02, 104, 110, 128; financial affairs and support, 23–24, 99, 104–05, 109–10, 139, 150, 165; genius and ingenuity of (*see also* style, descriptions of Beethoven's: ingenious), 16, 23, 26, 34, 40–41, 47–48, 57, 75–79, 86, 96, 101, 105–06, 118–19, 127–28, 142, 147, 152, 156, 165, 167, 170, 173, 189–90, 202, 205, 224, 229, 232; gifts received by, 101, 105, 110, 114–15; greatness of, 24–25, 37, 40, 48, 85, 88, 99, 116, 119, 123–24, 126–28, 140, 175, 183; as hero, 44–45, 77, 125; idealism of, 78; industry and diligence of, 37–38, 48, 78, 146–47, 158, 160, 173, 224; isolation and loneliness of, 16, 21, 59, 78, 90, 99, 102, 119–20, 128, 131; knowledge of J. S. Bach, 23–24; knowledge of Mozart, 135; late period, 97–98, 111, 119, 129–32, 140, 161; library of scores, 24, 114; lip reading by, 105; love and marital status, 103, 119, 122, 124; manuscripts by, 112–14; mental illness and madness of, 97–98, 119; middle period, 64; monuments to, 107, 111; mysticism of, 117; new paths taken by (*see also* style, descriptions of Beethoven's: innovative), 2, 43–44, 91, 94, 119, 127, 130–31, 138, 142, 175, 189, 224; personal appearance of, 35, 102, 104; pranks by, 102–03, 109; psychological characteristics of, 25, 28, 78, 99, 102–05, 110, 119–20, 122, 124, 127–28, 131, 138–39, 145, 147, 156, 159, 174, 224; reception of works of, 35, 37–39, 42, 44, 47, 59, 64, 74, 88–89, 97–100, 103, 106, 111–12, 119, 126, 129–33, 138, 153–54, 156–57, 159–60, 162, 164–74, 176–77, 180, 183, 185, 190, 199–201, 203–06, 214, 216, 222–23, 232–36; relationship between life and music of, 43–44, 90, 93, 119, 122, 128, 131; relations with people, 99, 104; romanticism of, 1–2, 17, 21–22, 40–41, 59, 71, 91, 95, 106, 111, 121–23, 161, 214–15; sight-reading skills, 23; spider story, 102, 108; and students, 101, 103–04, 109, 129, 198; talent of, 23, 35, 37, 119, 146; texts chosen by, 165–66, 221, 223; teachers and training of, 23–24, 26, 101, 113, 118, 126; travels by, 23–25, 34–35, 103; views on Cherubini, 33–34; views on Contini, 163; views on Goethe, 96; views on Handel, 120; views on his own works, 119, 161; views on Mozart's operas, 135; views on Wranitsky, 163; violin playing by, 101–02, 112; as virtuoso, 25, 36, 103
bird songs, 106, 110
Broadwood piano, 36, 103, 105, 109–10

cantatas, 165
Cartesian method, 9–10, 12
chamber music, 59
chorale melodies, 228, 230
choral music, 150
churches, 8, 60, 115–17
church music, 88, 115–17, 228, 230; secular elements in Beethoven's music, 123
clarinettists, 37
comparisons of Beethoven: to Apollo, 44; to C. P. E. Bach, 143–44, 177, 210; to J. S. Bach, 12–13, 193; to Berlioz, 133; to Byron, 122; to Cervantes, 42; to Clementi, 177; to Diogenes, 103; to Don Quixote, 132; to Goethe, 122–23; to Handel, 120; to Hercules, 44; to Homer, 127; to Haydn, 29, 35, 43–44, 63, 78, 107, 119, 123–24, 127, 157, 164–65, 171, 199, 203;

comparisons of Beethoven (*cont.*)
  to Jean Paul, 51, 54, 86, 96, 106,
  121–22; to Michaelangelo, 122; to
  Mozart, 2, 23–24, 28–29, 35, 37–38,
  43–44, 47, 59, 63–64, 66, 78, 86,
  91, 102, 107, 119, 123–24, 126–27,
  130–31, 138–39, 141, 148, 154, 157,
  164, 199, 203, 205–06; to rivers or
  sea, 42–43, 85–86; to Raphael, 117;
  to Reichardt, 219; to Ries, 77–78; to
  Schubert, 220; to Schwanberger, 210;
  to Shakespeare, 40–42, 106, 122–23;
  to Vogler, 25–26; to volcanoes, 42–43;
  to Wagner, 40; to Wölffl, 28–29; to
  Zelter, 219
composition: Beethoven's habits of, 21,
  78, 106; Beethoven's knowledge of,
  2, 23, 26, 37, 95, 119–20, 142, 164,
  200, 224; motivations for, 78–80,
  142, 183, 222; Beethoven's training
  in, 23–24; motivations for, 115; rules
  of, 3–4, 16. *See also* style, descriptions
  of Beethoven's: nontraditional
concert producers, 97
concert programming, 167, 169
concertos, 62, 88, 93, 152, 172, 187,
  210, 213
concerts, amateur: in Vienna, 150–51
concerts, private: *Hausmusik*, 7–8; in
  Bremen, 48–49; in Linz, 159–60; in
  Vienna, 167–68
concerts, public, 1, 3–4, 6–8, 15, 19;
  in Amsterdam, 202–03; in Basel,
  204; in Berlin, 155–57, 161–62,
  167–69, 171–73, 199, 216–17; in
  Edinburgh, 43–44; in Elbersfeld,
  77–78; in Frankfurt am Main, 200;
  in Germany, 55–56; in Leipzig, 37,
  196–97, 200, 214; in Magdeburg,
  152; in Mergentheim, 24–25; in
  Munich, 170, 203; in Paris, 125–27,
  133; in Prague, 134–35; in Rore, 39;
  in Stuttgart, 127–28; in Vienna, 27,
  45–47, 104–10, 162–67, 197–98,
  221–23
conductors and conducting, 30–31,
  81, 86, 162–64, 171–72, 204, 222;
  Beethoven's views on, 163
connoisseurs, 28, 35, 39, 46–47, 84, 89,

98, 105, 124, 146, 148, 164, 166,
  170–71, 191–92, 195, 199, 202, 212
conversation books, 105, 110
counterpoint (including fugue), 14,
  32, 57, 60–61, 75, 81, 93, 125;
  Beethoven's knowledge of, 23–24,
  113–14, 120; Beethoven's use of, 112,
  120, 132, 143, 168, 185, 190–95,
  212
court culture (including music chapels),
  7, 101
critics and criticism, 1–22, 25, 56, 58,
  64, 75–77, 80, 88–89, 97–98, 100,
  111–12, 118, 124–25, 129–30
currencies, xv–xviii

dance music, Beethoven's lack of skill
  with, 20, 216
dances and dancers, 60–61, 83, 215–16.
  See also minuets
deterioration of music, 58–59, 64,
  87–89, 92, 97–98, 106, 119. *See also*
  improvement of music
Distichs, 84–85
doctrine of affects, 3, 5, 9, 14, 19–20, 29,
  32–34, 66, 92–94, 179; maintenance
  of single affect in Beethoven's music,
  190. *See also* affective depictions
dramatic music. *See* theater music
duets, 216

editions of Beethoven's music: collected,
  204–05; first, 23–24, 26–27, 38–39,
  89, 109, 113–15, 117, 144–48, 153,
  157–59, 168, 172–78, 180, 196, 202,
  204–05, 215, 219, 227, 230, 233,
  236; second, 138–41, 148, 173–74,
  215, 217, 220, 223, 231, 233. *See
  also* score editions
Egyptian influence on criticism, 18
elegies. *See* laments
embellishment. *See* ornamentation
emotions. *See* doctrine of affects
Empfindsamer Stil. See sensitive style
England: Beethoven's views on, 105,
  120
Enlightenment, 1, 5, 11–18, 21, 53, 95
epic music, 31–32
epic poetry, 71
epigrams, 132

fantasy and fantasies, 2–3, 15, 17, 55,
    94, 133–34
fate, 64, 82, 99, 128
figurations, 102, 191, 194, 206, 228
fingerings, 194, 231
flute music, 216
form, 90, 93; and design of Beethoven's
    works, 71, 102, 106, 119, 161, 164,
    190. *See also* counterpoint; rondo
    form; sonata forms

galant style in Beethoven's music, 192,
    195
games, 49–52, 150
gendered criticism, 49, 99–100, 108–09,
    130, 143–44
genius, 29, 34–35, 41, 46, 50, 74, 77,
    84, 88, 94, 118, 193, 202, 232
German idealism, 75, 95
government, Beethoven's views on, 105
guitars, 55

harmony, 2, 13, 21, 34, 43, 80, 91–92,
    98, 105, 111, 119, 121–22, 125, 137,
    143, 145–46, 148–49, 156, 166–67,
    169–70, 173, 176, 185, 190–95, 199,
    203, 208, 211, 216, 224, 229, 236
harps, 55
hieroglyphics, 1–2, 17–19, 41
history, 91–94, 100
holy or divine, references to, 2, 42, 71,
    78–79, 120
horn players, 217
hymns, 50, 63, 100

idea(s) (content), 12, 34, 60–62, 66, 71,
    74, 90, 93–95, 126, 131; abundance
    and richness of, in Beethoven's music,
    2, 25, 28–29, 43, 48, 86, 99, 105–06,
    120, 142–43, 156, 163, 167, 199,
    200–01; Beethoven's development
    of, 34, 48, 69, 71, 106, 112–13,
    120–21, 131, 149, 162, 164, 170,
    174, 178, 192, 197, 199, 201,
    205–13, 222, 228–29, 236; diversity
    of, in Beethoven's music, 106, 191;
    piling up of, in Beethoven's music, 2,
    21, 131, 142, 145; undeveloped, in
    Beethoven's music, 44
imitation. *See* mimesis

improvement of music, 48, 56, 61, 64,
    75, 86–95, 106, 119, 131
improvisations by Beethoven, 25–26
    (1791), 28 (1799), 54–55 (1822), 102
    (as a boy), 134–35 (1798), 159–60
    (1812), 163 (1800), 185 (1803)
inconsistencies in Beethoven's music,
    122
inflation, xv–xvi, 109
influences: Albrechtsberger's on
    Beethoven, 113, 120; C. P. E. Bach's
    on Beethoven, 144; Beethoven's on
    future, 48, 100, 124; Beethoven's
    on other composers, 3, 86, 122;
    Beethoven's on students, 140–41,
    145; Beethoven's on symphony, 63;
    Handel's on Beethoven, 120; Haydn's
    on Beethoven, 102–03; Mozart's
    on Beethoven, 102, 126; Neefe's on
    Beethoven, 23; Sterkel's on Beethoven,
    102; Viotti's on Beethoven, 30
instrumental music, 2, 12–13, 17,
    29–30, 45, 60, 62, 86, 91–95, 99, 131
instrumental solos, 61–62
instrumentation and orchestration,
    62–63, 87; Beethoven's, 66–67,
    69–71, 74, 106, 121, 127, 149,
    163–64, 166–68, 177, 197, 200–01,
    206–13, 225. *See also* timpani
intervals, in Beethoven's music, 14,
    143–44, 150, 211. *See also* harmony
introductions, in Beethoven's music, 34,
    139, 148–49, 167, 178, 190, 230
Italian style, 3, 61, 75, 78, 219

journals, 1–22, 118. *See also names of
    specific journals in Index of Names*

keyboard music, 61
key characteristics, in Beethoven's
    music, 70, 177–78

laments, 33, 65, 100
librettists, 165
lieder. See songs and singing
listeners: Beethoven's music pleasing to,
    47–48, 51, 87, 119, 121–22, 130,
    138–39, 140–41, 143, 146, 149, 154–
    56, 164, 168, 170, 172, 174, 178,
    183, 189, 191, 196, 199, 208, 212,

listeners (*cont.*)

214, 218–20, 225, 231–32; difficulties of Beethoven's music for (*see also* style, descriptions of Beethoven's: obscure or incomprehensible), 2, 20–21, 41, 69–70, 90–95, 112, 130, 135, 137–38, 153–54, 156, 162, 168, 170, 174, 176, 196, 201–02, 236; and necessity of repeated hearings, 47, 111–12, 130, 142, 153–54, 196, 200, 219; transformed or overwhelmed by Beethoven's music, 37, 44, 51, 96, 100, 119, 121, 124, 126, 145, 209, 211

literary theory, 5, 8–9, 13, 33

logic, 10–12, 92

longing (as a concept), 1

lyrical music, 63

lyrical-epic music, 32

marches, 60, 217–18

melodies and themes, in Beethoven's music, 2, 13–14, 21, 34, 43, 46, 61–62, 65, 69, 72–74, 76, 91–94, 98, 119, 121, 146–49, 160, 164, 166, 170, 173, 178, 184, 187–88, 190, 199, 221, 228–30, 232

metaphysics, 10–11

middle class, 4, 7–8

mimesis, 2, 10, 12–13, 18

minuets, 62; in Beethoven's music, 64

modes (major and minor), in Beethoven's music, 141, 211–12, 230

modulations, in Beethoven's music, 21, 34, 99, 105, 119, 145–49, 173, 197, 199, 209, 211–12, 220

Moors, 73, 97

morality, Beethoven's views on, 104

motives and motivic unity, 131, 135, 206–08, 213, 230

movements, slower, in Beethoven's music, 119, 122

music education, 46, 74, 157, 171, 183

musical life and status of music: in Berlin, 59, 67, 75, 89, 98; in England, 57; in Germany, 55–56, 61; in Leipzig, 57, 89, 200; in Vienna, 6, 25–29, 38, 45–47, 57, 150–51, 153, 163–65, 202, 232. *See also* concerts, amateur; concerts, private; concerts, public

mythology, antiquity, and mythological figures, 12, 21, 26, 44, 47, 50–51, 54, 58, 60, 75, 77, 84–85, 102–03, 108, 121, 129, 132, 166, 224, 227, 235

naiveness (as a concept), 15, 50–51

naive music, 21, 31–34, 35

naive poetry, 33

Napoleonic wars, xv–xvi, 3–5

nationalism and patriotism, German, 14, 49, 55, 77–78, 84, 87, 97, 102–03, 106–07, 118–25, 182, 222–23

nature and natural laws, 2, 9–15, 17, 20, 46, 66–67, 79, 88, 91–94, 99, 106, 116–17, 121, 128; Beethoven's love of, 106, 117; figure in Beethoven's music, 1–2, 119, 121

nobility, 7; Beethoven's views on, 104; Beethoven's relations with, 103

noble simplicity, 21, 98. *See also* style, descriptions of Beethoven's: simple; style, descriptions of Beethoven's: noble

novel (*roman*), 2, 17, 19

objective music, 31–32, 92, 95

oboists, 166, 168–69

octets, 162

odes, 53, 63

operas, 13, 27, 31, 33, 38, 46–47, 52–54, 75–76, 93, 95, 129, 135, 150, 162; Beethoven's plans for, 40–41

opus numbers, Beethoven's designation of, 106, 139, 143–44, 188

oratorios, 56–60

orchestras, 7, 24–25, 37, 39, 55–56, 61–62, 67, 81, 102, 163, 166–67, 171, 196, 199–200, 213, 232; necessity for large, with Beethoven's music, 196, 204

organ music, 60

organ playing, by Beethoven, 23, 25, 102, 109, 113

organs, 55

organ style, Beethoven's overuse of, 143

organists, 23–26, 37, 55, 60–61, 151

ornamentation (including free embellishment), 12–14, 46, 61, 154, 213, 222; Beethoven's use of, 144 overtures, 37, 39, 56, 60–61, 75, 161–62, 172, 221

parody, in Beethoven's music, 218, 221
pathetic style, in Beethoven's music, 148
patrons and annuity, Beethoven's, 104, 109, 128, 225
pedagogical models and texts, 3, 15
perception, 10–12, 92, 94
performances, Beethoven's private and public: 24 (1791), 54–55 (1822), 103 (1791), 108–09 (1791), 159–60 (1812), 162–63 (1800), 164–67 (1803)
performers: advice for, 147, 154, 157, 174, 177, 191, 193–94, 219, 224, 229, 234; Beethoven's music pleasing to, 146, 160, 164, 178, 191; Beethoven's relations with, 163–64; requirements for, 141, 145, 173, 175, 177, 181, 204–05, 213, 234–35; difficulties of Beethoven's music for, 13, 39, 47, 56, 105, 110, 112, 137, 141, 143–46, 148–49, 153, 158, 162–63, 166–68, 170, 173, 176–77, 181, 187, 189, 191, 193, 196, 198–201, 205, 213, 224, 231, 233, 236; ease of Beethoven's music for, 174, 178, 182, 186, 214, 219–20, 225
philosophy, 1, 3, 5, 8–11
phrasing, in Beethoven's music, 14, 122, 190
pianist(s): Beethoven's reputation as a, 23–28, 103, 158–59, 165; Beethoven's views on, 25, 103; female, 27–28, 39, 103, 109, 151; male, 25–30, 36, 58, 76, 103, 108–09, 135, 151
piano and cembalo playing by Beethoven, 23–24 (1783), 24–25 (1791), 26 (1796), 28 (1799), 54–58 (1822), 101–03 (as a boy), 108–09 (1791), 134–35 (1798), 142 (1799), 146 (1799), 151 (1803), 158 (1802), 159 (1812), 163 (1800), 165 (1803)
piano music, 61, 150, 174, 187
pianos, 24–26, 39, 47, 55, 177, 213–14; Beethoven's use of, 210; Beethoven's views on, 24–25. *See also* Broadwood piano

poetry and poets, 7–8, 11–12, 14–17, 19–21, 42, 44–045, 48–54, 58–60, 92, 94, 100–02, 110–11, 132, 188, 202, 219, 226–27, 230, 233
politics, Beethoven's views on, 104
polonaises, 39
potpourris, 57
printing and publisher errors, 138, 144, 148, 159, 186, 194, 215, 218, 223, 225, 233, 235
printing successes, 128–29, 138, 154, 157–58, 171–72, 182, 194, 201, 204–05, 225, 230, 233, 235
program music, 66–67, 92, 178–80, 217–18
program music in Beethoven's music: battle music, 66–67, 216; birdsongs, 106; bloody battlefield of death, 70; country life, 161; dancing spirits, 172; death of a hero, 178; dew drop, 234; funeral procession, 82–83; funeral song and parade of lamenting prisoners, 74; games, 83; hero and the war, 67–69; hero's life and battle, 82; inner and outer life, 179; lovers' behavior, 83; Moors, 73; native dances, 83; pastoral music, 66–67; romantic stories, 111; *Romeo and Juliet*, 41; rustic scenes, 66; tightrope walkers, 217–18; wine festival, 83
public education, 15–16, 21
public taste, 7–8, 15
publishers, 23, 25, 30–31, 33, 113–14, 138–39, 157–58, 180, 233, 235

quintets, 87, 162

rationalism, reason, and logic, 9–10, 12, 15, 19–20, 74, 131
rehearsals, 168, 196–97, 200
religious experience, 2, 17, 115
religious or divine music, 8, 60, 78, 82. *See also* church music
requiems, 172
revolutions in music, 90–95, 98
rhetoric, 8–9, 11–12, 14, 148, 228
rhythm, in Beethoven's music, 14, 46, 102, 149, 191, 206
ritornello-concerto form, in Beethoven's music, 209

Beethoven: genius and ingenuity of),
2, 113, 153–54, 169–70, 175, 183,
189–91, 203, 223, 224; innovative,
64, 77, 86, 90–91, 95, 99, 119–22,
127; inspired, 96, 204; interesting,
174, 201, 231; intimate, 43, 63, 139,
190, 219; ironic, 42, 87, 96; Italianate,
219; labored or overworked writing,
145, 200, 236; lacking awkwardness,
189; lacking beauty, 137, 164, 185;
lacking bizarreness, 156, 166; lacking
definite character, 185; lacking
design, 97; lacking development, 44;
lacking economy of means, 119, 126;
lacking excess, 174, 205, 209; lacking
expressiveness, 192; lacking flow of
thoughts, 185; lacking inspiration,
132; lacking melody, 119; lacking
nature and naturalness, 21, 97,
145–46, 224; lacking nobility, 21, 97,
132; lacking ordered imagination,
44, 124; lacking originality, 119,
147–48, 185, 216, 225; lacking
pleasing harmonies, 216; lacking
proportion, 2, 127; lacking purity,
119–20; lacking simplicity of forces,
199; lacking variety, 192; learned, 2,
12, 97, 118, 120, 142, 145, 192, 205,
216; limited or less comprehensive,
119; lyrical, 63–64; manly, 99,
143, 178; mathematical, 98; noble,
141, 178, 205; nontraditional, 2,
14, 21, 43, 95, 111, 121–22, 126,
128, 138, 143, 145, 164, 167, 190,
202–03; novel-like, 2, 48; obscure
or incomprehensible, 1–2, 12, 17,
20, 28, 69, 41, 86, 97–99, 105, 111,
119, 127, 130, 137, 142, 168, 170;
ordered, 12, 34, 143, 164, 167, 174;
original, 20, 35, 41, 44, 48, 56,
78, 86, 90–91, 103, 106, 119–21,
127, 131, 135, 137–38, 141–42,
145, 147, 155–56, 158–59, 163–65,
168, 173–74, 178, 185, 187–88,
190–91, 196–97, 199–202, 204, 216,
218, 222, 225, 229, 231–34, 236;
overheated, 130; powerful, 2, 34,
37, 40, 44, 74, 80, 99, 105–06, 119,
121, 124, 126–27, 137, 142, 144,
148, 156, 167, 170–71, 173, 190,
196, 197, 200, 203–04, 209, 214,
219, 229, 234; profound, 37, 40,
43–44, 51, 78, 106, 123, 137, 145,
150, 156, 170, 190, 196, 201–02,
212, 222, 234; ridiculous, 187,
225; "romance-like," 73; serious,
37, 119, 139, 145, 150, 153, 173,
178, 185; shapeless, 44; simple, 1–2,
13–14, 183, 188, 219, 229, 231–32;
striving, 20–21, 44–45, 111, 131,
145, 164–65; sublime, 13, 34, 48,
73, 107, 106, 112, 123, 126, 148,
150, 156, 202; surprising, 73, 122,
147, 165, 168, 191, 199, 208, 212;
sweetness of, 219; tasteful, 26, 163;
tender, 106, 119, 124, 210, 219;
unified or organic (see also motives
and motivic unity), 1–2, 29, 34,
41, 63, 95, 120–21, 123–24, 141,
143, 147, 167, 173, 176, 189, 196,
205–10; uninteresting, 119, 145, 192,
225, 229; unique and uniqueness of
each work, 37, 43, 99, 102, 105, 116,
119, 124, 173, 203, 213; universal,
29; well-maintained character, 34,
143, 150, 174, 185, 190, 205, 209,
232; wild, 29, 44, 73, 80, 121, 127,
153, 168, 173–74, 178, 199–201
symphonies, 29–31, 33, 37, 39, 55–56,
59–64, 75–77, 88, 93–94, 97, 102,
162, 178, 187, 196, 200

taste, 14
tempo designations, in Beethoven's
music, 148
tension or expectation, Beethoven's use
of, 34, 96, 211
terpodions, 55
texture, 13
theater music, 7, 46, 91–93
theaters, 60, 122, 23, 150
theater works, 40–41
thematic development, 61
theology, 11
ticket prices, 165
tightrope walkers, 217–18
timpani, Beethoven's use of, 208–9
tonality, in Beethoven's music, 67, 122,
125, 167, 177, 189, 209–10, 212,
217, 229

Index of Beethoven's Works

Rondo (Op. 51, no. 2), 178, 231
piano four-hands
    Sonata (Op. 6), 140–41, 144
    Three Marches (Op. 45), 218–19
piano two hands
    sonatas and sonatinas, 95, 113, 119, 159
        Three Sonatas (Op. 2), 26–27, 139; No. 2, 134–35
        Sonata (Op. 7), 141–42, 144, 161
        Three Sonatas (Op. 10), 142–44; No. 1, 144; No. 3, 143–44
        Sonata ("Pathétique," Op. 13), 147–49, 161
        Sonata (Op. 22), 30, 149, 161, 173–74
        Sonata (Op. 26), 164, 176–80
        Two Sonatas (Op. 27), 164, 180; No. 1, 176–77; No. 2, 176–78
        Sonata (Op. 28), 180–81
        Three Sonatas (Op. 31), 187, 233; No. 1, 187; No. 2 ("Tempest"), 41, 187
        Two Sonatas (Op. 49), 231
        Sonata ("Waldstein," Op. 53), 161, 233, 234–35 (arr. for piano four-hands)
        Sonata (Op. 54), 76, 236
        Sonata (Op. 57), 76
        Sonata (Op. 101), 109
        Sonata (Op. 106), 161
        Sonata (Op. 111), 74, 76–77, 95
        Three Sonatas (WoO 47), 24–25, 27, 101–02, 109; No. 2, 149
    variations, 25
        Six Variations (Op. 34), 175, 188–89
        Fifteen Variations ("Prometheus," Op. 35), 175, 190–95
        on a Waltz by Diabelli (Op. 120), 101, 106, 110
        on a March by Dressler (WoO 63), 24
        on Righini's "Venni amore" (WoO 65), 101, 103, 109
        on a Russian Dance from Wranitzky's Das Waldmädchen (WoO 71), 222
        on "Une fièvre brûlante" from Grétry's Richard Coeur de Lion (WoO 72), 146, 180
        on "Ich denke dein" (WoO 74), 115

on "God Save the King" (WoO 78), 218–19

VOCAL MUSIC

MASSES AND ORATORIO
Christus am Ölberg (Op. 85), 57, 101, 105–06, 111, 118–19, 123, 150, 164–66, 197
Mass in C (Op. 86), 38–39, 101, 105–06, 118–19, 123
Missa solemnis (Op. 123), 77, 81, 101, 105–06, 110, 116–19, 123, 129, 132

WORKS FOR STAGE
incidental music
    Music to Goethe's *Egmont* (Op. 84), 40, 101, 105
    Music to Kotzebue's *König Stephan* (Op. 117), 115
    "Germania," Finale to Treitschke's *Die gute Nachricht* (WoO 94), 115
    Leonore Prohaska (WoO 96), No. 4, Funeral March, 177
opera
    Leonore-Fidelio (Op. 72), 38–39, 48, 54, 56, 77–78, 81, 86, 101, 105–06, 115, 118–19, 123, 125, 151

WORKS WITH LARGER INSTRUMENTAL ENSEMBLES
for chorus and solos
    Der glorreiche Augenblick (Op. 136), 112, 114–15
for solo voices
    Tremate, empi tremate (Op. 116), 115
    Elegischer Gesang (Op. 118), 118, 123, 125

WORKS WITH PIANO
songs, 113
    An die Hoffnung (Op. 32), 188
    Adelaide (Op. 46), 101, 105, 110, 219–23
    Six Songs by Gellert (Op. 48), 101, 105, 110, 228–30
    Eight Songs (Op. 52), 224, 225–27, 231–33